A. F. Bandelier

The gilded man (El Dorado)

And other pictures of the Spanish occupancy of America

A. F. Bandelier

The gilded man (El Dorado)
And other pictures of the Spanish occupancy of America

ISBN/EAN: 9783742834102

Manufactured in Europe, USA, Canada, Australia, Japa

Cover: Foto ©Andreas Hilbeck / pixelio.de

Manufactured and distributed by brebook publishing software (www.brebook.com)

A. F. Bandelier

The gilded man (El Dorado)

AND OTHER PICTURES OF THE SPANISH
OCCUPANCY OF AMERICA

BY

A. F. BANDELIER
AUTHOR OF MEXICO, THE PUEBLOS OF PECOS, ETC.

NEW YORK
D. APPLETON AND COMPANY
1893

PUBLISHERS' NOTE.

As compared with the peopling of our Atlantic seaboard, the first explorations of our Southwest by a white race have received comparatively slight attention, the minor consequences of the latter, and the inaccessibility of the early Spanish records, being the sufficiently obvious causes which have combined to prevent minute and exhaustive studies until within the past few years.

Dramatic and intensely interesting conditions have been revealed as Mr. Bandelier—whose work under the auspices of the Archæological Institute of America and on the Hemenway Survey has entitled him to stand first as the documentary historian of this region, and also to rank as the most exhaustive of its explorers—has brought the facts of this long-hidden history once more to the light. It is the history of a search for the Golden Fleece, which was full of strange and romantic episodes; a history of the progress of the cross and the sword, which was accompanied by deeds of superhuman endurance, dauntless courage, and a pitiless bigotry and ravening cruelty that drove even the gentle Pueblos to revolt, and to the attempted destruction and concealment of all traces of their conquerors. The Southwest is the land of romantic history, albeit the history is often dark and bloody, and the pictures

f Spanish exploration and domination which M
Jandelier presents in this volume are of profound i
erest. The legends of the mysterious Seven Citi
f Cibola, and of the elusive Gran Quivira, are s
orth clothed in no other romantic garb than that d
o the truth ascertained by a learned explorer ar
rchæologist; but the bare truth is so strange ar
10ving that it has needed no adornment. Direct
rom the records we have the final facts in the afte
ife of one of La Salle's murderers. In the true sto
f El Dorado—that is to say, The Gilded Man—the
s settled definitely a matter that has undergone i
eterminate dispute through three hundred yea
These several papers, with the others here presente
elected from the records of Spanish conquest on bo
ontinents of America, do not constitute a continuo
tor a complete history. Each, however, is comple
n itself; each probably crystallizes the subject that
mbraces; and the interest and historical value of t
ollection as a whole make it a necessary part
very library in which American history is adequate
epresented.

Owing to Mr. Bandelier's absence in Peru whi
his volume was passing through the press, he h
een unable to revise the proofs—a duty which M
Thomas A. Janvier, utilizing her familiarity wi
Mexican and Spanish historical literature, very obli
ngly has performed in his behalf. In accordan
vith her wish we add that to the inability of t
uthor to give his work this final revision must
ttributed any errors which may be found in the te

he Gilded Man:
    I.—Cundinamarca
    II.—Meta
    III.—Omagua
    IV.—The expedition of Ursua and Aguirre .
ibola:
    Introduction.
    I.—The Amazons
    II.—The seven cities .
    III.—Francisco Vasquez Coronado
    IV.—The New Mexican Pueblos
    V.—Quivira .
he massacre of Cholula (1519)
he age of the city of Santa Fé .

CHAPTER I.

CUNDINAMARCA.

WHILE the early Spanish adventurers in America are justly charged with neglecting the true interest of colonization in their excessive greed for treasure and thereby bringing harm to those parts of the Western Continent which they entered, it cannot be denied that their irrepressible seeking for the precious metals contributed directly to an earlier knowledge and a more rapid settlement of the country. The Spaniards' thirst for gold led them into adventures which excite admiration and wonder as expressions of manly energy, while they offer the saddest pictures from the point of view of morals.

In every age gold has presented one of the strongest means of enticing men from their homes to remote lands, and of promoting trade between distant regions and the settlement of previously uninhabited districts. We have received from the earliest antiquity the stories of the voyage of the Argonauts, of the

:pedition of Hercules after the golden apples of t[he] [H]esperides, and of the settlement of the Phœnicia[ns in] Spain, the gold of which they carried to the Syri[an c]oast. For gold the Semitic navigators sailed fro[m] [th]e Red Sea to Tarshish and Ophir.*

Portuguese seamen as early as the middle of t[he] [fif]teenth century brought gold from the west coa[st of] Africa; in order to find a sea-route to the gol[d la]nds of India, Vasco da Gama sailed around t[he C]ape of Good Hope; and in order to obtain a short[er ro]ute from Spain to India Christopher Columb[us v]entured out upon the Atlantic Ocean and the[n r]eached the new gold-land, America.

On Thursday, October 11, 1492, Columbus land[ed u]pon Watling Island, or Guanahani, one of the B[aha]ma group, and on Saturday, the 13th, he wrot[e:] "Many of these people, all men, came from the sho[re] . . and I was anxious to learn whether they h[ad g]old. I saw also that some of them wore little piec[es o]f gold in their perforated noses. I learned [by] [si]gns that there was a king in the south, or sou[th-]

---

* While we may look for the former treasure region [in S]umatra, the latest researches make it probable that Op[hir] presented not only Sofala, but also the coasts and inter[ior of] East Africa south of it, including Mozambique, Monon[om]pa, and the country of the ruins of Zimbabue (Mashonalan[d).] [T]his conclusion appears more credible than the opinion p[er]stently maintained by Montesino that Ophir was Peru. T[he di]fficulties of a long sea-voyage from Ezion-Geber to t[he w]estern coast of South America would be partly removed [if w]e could accept Professor Haeckel's hypothesis of a contin[ent] [of] Lemuria having once stood in the Indian Ocean, a[nd we] [w]ould also suppose the Western Atlantis to have existed [w]hich the natives of Australia sought in the eastern part the island, who owned many vessels filled with ld."*

This was the first trace of gold which the Euroans found in America. Cuba, where the Admiral xt landed, afforded him no gold, but he found the ecious metal so abundant in Hispaniola (Santo Do.ngo, or Hayti) that he was able, after he returned, write from Lisbon to his sovereigns, March 14, 93: "To make a short story of the profits of this yage, I promise, with such small helps as our inncible Majesties may afford me, to furnish them the gold they need."

Hispaniola continued till the first decade of the (teenth century to be the seat of gold production the newly discovered western land. The conseences of this gold-seeking to the unhappy natives e well known, and need not be dwelt upon. The)erations were continued on this island for only a ry short time. As a result of the fearfully rapid sappearance of the aborigines, the supply of labors began to fail, and the mines fell into disuse, alough, according to Herrera,† they furnished to the other-country, Spain, down to the discovery of exico, five hundred thousand ducats in gold.

The Admiral saw the mainland of South America r the first time on his third voyage, at Punta de acos, Trinidad, July 31, 1498, and found evidences gold on the coast of Venezuela. The expedition Ojeda in 1499 and 1500, although it sailed along

---

* Journal of the Admiral, published by Navarrete, from e *"Historia apologética de las Indias"* of Bartolomeo de Las isas. MSS. at Madrid.

ie whole northern coast to New Granada, yield
ily a small return, for after the largest pearls a
old pieces were turned into the royal treasury or
ve hundred ducats were left to be divided amo
ie hundred and fifty sharers. A few months l
ire Ojeda, an expedition had returned to Sp
om the same region which had attained cons
able material results, notwithstanding the sm
eans with which it had been undertaken. Chr
val Guerra and Pero Alonzo Nino, with a po
travel of fifty tons and thirty-three men, had cross
ie ocean to Venezuela and sailed along its co
om bay to bay, trading and bartering with t
atives, and had thus acquired much gold and m
an one hundred and fifty marks' worth of pea
hey brought the report that while gold-dust w
ire in the eastern part of the northern coast
outh America, the metal was more abundant t
rther west they went. When in 1500 Rodrigo
astidas of Santa Marta discovered the snow-cover
ot-hills of the Cordilleras, his first thought mig
ell have been that the noble metal which t
arlike Indians of the coast wore so abundan
s a decoration was derived from those dista
eights.*

While Ojeda was vainly trying to found a settl

---

* Emeralds may also have been shown to the Spania
en; for in the capitulation with Ojeda, on his second v
ge, July 5, 1501, islands are mentioned, near Quiquevac
1 the mainland, where the green stones were of which spe
ens had been brought to him. Quiquevacoa, or Coquivac
as the Indian name for the country around the Gulf

ment near Maracaybo, the great Admiral was industriously preparing for a new voyage of discovery. He sailed in 1502, and on the 17th of August of that year he landed, after meeting much tempestuous weather, at Truxillo in Honduras. Sailing along the Mosquito Coast, beaten day and night by severe storms, Columbus reached Porto Bello and Chiriqui. Gold was found in quantities at Chiriqui and Veragua, in the vicinity of the famous mines of Tisingal, which the French filibuster Ravenau de Lussan mentioned as late as 1698.* The various efforts of the Spanish to plant colonies on the Isthmus and in western New Granada † had only insignificant results till Vasco Nuñez de Balboa in 1511 assumed the direction of the colony in Darien, with a firm hand, but without any higher right, and with great sagacity immediately brought about closer relations with the surrounding Indian tribes. The tribe of Dabaybe on the Rio Atrato, who had many ornaments of gold, pointed to the west and south as the regions from which this gold came. Balboa, following the directions of the Indians, who hoped to get rid of their distrusted guests and send them to their nearest enemies, reached the coast of the Pacific Ocean on the 25th of September, 1543. There he seems to have heard a report‡ of a wealthy tribe which lived on the seacoast far to the south and used large sheep as beasts of burden. From this time forward the attention of the Span-

---

* The name of "The Rich Coast," Costa Rica, is still attached to that part of Central America north of Chiriqui.

† Ojeda and Diego de Nicuesa.

‡ Quintana, and Herrera, dec. i. lib. x. cap. iii.

iards was directed to the countries south of the Isthmus.*

Prescott says, in his "Conquest of Peru," that Balboa learned in this way of the riches of that kingdom. His authorities are Herrera, who says: "And this was the second report which Vasco Nuñez received of the condition and wealth of Peru;"† and the later Quintana. Pascual de Andagoya, who went in 1522 as far as Punta de Pinas, on the western coast of New Granada, says: "He had received there exact accounts through traders and chiefs concerning the whole coast to Cuzco."‡ Still, it may be doubtful whether this notice does not refer to the civilized tribes of central New Granada, who carried their salt over the beaten mountain paths to the cannibal inhabitants of the Cauca Valley and received gold in exchange for it. Without forgetting that the llama was never used as a beast of burden in New Granada, the supposition that accounts of Peru had reached the Isthmus, notwithstanding the great distance, involves nothing impossible. Prod-

---

* The discovery of Mexico by Córdova and its conquest afterward by Cortés affected the Spanish colonies south of the Isthmus very little. The influence of the colonization of the Mexican table-land extended no farther than to Yucatan, Guatemala, and a part of Honduras. The booty which the Spaniards gained there, partly in gold, was not great. The presents which the chiefs at Tenochtitlan sent to the seacoast to Cortés were lost at sea, and all the treasures which the Mexicans had accumulated in their great "pueblo" in the lagoon were ruined by the inundation during the retreat of July 1, 1519, or were burned during the subsequent attack.

† Decada i., p. 267.

‡ "Relacion de los succesos de Pedrarias Davila," etc.

ucts of nature and art, and reports of conditions and events in single countries, are alike carried to great distances through war and trade.

Although languages and dialects were separated from one another by uninhabited neutral regions, prisoners of war could tell of what was going on at their homes; the booty would include a variety of strange objects; and traders traversed the country in the face of numerous dangers, visited the enemy's markets, and carried their goods to them, with many novelties. This process was repeated from tribe to tribe; and in that way the products of one half of the continent passed, often in single objects, to the other half, and with them accounts of far-off regions, though changed and distorted by time and distance, into remote quarters.

The centers of this primitive trade were among those tribes which, being the most civilized, had the largest number of wants and the most abundant productions. They were the agricultural tribes, the "village Indians" of the higher races. These, although in America they never lived in a gold-bearing country, accumulated the metallic treasures of the lands around them, acquiring them by means of successful wars, or through an active and extensive trade. But the Spaniards, who had no taste for work, preferring chivalrous robbery, sought first the centres of trade and the treasure already laid up in them. The conquest of Mexico gave them evidence of the existence of such a centre in the central part of the Western Continent; but concerning South America there were only rumors and vague guesses.

Excepting the colonies on the Isthmus of Darien

and at Panamá, the Spanish settlements in New Granada and Venezuela made little progress. Panamá grew vigorously; ships sailed thence southward to the Pearl Islands and to the west coast of New Granada. The whole western slope of the Andes, from the Rio Atrato southward, the provinces of Antioquia and Cauca, were very rich in gold. But they were inhabited by savage and warlike tribes addicted to a horrible cannibalism, whose villages were rarely situated upon the coast, while access to them by land from Panamá was attended with great difficulties. The Spaniards on the western side of South America were therefore involuntarily led into making coast voyages, which in the course of time took them to Peru.

The Spanish enterprises in Venezuela, after the pearl fisheries on the island of Margarita were organized, were limited to making single landings, the chief purpose of which was barter, and especially man-stealing. This practice depopulated the coast, and embittered the natives to such a degree that they became dangerous enemies to all attempts at permanent colonization. By them the well-intended effort of the famous lieutenant Las Casas to found a colony at Cumaná was defeated with bloodshed in the year 1521. Only in Coro, on the narrow, arid isthmus that connects the peninsula of Paraguana with the country around Lake Maracaybo, Juan de Ampues succeeded in 1527, with seventy men, in founding a colony and establishing friendly relations with the Coquetios Indians around him.

The Spaniards had by their predatory expeditions excited the resentment of the Indians along the northern coast of New Granada, and those tribes, populous and rich in treasures accumulated by their trade with the interior, but little civilized, offered them a vigorous resistance. Their poisoned arrows were formidable weapons, and the thick woods gave them secure hiding-places and natural fortifications. Rodrigo de Bastidas, having founded a settlement at Santa Marta in 1525, returned to San Domingo in consequence of an outbreak among his men. His successors, Palomino, Badillo, and Heredia, tried without success to overcome the gold-rich tribes of northern New Granada. They could advance no farther than the valley of La Ramada. Palomino was drowned, and a bitter quarrel arose between Heredia and Badillo, the adjustment of which was left to the Emperor Charles V. Without regarding the claims of the two candidates, the Spanish Government appointed Garcia de Lerma governor of Santa Marta, with a new military force. At the same time the Emperor leased the Province of Venezuela, extending from Cape de la Vela on the west to Maracapanna, now Piritú, on the east, to the house of Bartholomäus Welser & Co., of Augsburg, and in 1529 Ambrosius Dalfinger and Bartholomäus Seyler landed at Coro with four hundred men, and took possession of the post for "M. M. H. H. Welser." Ampues had to yield, and the Germans became lessees of a large part of northern South America. They found the colony of Coro prospering, and the Indians in the neighborhood friendly. A story was current among these Indians of a tribe dwelling in the mountains to the south with whom gold was so abundant that they powdered the whole body of their chief with it. This was the legend of "the gilded man"—*el hombre dorado,* or, more briefly, *el dorado,* "the gilded." The story was based on a fact: a chieftain who was gilded for a certain ceremonial occasion once really existed, on the table-land of Bogotá, in the province of Cundinamarca, in the heart of New Granada.

According to Lucas Fernandez Piedrahita, Bishop of Panamá,* the district of Cundinamarca included nearly all eastern and central New Granada. The eastern Cordilleras bounded it on the east, it extended on the north to the Rio Cesar and the region of Lake Maracaybo, on the west to the Rio Magdalena, and on the south to Reyva. But the heart of the district, Cundinamarca, in its strictest sense, was the high table-land of Bogotá, once the home of "the *dorado.*" "This table-land," says Alexander von Humboldt, in his *"Vues des Cordillères et Monuments indigènes"* (Chute de Tequendama), on which the city of Santa Fé is situated, "has some similarity to the plateau that encloses the Mexican lakes. Both lie higher than the convent of St. Bernard; the former is 2660 metres and the latter 2277 metres above the level of the sea. The Valley of Mexico, surrounded by a circular wall of porphyritic mountains, was covered in the central part with water, for before the Europeans dug the canal of Huehuetoca the numerous mountain streams that fell into the valley had no outlet from it. The table-land of Bogotá is likewise surrounded by high mountains, while the perfect evenness of the level, the geological constitution of the ground, and the form of the rocks of

---

* *"Historia general del nuevo Reyno de Granada, 1688."*

Suba and Facatativa, which rise like islands from the midst of the savannas, all suggest the existence of a former lake-basin. The stream of Funza, commonly called the Rio de Bogotá, has forced a channel for itself through the mountains southwest of Santa Fé. It issues from the valley at the estate of Tequendama, falling through a narrow opening into a cañon which descends to the valley of the Magdalena. If this opening, the only outlet the valley of Bogotá has, were closed, the fertile plain would gradually be converted into a lake like that of the Mexican plateau."

On this high plain, whose even, mild climate permitted the cultivation of the grains of the temperate zone, lived, in small communities, according to their several dialects, the agricultural village Indians, the Muysca. Isolated by nature, for the highland that girt them on every side could be reached only through narrow ravines, they were entirely surrounded by savage cannibal tribes. Such were the Panches west of Bogotá, and in the north the semi-nomadic kindred tribes to the Muysca, the Musos and Colimas. Engaged in constant war with one another, the Muysca lived in hereditary enmity with their neighbors. While the Panches ate with relish the bodies of fallen Muysca, the latter brought the heads of slain Panches as trophies to their homes. Yet these hostilities did not prevent an active reciprocity of trade. The Muysca wove cotton cloths, and their country contained emeralds, which, like all green stones, were valued by the Indians as most precious gems. But their most valuable commodity was salt. In white cakes shaped like sugar loaves this necessary was carried over beaten paths west to the Rio Cauca, and north, from tribe to tribe down the Magdalena, for a distance of a hundred leagues. Regular markets were maintained, even in hostile territories, and the Muysca received in exchange for their goods, gold, of which their own country was destitute, while their uncivilized neighbors, particularly the Panches and other western tribes, possessed it in abundance. The precious metal was thus accumulated to superfluity on the table-land of Bogotá. The Muysca understood the art of hammering it and casting it in tasteful shapes, and they adorned with it their clothes, their weapons, and both the interior and the exterior of their temples and dwellings.

The Muysca lived in villages—"pueblos"—of which an exaggerated terminology has made cities; and their large communal houses, which were intended, according to the Indian custom, for the whole family, have been magnified into palaces. These buildings were made of wood and straw; but the temple at Iraca had stone pillars. Their tools and weapons were of stone and hard wood; but vessels of copper or bronze, such as the Peruvians possessed, have not been found among them, although a recent authority, Dr. Rafael Zerda, believes that they were acquainted with alloys. Their organization was a military democracy, such as prevailed throughout America. In each tribe the position of chief was hereditary in a particular clan or gens, out of which the *uzaque*, as he was called, was chosen. This chief, or uzaque, simply represented the executive power. As in Mexico, the council of the elders of the tribe acted with him in decision.

Concerning the religious ideas of the Muysca, as

well as concerning their language, so much has been published in recent times and since Herr von Humboldt directed attention to them in his celebrated researches ("*Vues des Cordillères,*" etc., and "*Calendrier des Muyscas*") that we refrain from superfluous repetition. Their language was probably similar to the Peruvian Quichua, but their numeral system was more like that of the Central American peoples. Their calendar combined with the Peruvian month of thirty days the double, civil, and ritual year of the Mexica. Besides the worship of the sun and moon (Bochica and Bachue or Chia), which was performed with stated human sacrifices, in which the Mexican rite of cutting out the heart was employed, there existed, as in Peru, a kind of fetish worship of striking natural objects. The numerous lakes of the plateau were holy places. Each of them was regarded as the seat of a special divinity, to which gold and emeralds were offered by throwing them into the water. In the execution of the drainage works which have been instituted at different places in more recent times, as at the lagoon of Siecha, interesting objects of art and of gold have been brought to light.

Among the many lakes of the table-land of Bogotá known as such places of offering, the lake of Guatavitá became eminently famous as the spot where the myth of *el dorado*, or the gilded man, originated. This water lies north of Santa Fé, on the páramo of the same name, picturesquely situated at a height of 3199 metres above the sea. A symmetrical cone, the base of which is about two hours in circumference, bears on its apex the lake, which has a circuit of five kilometres and a depth of sixteen fathoms. The bottom of the lake is of fine sand. Near this water, at the foot of the páramo, lies the village of Guatavitá. The inhabitants of this place about the year 1490 constituted an independent tribe. A legend was current among them that the wife of one of their earlier chiefs had thrown herself into the water in order to avoid a punishment, and that she survived there as the goddess of the lake. Besides the Indians of the tribe of Guatavitá, pilgrims came from the communes around to cast their offerings of gold and emeralds into the water. At every new choice of a uzaque of Guatavitá, an imposing ceremonial was observed. The male population marched out in a long procession to the páramo. In front walked wailing men, nude, their bodies painted with red ochre, the sign of deep mourning among the Muysca. Groups followed, of men richly decorated with gold and emeralds, their heads adorned with feathers, and braves clothed in jaguars' skins. The greater number of them went uttering joyful shouts, others blew on horns, pipes, and conchs. *Xeques*, or priests, were in the company, too, in long black robes adorned with white crosses, and tall black caps. The rear of the procession was composed of the nobles of the tribe and the chief priests, bearing the newly elected chieftain, or uzaque, upon a barrow hung with discs of gold. His naked body was anointed with resinous gums, and covered all over with gold-dust. This was the gilded man, *el hombre dorado*, whose fame had reached to the seacoast.*

* Zamora treats these ceremonies as fabulous, but they are vouched for by Piedrahita, Pedro Simon, and others, as having once existed.

Arrived at the shore, the gilded chief and his companions stepped upon a *balsa* and proceeded upon it to the middle of the lake. There the chief plunged into the water and washed off his metallic covering, while the assembled company, with shouts and the sound of instruments, threw in the gold and the jewels they had brought with them. The offerings completed, the chief returned to the shore and to the village of Guatavitá. The festival closed with dancing and feasting.*

Till about the year 1470 the tribe of the Tunja was the most powerful clan on the highland; at that time the Muysca of Bogotá † began to extend their dominion. Their chief, or *zippa*, Nemequene, overcame the Guatavitá Indians in the last decade of the fifteenth century, and made them tributary. With that he put an end to the ceremony of the *dorado*. The gilded chief had ceased to wash off his glittering coat in the waters of Guatavitá thirty years before Juan de Ampues founded the colony of Coro, but news of this change on the highlands of Cundinamarca had not yet reached the coast, and the *dorado* still continued to live in the mouths of the natives there.

Ambrosius Dalfinger, of Ulm, in Suabia, the new German governor of Venezuela, was the first to hunt upon the trail of the "gilded man." He left Coro in July, 1529, sailed across the Gulf of Venezuela, on the western coast of which he established the post of Maracaybo, and then pressed westwardly inland to

---

* A group of ten golden figures has been found in the lagoon of Siecha, representing the *balsa* with the *dorado*.

† Bacatá—the extreme cultivated land.

the Rio Magdalena. He was not aware that he was thereby encroaching upon the territory of the government of Santa Marta. No white man had ever entered these regions before him. Thick woods, partly swampy and partly hilly, covered the country, and warlike tribes, who often possessed gold, lived in the valleys. Dalfinger was a valiant soldier, who permitted no obstacle interposed by tropical nature, or resistance offered by the natives, to keep him back. He was, moreover, a rough, heartless warrior of a kind of which the European armies of the time supplied many examples. Gold and slaves were his object, and in pursuit of them he plundered the inhabited country, and then devastated it in so terrible a manner that even the Spanish historians relate his deeds with revulsion. The rich valley of Cupari was wholly overrun and partly depopulated. When in 1529 Dalfinger reached the Magdalena at Tamalameque, he found the stream in flood, and the Indian villages surrounded by water, so that he could not get to them; he then turned up the river toward the hills. Herrera says: "He went up the country, keeping by the river and the hills, to the Rio de Lebrija, the windings of which he followed as closely as possible. And when the way became barred by the numerous lagoons he went up into the hills, where he found a cool region (*tierra fria*) thickly populated. He was forced to fight with the people, and suffered severely from them."[*] He had here in all probability reached the edge of the plateau of Bogotá, and the Indians before whose resistance his weakened army had to yield were the Muysca, to

[*] Dec. iv. lib. iv. cap. i., p. 101.

whose linguistic stem the *dorado* had belonged. Dalfinger wintered at the foot of the hills. The next year (1530) he continued his murderous campaign of plunder on the right bank of the Magdalena, till in the Ambrosia Valley the natives inflicted a second defeat upon him. Then he, with his troops, diminished to a few more than a hundred men, retreated to Coro, where he arrived about May. He brought with him 40,000 pesos in gold. He had already sent 30,000 pesos to Coro the year before, but both the treasure and its escort had been lost in the forest.*

From the settlement of Santa Marta, on the northern coast of New Granada, the Spaniards advanced in the meantime very slowly toward the south. The periodical overflows of the Magdalena, the thick

---

* Dr. Clements R. Markham supposes, following Oviedo y Baños ("*Historia de Venezuela,*" 1728), that Dalfinger died from a wound in 1530; but this appears to be erroneous, as is the assertion, too, of the same author that Dalfinger got no farther than the Rio Cesar. As to the latter point, Herrera, who is very exact in relating the deeds of the Europeans, mentions very plainly his reaching the cool country (*adonde halló tierra fria*). Dalfinger's death can hardly have taken place before 1532. Nicolaus Federmann, Dalfinger's provincial successor, says that he went to San Domingo in 1530 to be cured of a fever. When Federmann returned, in 1532, from his first expedition (southward to the plain of Meta), the governor was still living. Herrera's statement (dec. iv. lib. ii. cap. ii.) that Dalfinger died at Coro in 1532 is the probable one. Federmann went back to Europe, but we shall see him later seeking for the *dorado*. Hans Scissenhoffer (Juan Aleman) succeeded him as governor of Coro, but died soon afterward without having undertaken anything. His successor, Georg von Speyer, was likewise inactive till the year 1535.

woods of the interior, the resistance of the exasperated Indians, and, above all, the previous devastation of the inhabited districts by Dalfinger, created extremely formidable obstacles to their progress. Tamalameque, which Luis de Cardoso captured in 1531, was, till 1536, the most southern point which the Spaniards could reach from Santa Marta or Cartagena.

In the meantime reports had been brought from the western coast of South America which caused great excitement in all the Spanish colonies in America, and even in the mother-land itself. The coasting voyages southward, initiated by Pascual de Andagoya in 1522, were continued by Francisco Pizarro in 1524. The accounts which he received concerning the southern country (Peru) on his first expedition determined him on his return to Panamá to lay out the plans for a larger enterprise, and on March 10, 1526, an agreement was made between him, Diego Almagro, and the licentiate Gaspar de Espinosa, in which the subsequent conquest of Peru was designated as a "business." On a third voyage, in 1528, Pizarro touched at Tumbez, in Quito, and saw the stone houses, the llamas, the emeralds, and the gold of the land of the Quichua. Three years later the actual descent upon the Peruvian coast began, and events succeeded one another with surprising rapidity. On the 15th of November, 1532, the Capac Inca Atahualpa was a prisoner of the white men at Cassamarca. The weak bonds which held together the government of the Quichua tribe were broken at once, and every chief, every subjected district, acted independently. Huascar Inca, the regularly chosen chief in Cuzco, was murdered at his brother's command; the Apu Quizquiz tried in vain to defend Cuzco; the Apu Rumiñavi fled to the north, whither Sebastian de Belalcazar pursued him as far as Quito, worrying him with bloody battles; and the Inca Manco Yupanqui surrendered to the Spaniards. The conquerors found the whole land open to them almost without having to draw the sword, and their spoil in precious metals was immense. According to the partition deed which the royal notary, Pedro Sancho, drew up at Cassamarca in July, 1533, Atahualpa's ransom, as it was called, amounted to 3,933,000 ducats of gold and 672,670 ducats of silver. The plundering of Cuzco yielded at least as much more. In the presence of such treasure the recollection of the riches of Mexico grew faint. A gold fever seized the Spanish colonists everywhere in America, and every one who could wandered to Peru. The existence of many of the settlements was thereby endangered. The leaders and founders of those colonies could not look on quietly while their men were leaving them to hasten into new lands of gold. In order to retain them they were obliged to make fresh efforts to find treasures in the vicinity, and occupation that would attach them to the country.

Georg von Speyer fitted out a campaign from Coro southward into the plain of the Meta. In Santa Marta, where a new governor, Pedro Fernandez de Lugo, adelantado of the Canary Islands, had arrived in 1535 with a reënforcement of twelve hundred men, an expedition was organized to ascend the Rio Magdalena to the highlands—those highlands concerning which vague accounts were afloat, and from which came the white cakes of salt that were found in the possession of the Indians of Tamalameque.

This expedition was divided into two parts. One part was to ascend the river in a number of brigantines, and was commanded by Lugo himself. The other division was to proceed inland from Santa Marta to Tamalameque on the right bank of the river and there meet the brigantines. The command of this division was given to the governor's lieutenant, the thirty-seven-years-old licentiate Gonzalo Ximenes de Quesada of Granada, afterward rightly surnamed *el Conquistador*. Under his leading were six hundred and twenty foot-soldiers and eighty-five horsemen. Both divisions started on April 5, 1536, but the flotilla, badly directed and overtaken by storms, never reached its destination. Some of the carelessly built boats went to the bottom, and all but two of the others returned to Cartagena in a damaged condition. Lugo died before a new flotilla could be collected; the building of new vessels was given up after his death; and the land expedition under Quesada, left alone to its fate, was gradually forgotten at the coast.

Before Quesada lay dense woods, in which lived once wealthy Indian tribes, who were now shy and hostile. A way had to be cut through the luxuriant tropical vegetation of these forests. They afforded the Spaniards but little food, while they abounded in poisonous reptiles and insects, with treacherous swamps in the lowlands, out of which rose dangerous miasms. The once fertile valleys were deserted; an ambuscade was often lying in wait in the forest border that girt them; and instead of nourishing fruits the Spaniards received a rain of poisoned arrows. Dalfinger had, indeed, previously accomplished a similar march, but in his time the country was populated, and he could support his men on the stored provisions and ripening crops of the natives. Quesada found only the wastes which his predecessor had created; every day some of his men fell ill or succumbed to the hardships. The Indian porters soon died because of them. Their services had become of little value, for there were shortly no more provisions for them to carry. The energy, quiet consideration, and self-denial of the leader had then to be brought into play to keep up the courage of his men.

Quesada justified the trust which his former superior had, perhaps without particular forethought, placed in him. He never spared his own person, and he did all he could for his men. If a rapid stream was to be bridged he was the first to lay the axe to the trees of which the bridge was to be built. He carried the sick and feeble in his own arms through swamps and across fords. He thus, by devotion combined with strictness in discipline, controlled his men so that the exhausted company followed him without demurrer to Tamalameque, where they expected to find the boats. The Rio Magdalena was in flood, and its shores were overflowed for miles. Instead of the expected flotilla loaded with provisions, Quesada found only two leaky brigantines, and a hundred and eighty famishing men. The disappointment was bitter; he felt as if he were abandoned. But the round cakes of salt that came from the mountains in the south had reached this region, and Quesada determined to follow the paths over which they had been brought. A retreat by land would, at any rate, involve sure destruction. Again his weary men followed him, and he reached Latora, one hundred and fifty leagues from the mouth of the Magdalena. Eight months had passed since he had left the coast, and his march had been disastrous, but the worst seemed to be yet awaiting him at this spot. A wooded, uninhabited waste of waters encompassed the force, and the swollen river cut off alike all advance and all retreat. Attempts to move the brigantines up the stream were vain; they could not be taken more than twenty-five leagues. Despair then overcame discipline. The men, dejected and weeping, besought their leader to send them back in the brigantines by detachments to the coast, and to give up an enterprise which had so far brought them, instead of gold, only misery, hunger, and death. The moment was imminent in which every bond of respect for their leader seemed about to be broken, when the captains Cardoso and Alburazin returned to the camp after several days of absence and reported that they had discovered a river flowing down from the mountains, and ascending it had come to a spot where traces of men could be seen. On the strength of this story Quesada was able to silence his men's complaints and gain time to make further research in the direction pointed out by his captains. Captain San Martin found, twenty-five miles farther up this mountain stream, a trodden path leading up into the mountains, and along it a number of huts which contained salt. Quesada himself started off with his best men and found the path, but fell ill and was obliged to halt. Antonio de Lebrixa went on to the mountains with twenty-five men, and came back with the welcome intelligence that he had found there a fertile plain inhabited by men who lived in villages and went about clothed in cotton. Quesada hastened back to his camp at Latora, put the sick and weak upon the brigantines, and sent them back to Cartagena. In the beginning of the year 1537 Quesada, at the head of one hundred and sixty-six of his most effective men, stepped upon the plateau of Cundinamarca, the former home of the *dorado*. He had lost more than five hundred men by hunger, illness, and exposure.

The sight of the first villages on the plateau satisfied the Spaniards of the wealth of the country. The people imagined that the strangers were man-eating monsters and fled to the woods, but left behind them a quantity of provisions, which were very acceptable to the half-starved Spaniards, and some gold and emeralds. The Indians posted themselves on the defensive in a ravine near Zorocota. Quesada tried unsuccessfully to storm their strong barricade. In the evening, after both sides had returned, tired with fighting, to their camps, two of the Spaniards' horses broke loose and ran, chasing one another, over to the natives. The Indians, frightened by the strange beasts, fled into the woods. The Spaniards found the large village of Guacheta deserted, the inhabitants having taken refuge among the rocks overlooking it. In the midst of the place was an old man stripped and bound to a stake, as an offering of food to the whites. They unbound him, gave him a red cap, and sent him away. Thereupon the men on the rocks, supposing that they considered him too tough, cast living children down to them. Seeing that these little ones, too, were not touched by the strangers, they sent down from the heights a man and a woman, both stripped, and a stag, bound. The Spaniards sent back the man and woman with small gifts, and kept the stag. The Indians upon this were reassured, left their place of refuge, came down from the rocks, and gave themselves up to the white men. This was on March 12, 1537. Quesada followed the wise policy of conserving the strictest discipline. He caused one of his men who had stolen cloth from an Indian to be hung. This course secured him the good-will of the natives, so that many places received the Spaniards as liberators; for the country they had so far passed through was tributary to the Muysca of Bogotá, and, as was the case everywhere among the Indians, the subjected races hated the conquering tribe. The people were therefore not at all loath to point out to the strangers by signs the direction of Mucqueta, the chief town of Bogotá, near the present Santa Fé, where, they intimated to the eager Spaniards, emeralds and gold were plentiful. The rulers of Bogotá witnessed with apprehension the approach of the strangers, and their braves having assembled for a campaign against Tunja, the whole force, in which there were five hundred uzaques, or chiefs, alone, turned against the Spaniards. The Muysca fell upon Quesada's rear-guard near the Salines of Zippaquira, their xeques, or priests, carrying in front the bones of deceased chieftains, while in the midst of the host was the head chief of

Bogotá, Thysqueshuza, on a gilded barrow. The first assault having been repelled by the Spaniards, the Indian warriors scattered in every direction; the zippa leaped from his barrow and fled to the woods, and each chief hastened back with his men into his village. Quesada took possession of Muequeta without meeting resistance, for the power of the tribe of Bogotá was broken forever. But he did not find the treasure he was in search of and had expected to obtain. The place had been stripped of everything valuable, and the conqueror surveyed the bare and empty rooms with no little disappointment. Every attempt to put himself in communication with the fugitive zippa miscarried, while no promises of reward, no torture, could extract from the Indians of Muequeta the secret of the spot whither the treasure had been taken. Muequeta became Quesada's headquarters, and thence he sent out scouting parties to explore the country. A few villages surrendered to the Spaniards, but others, like Guatavitá, the home of the *dorado*, resisted them strenuously, and hid their gold or threw it into the lagoons of the páramos. The region subjected to the Spaniards in this way grew continuously larger, for the Muysca never offered a united resistance. The dissensions and the mutual hatreds of the smaller tribes contributed quite as much as the superiority of their own weapons to the victory of the conquerors. Out of hostility to that clan a rival uzaque informed a Spanish scouting party of the great wealth of the powerful tribe of the Tunja. Quesada himself went against them, and so quiet was his march that the uzaque of Tunja and all the chiefs of the tribe were surprised in their council-house. Quesada was about to embrace the chief, but the Indians looked upon this as an offence, and threw themselves, armed, upon the Spaniards. A savage combat ensued, within and without the council-house. By sunset the village of Tunja was in the possession of the whites, the uzaque was a prisoner, and the pillage was fully under way. The booty, when piled up in a courtyard, formed a heap so large that a rider on horseback might hide himself behind it. "Peru, Peru, we have found a second Cassamarca!" exclaimed the astonished victors.

The Spaniards were less fortunate in Duytama than in Tunja. They were not able to capture the fortified position; but they anticipated a rich compensation for this failure when they beheld the glitter of the golden plates of the large town of Iraca. The Sugamuxi of Iraca submitted, but a fire broke out, through the carelessness of two Spaniards, during the pillage of the great temple of the sun, and consumed the whole building with all its treasure of gold and emeralds. Quesada returned to Muequeta, where the spoil was divided, and the royal fifth was set aside. Although it is certain that much gold had been stolen or lost or hidden by individuals, and the treasures of the wealthy tribes of Bogotá and Iraca had all disappeared, the prize was still worthy of the home of the *dorado*. It was officially valued at 246,976 pesos in gold and 1815 emeralds, among which were some of great value.

The conquerors of Cundinamarca had, however, not yet found the *dorado* himself. Exaggerated stories were still current of Muysca chiefs rich in gold, and it was said that the fugitive zippa of Bogotá lived in the mountains in a golden house. That chief was hunted out and murdered in his hiding-place, but his death did not bring to light the gold of Bogotá. One reconnoitring party of Spaniards looked down from a mountain summit eastward upon the plain of the Upper Meta, and another party brought in a report that there or in the south lived a tribe of warlike women who had much gold. In this way the myth of the Amazons became associated in 1538 with the tradition of the *dorado*.

Quesada felt himself too weak to go in search of the origin of these reports; it was necessary first to secure the conquered country. In August, 1538, therefore, the foundation of the present city of Santa Fé de Bogotá was laid, not far from Muequeta. Quesada intended then to go in person to the coast and obtain reinforcements; but before he could carry out this design news was brought to him from the south that caused him to delay his departure.

He was informed that a number of men like his own, having horses, had come down out of the Cauca Valley into the valley of the Magdalena. A few days later it was said that this troop had crossed the Magdalena and was advancing into southern Cundinamarca. It was the force of the conqueror of Quito, Sebastian de Belalcazar, who, after driving the Peruvian Apu Rumiñavi out of Quito, and by his intervention making Pedro de Alvarado's landing at Manta harmless, had gone northward through Pasto to Papayan. An Indian from New Granada had already, according to Castellano, told him in Quito the story of the gilded chieftain, and had thus induced him to undertake this march. From Papayan he had proceeded along the Upper Cauca to the tribes of Anzerma and Lile, which were rich in gold but addicted to the most abominable cannibalism, and thence following the path on which salt was brought down from the mountains to the high tableland of the interior.

Quesada had hardly received this news when it was also reported to him that white men with several horses were approaching from the east out of the plain of Meta, and were coming up through the ravines of the mountain. These men were the German Nicolaus Federmann of Ulm and his company. On his return from Europe Federmann had received a position as lieutenant of Georg von Speyer in Coro. His chief was engaged in a campaign in the southern plains, and Federmann was to have gone after him with reënforcements, but had faithlessly struck out for the mountains, and was following on the track of Dalfinger to the home of the *dorado*.

Thus, led thither by the same inducement, Quesada from the north, Belalcazar from the south, and Federmann from the east, found themselves at the same time on the plateau of Cundinamarca. The positions which the three Spaniards took formed an equiangled triangle, each side of which was six leagues long. Each leader had the same number of men—one hundred and sixty-three soldiers and a priest. None of them had been aware of the vicinity of the others, and therefore each of them thought he was the discoverer of the country. A fatal conflict seemed inevitable, but the encounter, which might have provoked a rising of the Indians and a massacre of the Spaniards, was averted by the wisdom of Quesada and the mediation of the priests. The three leaders agreed to submit their claims in person to the Spanish court, and in the meantime to leave all their forces on the plateau in order to hold the conquered land. The three—Gonzalo Ximenes de Quesada, Sebastian de Belalcazar, and Nicolaus Federmann—then departed from Bogotá and proceeded together to Spain. Federmann was destined never to see America again, for the Welsers would not overlook the treachery which he had committed against his commander, Georg von Speyer. Quesada suffered the basest ingratitude from the Court. Nine years passed before he was allowed to return to the scene of his activity, and he received as the only reward for his great services the title of Marshal of the new kingdom of Granada.

The brother of the conqueror, the avaricious and cruel Hernan Perez de Quesada, remained at Bogotá as the commanding officer of the Spaniards. He completed the subjugation of the Muysca. The unhappy natives suffered exceedingly cruel maltreatment, for the sake of gold, from him and his barbarous lieutenants. No means was too violent or too immoral if gold could be got by it. Hernan Perez made an unsuccessful attempt in 1540 to drain the lake of Guatavitá in order to recover from it the gold of the *dorado;* but four thousand pesos was all the return he realized from the experiment. The Muysca, plundered and plagued by the whites amongst them, and warred upon on their borders by the Panches and Musos living around them, who were not subjected to the Spaniards till some time afterward, went down almost irresistibly to extinction. Their vigor was broken, and they had no hope of consideration or forbearance from their rulers. When the former Sugamuxi of Iraca was told that a new governor had come who was a friend to the Indians, he asked a Spaniard if he believed the river was going to flow upstream; when the white man answered this question in the negative, the chief responded, "How do you suppose, then, that I am going to believe in the existence of a Spanish officer who will feel and act justly and reasonably toward us?"

With the conquest of Cundinamarca was secured the last great treasure of gold that awaited the Spaniards in America. Their wild greed was, however, doubly excited by their success so far, and they thirsted for more and greater. The Minorite monk, Fray Toribio of Benevento,* wrote with truth in 1540: "And gold is, like another golden calf, worshipped by them as a god; for they come without intermission and without thought, across the sea, to toil and danger, in order to get it. May it please God that it be not for their damnation." Then rose again, like an avenging spirit, the legend of the gilded chieftain, in the still unknown regions of the South American continent. Transplanted by the over-excited imagination of the white men, the vision of the *dorado* appeared, like a mirage, enticing, deceiving, and leading men to destruction, on the banks of the Orinoco and the Amazon, in Omagua and Parime.

* Called Motolinia, "the poor." "*Historia de los Indios de Nueva España.*"

CHAPTER II.

META.

As we have mentioned, the conquest of New Granada by Gonzalo Ximenes de Quesada concluded, as to the whole of Spanish America, that series of extraordinary discoveries of precious metals in the possession of the natives which exercised so sudden an influence on the value of gold, among European peoples in particular. When the Peruvian spoil was divided at Cassamarca in 1533 the peso, which contains about the same quantity of metal as our dollar, had an exchangeable value nearly the same as that of a pound sterling, or $4.85; but by 1553 its value had declined, according to the learned Mexican student, Orozco y Berra, to $2.93, or about forty per cent. During these twenty years Mexico alone yielded in gold and silver together 1,355,793 pesos. The four ships which arrived in Spain from Peru on the 5th of December, 1533, and the 9th of January and 3d of June, 1534, carried, without including golden vessels and ornaments, 708,590 pesos in gold and 240,680 pesos in silver. The spoil of New Granada amounted to 246,972 pesos in gold alone. These examples, drawn from two years only in South America, show clearly that the great depreciation of the precious metals we have just cited is to be ascribed principally to the findings in Peru and New Granada. .The value of silver fell about eighty-four per cent. in Europe between 1514 and 1610, a fall which was caused by the working of the silver mines of Potosi in Bolivia. These yielded, between 1545 and 1564, 641,250,000 pesos or piastres in silver. The discovery of New Granada had an especial effect on the value of emeralds.

It cannot be denied that this sudden depreciation of the metallic media of exchange had a great influence on the demand for them, while it covered the search for them with the mantle of a legitimate want. The need of specie was evident, and the less the material of which coins were made was worth, the more of it must be had. To this was added the fact that the simple necessities of life on which Europeans depended for existence were at first not to be got, for example, in Peru. The first horses sold there brought 6000 pesos (equivalent to at least $28,000 in present values); and in 1554 Alonzo de Alvarado offered in vain 10,000 pesos, or $29,300, for an ordinary saddle-horse. Between thirty and forty pesos were paid in Cassamarca soon after the division of the spoil for a pair of half-boots, and forty or fifty pesos for a sword. The first cow was sold in Cuzco in 1550 for two hundred pesos. Nine years later the price of a cow had fallen to seventeen pesos. Wine began to be cheaper about 1554, when a ship landed at Truxillo with two thousand casks; the first cask was sold for six hundred ducats, and the last one for two hundred ducats.

Still, no explanation or excuse can be found in these extreme instances for the reckless, passionate eagerness with which the Spaniards, without waiting to secure one treasure, pursued the visions of others.

The transactions and expeditions subsequent to the conquest of New Granada, of which the *dorado* was the object, depended on such fancies.

Before describing the second period of the search for the *dorado*, let us return to the fourth decade of the sixteenth century and take a view of a number of enterprises carried out at the same time with the conquests of Peru and New Granada, by the aid of which we may be better prepared in historical and geographical knowledge for the understanding of later events. The regions on which we have to fix our attention for this purpose are the present republic of Venezuela and southeastern New Granada.

While Dalfinger was engaged in his arduous expedition to the Magdalena, considerable attempts were begun to found colonies on the northeastern coast of the South American continent. Antonio Sedeño, *contador* of the island of Puerto Rico, was a wealthy and prominent man. One of his contemporaries, Gonzalo Fernandez de Oviedo y Valdés, says of him that "under the pretext of serving God and his king he hoped, through what he possessed and through his estates on the island of St. John, to acquire a larger property on the island of Trinidad and on the mainland, and greater honor. But it did not turn out to the advantage of his purse, for while he despised what he had, he pursued the schemes of his fancy. . . . This lust for ruling and for being more than others caused him to lose his property, and, what was more, his time too, and exposed his body as well as his soul to great danger and trouble." * Sedeño sought and obtained the appointment of governor

* "*Hist. gen. y nat. de Indias*," lib. xxiv. cap. i.

of Trinidad, with the design of "building a strong house there" (*de labrar una casa fuerte*),* of which he should be the *alcalde*. But his concession did not extend beyond the island. Nevertheless, having left San Lúcar de Barrameda on the 18th of September, 1530, with seventy men, Sedeño's first act after reaching Trinidad was to take formal possession of it and then pass over to the mainland. There, on the Gulf of Paria, he built, outside of his province, and contrary to his commission, the "strong house" which he had contemplated building in Trinidad. This act, apparently insignificant in itself, was of great importance for the future. Sedeño left a small garrison in the "strong house," and sailed to the Antilles to procure reënforcements. He hoped that he had in the meantime secured undisputed possession of the mainland, even though it was without higher sanction. But without his knowledge a former companion of Cortés, Diego de Ordaz, the same person to whom is ascribed the first ascension of the Mexican volcano Popocatepetl, had obtained in Spain a concession for the colonization of the then very indefinite district of Marañon on the mainland. This concession was granted in 1530, and included permission to occupy the coast from the territory leased to Welser & Co. to the mouth of the Marañon, and to erect four fortresses. An allowance of 725,000 maravedis a year was set aside for him, while he had also an assured income from Mexico of between 6000 and 7000 pesos. Ordaz fitted out two ships and a caravel in Spain at his own cost, and sailed from

* Herrera, dec. v. lib. ii. cap. i.

San Lúcar de Barrameda with four hundred and fifty men on the 20th of October, 1531. Although an additional caravel joined the squadron at the Canary Islands, and the aggregate force was increased to six hundred men, yet, in consequence of heavy storms, the Admiral's ship was the only vessel that came in sight of the South American coast, near the mouth of the Amazon.* Ordaz sailed on thence northward along the coast to Paria, where he found the fort built by Sedeño. He captured this post by assault, regarding it as belonging to his concession, and kept it for a further base of operations. Ordaz thought so little of the region of the mouths of the Amazon and of the coast of southern Guiana that he abandoned all attempts there and decided to turn to the nearer-lying mouths of the Orinoco. He fitted out a flotilla of seven galleys from Paria, with which, with two hundred and eighty men and eighteen horses, to explore the thickly wooded labyrinth of the delta of that river.

The fleet was worked with great difficulty through one of the numerous channels up into the principal arm of the river. The relations of Ordaz with the Arnaks,† the scattered inhabitants of that swampy, unhealthy wilderness, were for the most part of a tolerably friendly character. But when the tribe of Baratubaro refused to furnish him provisions he

---

* The knowledge of this river was so imperfect at this time that we cannot be sure this statement is correct, although Herrera says (dec. iv. lib. x. cap. ix.): "Diego de Ordás reached the Rio Marañon with the intention of beginning his explorations there."

† From *arna*, tiger.

punished them severely for it. Sailing up the principal stream, he at length came to the falls of the Orinoco, near Atures and Maypures, since made famous by Alexander von Humboldt, where the miles of rapids and small cataracts by which the course of the river was broken made further navigation impossible. Before this the officers of the expedition had vainly tried to persuade Ordaz to abandon his boats and press into the interior. Now it was necessary to leave the boats. On the right extended a broad savanna, on which a hostile encounter took place with the Indians. They informed Ordaz that the river flowed from a large lake which lay in the midst of high and rugged mountains. The way thither lay through a province called Meta, which was thickly populated and rich in gold. Silver, which the Spaniards showed the natives, was not known to them, but they recognized gold at once as the substance that was abundant in Meta. They pointed to the west as the direction in which this land was to be found. Unfortunately, the river was falling so rapidly that Ordaz would not venture to march inland. Unwillingly he had to embark again and begin a dangerous and laborious retreat. Eighty of his men died from the hardships of the voyage; with the rest, ill and despondent, he reached Paria. His purpose was, since the Indians near the falls of the Orinoco had spoken so highly of the wealth of Meta, to march overland thither from the northern coast of Venezuela—the Gulf of Cariaco. He left a little colony of a hundred souls at Paria, and sent a part of his force under Alonzo de Herrera to Cumaná, following it himself eight days later. To his surprise he was received at Cumaná with cannon-shots, and was informed that his men were on the island of Cubagua, and that the post belonged to that jurisdiction. Greatly astonished at this unexpected communication and at his hostile reception, he crossed over to Cubagua, where most unpleasant information was imparted to him. During the period of nearly two years which Ordaz had spent on the Orinoco Sedeño had been informed of the occupation of the post he had established at Paria. He at once appealed to Spain against what he styled a violent attack on his rights. He cited the terms of Ordaz's concession, which, indeed, confirmed to him the coast from the Marañon to the limits of Welser's leasehold, but defined the length of the coast-line as two hundred leagues from the mouth of the Marañon. Sedeño insisted that under the latter clause Paria was outside of that concession, and therefore contested the right of Ordaz to occupy the post there. The contention was in many respects characteristic of the times. It especially illustrates the vagueness of the geographical ideas of the period, which estimated the distance from the easternmost point of the German concession in Venezuela to the mouth of the Amazon as only two hundred leagues. The Crown decided in favor of Sedeño so far as to order Ordaz to restore to him the property he had seized, and to satisfy himself with the prescribed two hundred leagues of coast, which he could choose either "from the Cape of La Vela toward the Marañon, or from the Marañon toward the Cape of La Vela," as he might prefer.* Ordaz was

---

* Herrera, dec. iv. lib. x. cap. x.

further ordered to restore to the jurisdiction of the city of New Cadiz, on the island of Cubagua, the coast of Cumaná, which he claimed. The inhabitants of Cubagua had joined with Sedeño against Ordaz, and when the latter came upon the island he found that his people had been dispersed, and his lieutenant, Alonzo Herrera, was held a prisoner. Ordaz all at once found himself alone, and grieving bitterly over his loss, sailed for Spain, in order to contend there for his claims, and if possible to organize a new expedition. Death overtook him on the ocean in 1533, and the waves were his grave.

Of all their laborious enterprises, there was left to the party of Ordaz only the post in Paria. Sedeño seized this also, and thus seemed to make himself sole heir of the scanty acquisitions of his unfortunate rival. The chief of them was, so far as the interests of the time were concerned, a name—Meta; signifying the intangible, enticing vision of a land of gold, which was to be found west of the Orinoco. But before Sedeño could enter upon the pursuit of this vision a bitter quarrel arose between him and his confederates at Cubagua over the ambiguous decision of the Crown already mentioned. The control of the island of Trinidad cost him much labor and a large sum of money, and when he landed at Paria on his return thence he found that the island of Cubagua now claimed that post.

It is aside from the purpose of this sketch to consider the controversies and contentions, continuing till the end of 1534, between Sedeño and the administration of Cubagua, of which the "strong house" in Paria, called by Oviedo "the house of discord" (*casa de discordia*), was the object. In consequence of them Sedeño was put in prison. Nothing was accomplished on the mainland, because each party alternately stood in the way of the other engaging in any important enterprise; but man-stealing was carried on on the northern coast of Venezuela, as before from Cubagua and Margarita, without hindrance. Notwithstanding the complete miscarriage of the enterprises of Diego de Ordaz and his death, a number of men and officers at Paria remained faithful to the memory, at least, of his plans. They had indeed to submit to the authority which was exercised alternately by Sedeño and the people at Cubagua, but they never gave up the hope of making use on their own account of the information which they had collected on their memorable campaign to the falls of the Orinoco. Alonzo de Herrera, the former prisoner at Cubagua, afterward Sedeño's associate, finally acquired and maintained the command of the "house of discord" on the mainland at Paria.

Among the few comrades who had sailed with Ordaz was Geronimo D'Ortal, his treasurer, who reached Spain, and obtained from the Crown a concession, as successor of the deceased Ordaz, to occupy and administer Paria. The report of this arrangement soon reached the West Indies, and produced no little commotion there. Sedeño, leaving Trinidad, sailed for Margarita, but his former allies of Cubagua pursued him there and compelled him to go back to Puerto Rico. In revenge, he determined to join with D'Ortal, as soon as he should arrive, against the people of Cubagua.

D'Ortal arrived in Paria with two hundred men in October, 1534, and was joyfully received by Alonzo de Herrera and his company of about thirty men. He at once began preparations to explore the Orinoco, and "find there that province of Meta, of which he had learned through the natives that it was a land of great wealth."* But, mindful of the experience of his predecessors, he sent thither only a part of his force (one hundred and thirty men) under the command of Alonzo de Herrera, with nine galleys and a caravel. Herrera was to establish himself at the upper end of the delta of the Orinoco, among the Aruas (Waruas or Aruaks), while D'Ortal should wait in Paria for the arrival at the West India Islands of the reinforcement of a hundred men, which Juan Fernandez de Alderete was to bring him from Spain. The reinforcement came to Cubagua, and D'Ortal went there to receive it. Then, in the year 1535, he returned to Paria.† Thence he went to Trinidad, and sent a detachment of his men back to the coast to unload a ship that was waiting there with provisions. Ten leagues from Trinidad they found three small boats, and in them, to their no little surprise, the dwindled remnant of the expedition of Alonzo de Herrera.

That valiant and adventurous officer, of whom Oviedo says that "he knew much better how to kill

---

* Oviedo, lib. xxiv. cap. vii.

† According to Oviedo there were two San Miguels: the "house of contention," where D'Ortal landed, "*en aquel golpho é costa de Paria*" (lib. xxxiv. cap. viii.); and the later San Miguel de Neveri, east of Piritú. Oviedo and Herrera do not agree concerning the latter post.

Indians than to govern them," had gone up the Orinoco to the Rio Apure (Carao), and thence—where he was assured that "Guiana lay behind him and Meta before him," and the reports of the wealth of the latter region were confirmed—"to a bay or arm of the sea, which empties into the same river Huyapari, and is called the bay of Meta." * In twenty days he reached "the mouth of that bay," which seems to be nothing else than the mouth of the Rio Meta. It was the rainy season, the streams were very high, and the boats had to be drawn with ropes. The water often came up to the breasts of the towing men, and it was only with extreme toil that they succeeded in advancing in forty days twenty leagues westward up the Meta. Oviedo, a contemporary whom we have often cited, says of this incident: "I do not believe that any of those who took part in this expedition would have taken so much trouble to get into Paradise." By the end of the forty days the current had grown to be so strong that farther advance on the river, even by towing, became impossible. The whole country was inundated;† yet a hundred men left the boats and tried to press, through these plains converted into a series of lagoons, farther west to Meta. Most of the scattered inhabitants had fled, but they at last met an Indian woman who understood the dialects they had so far heard. She promised to conduct the Spaniards to a large village, but warned them that its

* Huyapari was one of the many names of the Orinoco. It is also written Biapari and Uiapari.

† The height of water in the Orinoco in the interior of Guiana varies from twenty-eight to thirty-four feet annually.

4

inhabitants would certainly eat up the Christians, seeing they were so few. When she had told enough falsehoods to the whites, Herrera had her hanged "in thanks for her work, and since he was groping around, as it were, in the dark, he thought he might find the way better by means of this kind of holy torch, or by this good act. No wonder that an equally speedy and still sadder death fell upon him and others." *

The country assumed a more favorable aspect fifteen or twenty leagues from the point where the boats were left. The dry spots, which had hitherto only rarely shown themselves out of the boundless waters, became more evident, and upon them were vestiges of food plants, such as maize and yucca. The troops halted at a group of twelve huts, and sent thence some provisions to the sick and dying who had been left on the boats. The rest at this place was, however, of short duration, for the Indians soon attacked the camp by night. The assault was repulsed, but Alonzo de Herrera and three other Spaniards were mortally wounded, and died soon afterward in violent delirium from arrow poisoning. All the horses but one were killed in the fight, and the men were obliged, after returning to their boats, to use this one for food. The return voyage was speedily made, and they reached the Orinoco in fourteen days. Their leader was Alvaro de Ordaz. Willingly complying with the wishes of his men, he decided to leave this river as quickly as possible and return to Paria. Hunger and privation of every kind, hostile attacks and illness were diminishing the company nearly every

* Oviedo.

day, so that the remnant, which, as already mentioned, met D'Ortal's men at the seashore, formed only a little band of haggard sufferers. Their accounts showed that D'Ortal had abandoned the Orinoco in order to approach Meta overland from the north, from the Gulf of Cariaco. The conflicts of which the post at Paria was the occasion were renewed this time about the coast-land between Cumaná and the Rio Neveri. Three parties were jealously keeping watch upon one another, and, wherever it was possible, barring one another from the interior. Sedeño had at first united with D'Ortal, and then separated from him. Opposed to both were the "men of Cubagua," whose chief interest was to hold the coast for the preservation of their own existence, and for the prosecution of the traffic in men.

The expedition to the south, begun by D'Ortal in 1535, entirely miscarried. He tried to reach Meta, first by single reconnaissances, and then in a general campaign. But his men rose against him on the Orinoco, which he possibly struck below the Rio Apure.* A part of them wandered away, and we shall find them again later on in Federmann's following. The rest went back to the coast, where they delivered their commander up to justice. He remained a prisoner sixteen months, although his only crime was misfortune; and when he was released he had lost all desire for further campaigns, and "determined to marry." "And as his purpose was a good one," Oviedo says, "God gave him a good wife, a respectable and virtuous widow of suitable

* Oviedo, lib. xxiv. cap. xv.

age, who had means ... enough for him to live decently in our city of San Domingo on the island of Hispaniola, with more security and fame than could come to him in all these wars, or in hunting the fabulous riches of Meta, of which no one knows anything to this day, or can find the way there without its costing yet more human lives and leading to other troubles. To this point has our story come, this month of August, in the year one thousand five hundred and forty-five." * This event took place in 1536.

The map which Oviedo made about 1545 of the regions successively traversed by Ordaz, Herrera, and D'Ortal defined the results of all these expeditions better than any description could do. The fancied golden empire had not been found north of the lower course of the Orinoco and east of the territory given to the Welsers. It was the fortune of the Germans in Venezuela to determine what was the foundation of the myth which had thus transplanted itself into the eastern region of northern South America.

While Ambrosius Dalfinger was still lost on his campaign towards the Magdalena, the Welsers sent to Coro to his support a division of soldiers, with twenty-four German miners, under the command of Nicolaus Federmann, a burger of Ulm. This reinforcement probably arrived at Coro in June, 1530. Immediately afterward came another reinforcement upon three ships, and with it an agent of the Welsers, Hans Seissenhoffer, who was made governor in Dalfinger's absence. Federmann, who seems to have been a capable, crafty, and energetic man, became Seissenhoffer's lieutenant. On account

* Oviedo, lib. xxiv. cap. xvi.

of these changes the Spanish officers were withdrawn from Coro, an act which seems to have produced a great bitterness, especially against Federmann. When Dalfinger unexpectedly returned a short time after this, Seissenhoffer resigned his position, but Federmann remained—"as lieutenant of the governor and captain general, as which the whole army recognized me." *

Dalfinger brought back only vague accounts and a relatively considerable quantity of gold. He had not found the *dorado*, and had again withdrawn from the northeastern border of Cundinamarca. He did not tarry long at Coro, but sailed to San Domingo for the recovery of his health, leaving Federmann in his place. Federmann says: "Finding myself now in the city of Coro with a number of men who were unoccupied, I determined to undertake a campaign into the interior toward the south or the Southern Sea, in the hope of finding something profitable." He left the coast on the 12th of September, 1530, with "one hundred and ten Spaniards on foot, and sixteen on horseback, and a hundred Indians." His geographical notices are so extremely vague that we can follow him only a little way on this remarkable campaign. His estimates of distances are entirely untrustworthy, and the names of the Indian tribes which he met are often hardly recognizable. He reached

* "*Relacion de Nicolaus Federmann le Jeune*," cap. ii. Translated by Ternaux-Compans. The original was printed at Haguenau in 1557. We here follow almost exclusively the story of Federmann himself. Oviedo does not mention Federmann's next campaign, but says that he was in Coro during the rest of Dalfinger's life. Herrera also says nothing about it. Hence his own account is our only authority.

the Rio Tocuyo in northwestern Venezuela on the 1st of October, crossed it, and went south in search of a tribe of dwarfs called the Ayemanes. He met these little people,* who, he says, averaged five "palmos," or three and a half feet in height, and were well shaped.† Thence he went south, from tribe to tribe, across the district of Barquicimeto, to the Cuybas, near Truxillo, and the Cuyones, against whom he could not make headway, and was obliged to turn toward the west. The farthest point he reached was Itabana, situated on a river which he calls the Coaheri, and which was perhaps the Apure. Here he turned back, and arrived again in Coro March 17, 1531. The material results of his journey were small. The country he passed through consisted by turns of rugged sierras and savannas. The tribes, warlike and partially cannibal, were nomadic or half-sedentary people, and his contact with them was usually of a hostile character. He obtained some gold (3000 pesos) from a tribe near Barquicimeto; and there, too, a report was current of a country rich in gold in the direction of the "Southern Sea." The whole campaign was a mere reconnaissance, but was at the same time to Federmann himself a preparatory school for his subsequent great expedition. Federmann went to Spain from Coro, and on the death of Dalfinger, shortly afterward, obtained the position of governor of Venezuela. But the Spanish colonists there protested most earnestly against his appointment, and in order to satisfy

* Probably near the present Barquicimeto.
† We should add to this that nobody but Federmann mentions these dwarfs.

them without offending the Welsers the Cardinal de Siguenza recalled him after he had started, and Georg von Speyer was sent as governor to Coro. Federmann followed him privately, and Von Speyer, appreciating his energy and knowledge of the country, made him his lieutenant, about the year 1535.

A dispute was then going on between the provinces of Venezuela and Santa Marta concerning the possession of the valley inhabited by the Pacabueyes Indians, south of Cabo de la Vela, between the lake of Maracaybo on the east and the Sierra Santa Marta on the west. In order to put an end to this contention, Georg von Speyer despatched Federmann thither, with instructions to occupy the country, hold it by force of arms against "the people of Santa Marta," and then proceed farther west. After Federmann's departure on this errand, Georg von Speyer himself began a campaign southward. He seems to have been led to this enterprise by some indefinite reports, and to have considered the expedition to the west, which he entrusted to his lieutenant, as a secondary affair. He had doubtless heard of Meta. Georg von Speyer, following a vanguard which he had sent forward, left Coro May 13, 1535, and reached the vicinity of Barquicimeto by the middle of July. He there found his vanguard in full retreat, it having been beaten by the Cuybas Indians, the same whom we met on Federmann's first journey holding the country around Tucuyo. They were a warlike tribe, and, according to Herrera, cannibals, but also gave some attention to agriculture. Von Speyer, whose whole command now consisted of three hundred and sixty-one men, with eighty horses, easily overcame the Cuybas, but his men soon felt the effects of the unhealthy climate of the country, with its rivers everywhere out of their banks, so much that he was obliged to give up the march to the south and proceed southwesterly, along the mountains on his right. Thus he followed Federmann's former route. The health of his men became so critical when among the Cuyones Indians, eight days' journey from the Cuybas, that he could go on with only one hundred foot soldiers and thirty horsemen. He left the rest of his men behind, as being in no condition to march, under Francisco de Velasco. The country east and south being flooded, he could do nothing else than follow the southwestern slope of the sierra. Occasional raids into the mountains procured maize and salt. In a short time he was joined by most of the men he had left behind, who had recovered; but soon afterward he had to leave one hundred and thirty sick under the command of Sancho de Murga. The place where this occurred was, according to Oviedo, about one hundred and seventy leagues from Coro.

With a hundred and fifty foot and forty-nine cavalry, Von Speyer reached and crossed the Rio Apure, the great northern tributary of the Orinoco, on the 2d of February, 1536. To that point we hear of no clue leading him, of no new accounts brought to him, which might have excited the hope of a liberal reward. Like Quesada, he pursued with iron tenacity a vague purpose, that of searching the south. His experiences were all discouraging. The country, though rich in its profusion of tropical vegetation, gave him no gold. The western sierra was dreary and rugged, the eastern plains were unhealthy wastes of flooded marshes and inundated woods and prairies. The vast region was only sparsely inhabited by wild Indian tribes. While the endurance, the careful direction, and wise leading which he displayed during this first period of his campaign stamp him as one of the greatest captains of the time in America, his mild and discreet behavior toward the aborigines likewise marks Georg von Speyer as a man of honorable disposition. Even the Spanish writers agree in this. Although, unhappily, too little appreciated, he is one of the noblest figures of the Spanish conquest.

Pursuing his unhopeful way toward the southwest, he crossed the upper part of the Casanare. The Zaquitios Indians inhabiting the slope of the sierra were friendly and well disposed, and told him that on the other side of the mountains, on an unwooded plateau, dwelt a tribe rich in gold, who had tame sheep. Two moons farther in that direction was a chieftain named Caziriguey, who ruled over many people, and had a great temple. While the direction in which this rich land was said to lie (west) undoubtedly pointed to Bogotá, the story of the "tame sheep" makes it certain that knowledge of Peru had penetrated to this place, which was in northeastern New Granada. The Zaquitios offered to show Georg von Speyer the pass through which he could reach that plateau, and he eagerly accepted the service. Oviedo says: "This information gratified, strengthened, and encouraged the governor and the Spaniards so much that all the hardships they had endured were forgotten, and the way lying before them appeared as safe and easy as the streets of Valladolid and Medina del Campo."

But they searched for the pass in vain. Having arrived at the foot of the sierra, they were attacked by night in a village. A desperate battle took place, and although after two hours victory rested with the whites, they gave up further advance in that direction, and again followed the slope of the mountain toward the south. They had now entered the territory of a powerful tribe of Indians, which was then widely spread between the sources of the western tributaries of the Orinoco and the Cassiquiare, but is now confined to the shores of one branch of the Rio Negro. This tribe was that of the Uaupés.

No other branch of the South American aborigines affords so complete an example of that peculiar form of social organization which Mr. Lewis H. Morgan has shown to have existed among the Indians of the whole United States, as the Uaupés. They are, and were in the sixteenth century, village Indians of a low type. Their houses, built of wood, with gable roofs supported on upright posts, form large parallelograms, one hundred and fifteen feet long, seventy-five feet wide, and thirty feet high. The entrance, eight feet high, on one of the gable sides, is curtained with a mat. Several families inhabit a communal building of this kind, and choose from among themselves the "tushaúa" or chief of the house. The Uaupés were divided into a number of *gentes* (probably about thirty), and the names of twenty-one of them are well known.*

---

* They are: Ananas; Cobéus (man-eater); Piraiurus (fish-snout); Pisas (net); Tapurus (tapir); Uaracus (fish); Tucunderas (ant); Jacamis (trumpet-bird); Mucuras (opossum); Taiassus (hog); Tijucos (mud); Arapassos (woodpecker);

The Uaupés plant and cultivate maize and manioc, and have in later times raised besides sugar-cane and tobacco. They are skilful fishermen, and their canoes, hollowed out of logs, are often forty feet long. Both sexes go entirely naked, but the men wear a crown of feathers on their heads. Their houses are also used as burial-places for the dead. They received Von Speyer in an unfriendly manner, painted in black, and opposing the Spaniards with spears, bows and arrows, and clubs, under the protection of large shields of tapir-skin; but they could not resist the firearms and cavalry of the white men.

Von Speyer was forced to make a slow retreat, more by the violent rains than by the resistance of the Uaupés. Raging torrents pouring down from the mountains in the west often prevented his movements for days at a time. He heard again there, however, the name of Meta, and learned that he was near the source of that river. He was assured that civilized tribes having much gold dwelt there, and he determined to seek those tribes first of all.

Having returned to the country of the Zaquitios, he sent a detachment farther back to bring up the rest of his troops, whom he had left in the rear, sick. But they were not found. Following the route of their commander, they had gone on to the Apure, and

Tucanas (pepper-eater); Uacarras (crane); Ipecas (duck); Gis (axe); Coua (wasp); Corocoro (green ibis); Armadillos (armadillo); Tatus; Penimbucas (ashes). These names are somewhat similar to the designations which the Iroquois chose for their gentes, and prove, by the use of the names of peculiar animals, that the tribe of the Uaupés was certainly formed or divided up within tropical America.

then, giving him up, had returned to Coro. There were left to Von Speyer one hundred and forty men and forty-four horses. With these he went forward again to the Uaupés, and finally reached the sources of the Meta. The Uaupés who inhabited this region had some gold of twenty-two carats and some fine silver, but he was told that the rich tribe he was looking for dwelled beyond that country, on the other side of the western mountains. He tried in vain to push into the mountains; their inaccessible cliffs repelled every effort. He heard here of white men who some time before had tried to reach the Meta from the east with boats.*

Georg von Speyer was persuaded by his captain, Estevan Martin, to go farther south. Bloody conflicts took place with the Uaupés before he crossed the Rio Guaviare (or Boayare). On the other side of this river, Diego de Montes, "cosmographer and a man skilled in the use of the astrolabe," determined the latitude—2° 40'. The western mountain range here took a southwesterly direction; Von Speyer was on the borders of Ecuador. The hope rose again that by proceeding along that chain he could find a pass. Estevan Martin encouraged his hopes, and the Uaupés pointed thither to the strange tribe of the Chogues as being at the gateway to the land of gold. But after crossing the Rio Caqueta (also called the Japura) in northern Ecuador, a detachment sent out under Estevan Martin to ascend that stream was attacked by the Chogues, and its leader was slain. Von Speyer at once avenged the death of his associate, and explored the course of the river to the

* This story related to the unfortunate expedition of Herrera.

mountains, but was not able to cross them anywhere. His men were now exhausted, and yielding to their entreaties and remonstrances, he began a retreat on August 10, 1537, with one hundred and thirty men, of whom hardly fifty were fit for service. He had got to one degree north of the equator, and his road, if he had succeeded in crossing the mountains, would have led him to Pasto, between Quito and New Granada.

The advance had been continued through twenty-seven months; the retreat over the same road occupied more than nine months. The Guaviare detained him several days. He was surprised to learn when near the Rio Apure that his lieutenant Federmann had been there two months before, a fact he could not account for, because he had supposed Federmann to be engaged in the northwest. Without delaying longer he continued his march, and finally arrived at Coro, May 27, 1538, after an absence of three years.

While the material returns of this extraordinary campaign (5518 pesos in gold) were so small that it must be considered a total failure as to that object, the geographical results were of great value for later times. Besides visiting all the western tributaries of the Orinoco, the llanos of Casanare and Zaguan, the northwestern branches of the Amazon, and the eastern slope of the Cordillera of Pasto, Georg von Speyer's expedition gives us our earliest data concerning the ethnography of these regions. The campaign was also of the greatest importance for the special object of our research. Ordaz, Herrera, and D'Ortal had heard the story of the riches of Meta on the lower and middle Orinoco and in western Venezuela, and had sought for them. The result of their arduous campaigns was that the treasure was not to be found in those districts, that its seat was to be sought farther west, in the mountains in which the river rises, near a great lake. Georg von Speyer had now traversed the whole of western Venezuela and western New Granada, had reached the source of the Meta, and had thereby made it evident that the story of Meta referred to the treasures of New Granada, and was the echo, in another shape, of the legend of the *dorado*, which had been transported to the lower Orinoco. The gilded chieftain had vanished from the picture, and only the indefinite idea of a tribe in the highlands rich in gold was left; to this was joined the recollection of a lake, afterward transformed into the great "lagoon of the *dorado*," which we shall find again in "Parime." While Georg von Speyer was thus unwittingly determining the true character of the myth, his able but faithless lieutenant had found the real home of the *dorado*—the plateau of Cundinamarca.

Instead of proceeding westward, as his commission required, Nicolaus Federmann had hardly learned that Von Speyer had gone south when he followed in nearly the same direction, but more toward the southeast. Arriving in the vicinity of the Orinoco east of the Apure, he met the mutinous soldiers of the troop of Geronimo D'Ortal, and incorporated them with his own company. Then he turned toward the west, crossed the Meta, went on to the foot of the mountains, and after he had ascertained that Von Speyer was retreating, pressed boldly into the sierra.

Where his chief had failed, he succeeded; he crossed over the steep mountain, and, as we have recorded in the first part of the "*Dorado*," reached the plateau of Cundinamarca. But he had come too late. Quesada, as we know, had anticipated him. Federmann bitterly deplored the fact in his letter of August 1, 1539, from Jamaica to Francisco Davila. He charged the dead Dalfinger, as well as the then still living Georg von Speyer, with incapacity and want of courage, because "they might otherwise—the one eight years, the other three years before—have secured the wealth which now the people of Santa Marta had taken." In this letter, which Oviedo has preserved in abstract, Federmann wrote: "The stories about Meta are not wholly false, for that river does rise in the mountains that border the plain; and the House of Meta which was sought for so long is the Temple of Sogamosa, the holy objects in which the people of Santa Marta have now carried away in sacks." These words of an important eye-witness prove that it was the legend of the *dorado* which, transferred to Meta, distorted and diluted in many ways and spread throughout eastern South America, stimulated the bold enterprises we have sketched. If we dwell a little longer on some of these enterprises, it is, first, because they are so little known—in no case so well known as they ought to be; and second, there is associated with them, especially to the German public, a direct interest in the deeds of the Germans in South America. We shall, in the third part of the "*Dorado*," again, and for the last time, meet Germans in pursuit of the gilded chieftain.

CHAPTER III.

OMAGUA.

THE licentiate Juan de Castellanos, in his *"Elegias de Varones Illustres de Indias"* (1589), sang the legend of the *dorado* as it was current in Quito in 1536:

> When with that folk came Annasco,
> Benalcazar learned from a stranger
> Then living in the city of Quito,
> But who called Bogotá his home,
> Of a land there rich in golden treasure,
> Rich in emeralds glistening in the rock.
>
> . . . . . .
>
> A chief was there, who, stripped of vesture,
> Covered with golden dust from crown to toe,
> Sailed with offerings to the gods upon a lake,
> Borne by the waves upon a fragile raft,
> The dark flood to brighten with golden light.

In these words of a poet who can make far more pretension to historical accuracy than his contemporaries Erxcilla and Martin de Barco * lies a significant confirmation of the thesis maintained in our chapter on Cundinamarca: that the fame of the *dorado* had penetrated southward. Belalcazar's contemporary Oviedo declares positively that much was said in those regions of a great chief called "Dorado." Herrera, although not really contemporary (he was born in 1549), but one of the best authorities con-

* The former sings in "Araucana" of Chili; the latter of La Plata in "Argentina."

cerning Spanish America, says that an Indian in La Tacunga, from Cundinamarca, told Belalcazar much concerning the wealth of that country, and of a chief reigning there, "which was the cause of many undertaking the discovery of the *dorado*, who had till then appeared to be a phantom."* Concerning the nature and form of what was said of this *dorado*, Castellanos gives us the version we have quoted, which is confirmed by Oviedo, who says:

"When I asked why this prince or chief or king was called *dorado*, the Spaniards who had been in Quito and had now come to San Domingo (of whom there were more than ten here) answered, that, according to what had been heard from the Indians concerning that great lord or prince, he went about constantly covered with fine powdered gold, because he considered that kind of covering more beautiful and noble than any ornaments of beaten or pressed gold. The other princes and chiefs were accustomed to adorn themselves with the same, but their decoration seemed to him to be more common and meaner than that of the other, who put his on fresh every morning and washed it off in the evening. . . . The Indians further represent that this cacique, or king, is very rich and a great prince, and anoints himself every morning with a gum or fragrant liquid, on which the powdered gold is sprinkled and fixed, so that he resembles from sole to crown a brilliant piece of artfully shaped gold."

While these notices afford sufficient and circumstantial evidence of the existence of the legend south of Bogotá, it is a remarkable fact that the story was

* Dec. v. lib. viii. cap. xiv.

found, in an identical form, without any connection with this, and without any local relation, on the northern coast of South America; as has been already remarked in treating of Cundinamarca.* In both cases the seat of the *dorado* was located at Cundinamarca, although in one case this lay north, and in the other case directly south. We have further seen (in the second chapter) that accounts of a golden "Meta" were spread through all northeastern South America, to the lower Orinoco. Following the footsteps of those who pursued these reports, we found their origin again to be in New Granada, in the plateau of Cundinamarca; and that story of Meta was proved to be an echo of that of the *dorado*, faintly resounding in the farther distance. Also among the aborigines of that plateau itself existed a detailed tradition of the sacred ceremonial ablution of the chief of Guatavitá.† The lake still exists on the Bahlen Páramo, and at the beginning of this century the remains of ladders were still visible, which could not have been brought to the isolated mountain-top without a purpose. Many treasures of considerable value have been taken from this lake, among them a group of golden figures of antique Indian manufacture, which we have already mentioned, and concerning which the chronicler Don Rafael Zerda says: "Undoubtedly this piece repre-

---

* Father Gumilla says likewise in "*El Orinoco ilustrado*," etc. : "Reports concerning the gilded king were current from the earliest times of the conquest at Santa Marta, as well as on the coast of Venezuela."

† As Fray Pedro Simon records in the fragment of his "*Noticias historiales*" printed by Lord Kingsborough.

sents the religious ceremony which Zamora has described, with the cacique of Guatavitá surrounded by Indian priests, on the raft, which was taken on the day of the ceremony to the middle of the lake. It may be, as some persons believe, that Siecha lagune, and not the present Puatavitá, was the place of the *dorado* ceremony and consequently the ancient Guatavitá. But everything seems to indicate that there was really once a *dorado* at Bogotá."

We refer to this fact in order to clear up as fully as possible the question of the historical probability of the *dorado*, and to prepare the way for further discussion of the subject. The personal *dorado* has vanished, but his elusive shade still floats before us. The valiant figures of the conquest, knights who were little inferior in bravery and adventurous spirit to those of the Round Table, went in pursuit of him. Their career, begun with violence, ended usually in crime, and the generation which called forth and bore the great figures of Cortés, Pizarro, Quesada, and Georg von Speyer expired in the iniquities of Carvajal and the revolting monster Lope de Aguirre. We specify the last in order to mark with his end the close of the second period of the search for the *dorado*, for in him all the passions of the conquest blazed up again into a lurid flame.

Our narrative must this time be a chronological one, beginning in the year 1535, when Sebastian de Belalcazar, freed through negotiations from the threatening presence of Alvarado, who had landed from Guatemala, was at liberty to give his mind to establishing and further extending Spanish rule in Quito. It was on an expedition which the Spaniards sent out from Quito to explore the region that Louis Daza met the Indians who told the story of the *dorado*. The immediate result of this was the slow advance of Belalcazar to the north in 1538, which took him, as we have seen, by Pasto, Popayan, Cali, etc., to the Rio Cauca, and over the cordillera to Neyva, and then to Cundinamarca—a march which is usually described as an act of insubordination on his part. It took place, at all events, without the knowledge of Belalcazar's chief, Francisco Pizarro, who was no little exasperated by it.

On the other hand, it may not have been unpleasant to the cunning, although mad, conqueror of Peru to be relieved in this way of a subordinate who was his equal in craft and not far behind him in skill and energy. He therefore immediately sent his brother, Gonzalo Pizarro, to Quito to take the chief command there.* Gonzalo was, according to his instructions, more solicitous to prevent Belalcazar's possible return than to pursue him; and when he learned, in 1539, that Pascual de Andagoya and Jorge Robledo had occupied southern New Granada (Cauca), while Belalcazar had gone on "to find the valley which was called the Valley of the Gilded One,"† he, considering himself secure against the return of his formidable companion in arms, determined upon an expedition on his own account.

* In this act he abused his powers, which only permitted him to concede the whole government of Peru at pleasure, while single districts were put under the direction of commanders who could not be changed by him. See Herrera, dec. vi. lib. iii. cap. xi., and lib. viii. cap. vi.

† Herrera, dec. vi. lib. viii. cap. vi.

A version of the *dorado* legend lay at the bottom of his motives in this undertaking. Gonzalo Diaz de Pineda had, about 1539, gone to the village of Quixos, situated southeast of Quito, in the woods of the Upper Rio Napo (called by the chroniclers of the time Rio de la Canela), and had there found the cinnamon tree (*Nectandra Cinnamomoides* of the order *Lauraceæ*).* He also heard there of the Indians— Cofanes, Jibaros, Huambayos, etc.—and further, "that there were wealthy regions, in which the people went round adorned with gold, and where there were no mountains or woods." This was a reference to the plain, a confused echo of Meta, and gave a new stimulus to the anticipation that the spices of the Orient, then monopolized by the Portuguese, might be found in America.

Gonzalo Pizarro determined, without making any closer inquiry—a trait of the times as well as of his own personality—to follow up this story. He left Quito with 220 men on foot and on horse,† and proceeded toward Zumaco, beyond the Sierra, to press thence into the thick woods which encompass all the tributaries of the Amazon east of the Andes. It would lead us too far away to follow him on his march, which is known as the "Journey to the Cinnamon Country." It was an impotent groping around in a tropical wilderness, where, surrounded by an overwhelming profusion of impenetrable vegetation, man had to give up every other purpose

---

* It was probably the black cinnamon which Balmont de Bomaré in his "*Dictionnaire d'Histoire Naturelle*" of 1765 calls "*Canelle geroflée, Capelet ou Bois de Crabe.*"

† Oviedo says 230; Zarate, 200, and 4000 Indians.

than that of maintaining himself, and might in the end consider that he had done well if he escaped with his life. All their horses perished, and also the Indians; and the condition of the miserable remnant of the troop when it appeared again, on the table-land of Quito, after two years' absence, is thus described by the contemporary Augustin de Zarate, who came to Peru in 1543 as royal treasurer: "All, the General as well as the officers and men, were nearly naked, their clothes having been rotted by the constant rains and torn besides, so that their only covering consisted of the skins of animals worn in front and behind, and a few caps of the same material. . . . Their swords were without sheaths, and all eaten up with rust. Their feet were bare and wounded by thorns and roots, and they were so wan and wasted that one could no longer recognize them. . . . They threw themselves upon the food with so much eagerness that they had to be held back and to be gradually accustomed to the taking of it."* Such was the ending of the campaign to the cinnamon country.

It would be unjust to hold Gonzalo Pizarro responsible for this failure. The numerous rivers in these forest wildernesses are the only highways practicable to man, and his plan was from the beginning to use for his further movements one of the tributaries of the Amazon—that is, one of the streams issuing from the eastern slopes of the Andes; of the existence of the Amazon itself, as well as of its magnitude, he had no knowledge. For this purpose he had ordered his lieutenant, Francisco de Orellana (a native of

* "*Historia del Descubrimiento y de la Conquista del Peru.*"

OMAGUA. 63

Truxillo in Estremadura), to follow him on the Rio Napo with a bark * and provisions. But the stream carried his unwieldy boat much faster than the men could march, who were obliged to cut their way along the shore. Hence Orellana, with fifty-three men, including two priests, was soon far in advance of the main division. It was not possible to go back against the swift current. He halted, but the longer he waited the harder his situation became. The provisions were exhausted, the bonds of subordination became relaxed, and still no signs were perceived of Pizarro, who with the best will could not overcome the impediments interposed by nature. Thus all the precautions the able commander had taken were in the end nullified.† The impression prevailed from this time ‡ that Orellana had treacherously deserted Pizarro—an impression which, in my opinion, is not well founded. The natural difficulties were of such a character that Orellana could not wait for Pizarro. His only hope for existence lay in his giving himself up to the stream for an indefinitely longer voyage. Thus Orellana went on down to the Amazon. The magnitude of the immense river increased the longer he trusted himself upon it. It is known that Orellana passed the mouth of the Amazon on his wretched vessels, and thence committing himself to the sea, arrived at Cubagua on the 11th of

---

* "*Une Barca llena de Bastimento.*"

† Fray Gaspar de Carvajal, a Dominican, who went in Orellana's voyage, says that the current was so strong that they travelled twenty-five leagues a day.

‡ On which a contemporary, Gómara, in his "*Historia General de las Indias,*" division, "*Rio de Orellana,*" lays special emphasis.

September, 1541. The accounts of the details of his remarkable voyage do not agree, and it is not germane to our purpose to discuss them. The chief result of it was that the proportions of the gigantic stream which divides South America into a northern and southern half were at last appreciated, and that exaggerated notions were spread over Europe concerning the rich countries that lay north of the Amazon. The fable of the Amazons survived from classical antiquity as one of the cycle of myths that were credited or held possible. Orellana's chronicler, the Dominican Carvajal, transplanted it to the banks of the great South American river. This has been charged against him as an offence.

If we examine his account carefully, we shall find two distinct matters in it. One, relating what he witnessed himself, is simply a statement that below the mouth of the Rio Negro women took part in the fighting against the Spaniards; and that seems very plausible. The other matter comprises the account by a captive Indian of a tribe of Amazons rich in gold living north of the river. Tales of that kind were often imposed by the natives upon the Spaniards. The story bears immediately on the object of this work only to the extent that the Amazon River henceforward formed the southern boundary of the mythical region within which the *dorado* could still find a place.*

---

* The later Peruvian fable of the Paytiti is connected, as Von Humboldt has justly remarked, with the last concerted efforts of the Inca tribe to hold its position on the upper tributaries of the Amazon, and has therefore no connection with the real *dorado* legend.

Almost contemporaneously with this hazardous expedition, the starting-point of which lay south of Cundinamarca, and immediately after the departure of Gonzalo Ximenes de Quesada from Bogotá for Spain, Quesada's brother, Hernan Perez, who had remained on the high plateau as commander, determined to attempt a campaign to the west. The occasion of this resolution * was a report that great wealth of gold, silver, and emeralds was to be found on the slopes of a mountain west of New Granada. He left New Granada on the 1st of September, 1541, with 270 men and 200 horses, and went as far as the region which Georg von Speyer had fruitlessly traversed before him—the country of the Uaupés and Chogues in northern Ecuador. Hunger and suffering were his companions, but gold, which he sought so eagerly, he did not find. He returned after sixteen months, with his object unaccomplished. He had found neither the "House of the Sun," of which his far nobler brother had heard,† nor the Amazons, although, as we have already said in "Cundinamarca," the latter myth was also current in New Granada. We only refer passingly to this unfortunate expedition, and return to Coro, on the northern coast of Venezuela, where, as we mentioned at the close of "Meta," the Germans were preparing for new enterprises in the interior.

Georg von Speyer had not been discouraged by the failure of his march to Meta, but his bodily strength was broken. Yet he had hardly arrived in

---

* Herrera, dec. vii. lib. iv. cap. xii.
† Oviedo, lib. xxvi. cap. xxx.

Coro again when he sent some of the little gold* included in the spoil to San Domingo, to buy horses and other supplies necessary for fitting out a new expedition.† But he died before he was able to begin this campaign, at Coro, probably near the end of October or the beginning of November, 1540. Oviedo says: "May God be merciful to him, for truly, though I had little to do with him, he appeared to me worthy of his office, and I believe if he had lived that God and their Majesties would have gained through him. For, besides being virtuous and prudent, he was in the prime of life, and had acquired an amount of experience that would have made him a desirable leader in other enterprises."‡

The death of Von Speyer left the Welser grant in Venezuela without a director. Such a contingency had been, however, provided for. The Bishop of San Domingo, Rodrigo de Bastidas, had authority

---

* According to Oviedo (lib. xxv. cap. xvi.), 1262 pesos for the men and 1700 pesos for Von Speyer.

† Oviedo quotes from a report of Von Speyer's dated Coro, October 9, 1538, which has not since received any attention. Possibly it no longer exists.

‡ Benzoni, "*Storia di Nuovo Mondo,*" etc., says that Von Speyer came to a tragical end, and was murdered in bed by the Spaniards. There is no further evidence on this point. Benzoni was in America, it is true, from 1541 to 1556, but his statements have not nearly the value of those of Oviedo, who was very much interested in Von Speyer, was personally acquainted with him, and would at least have spoken of such a crime with indignation, especially as Benzoni himself says the King of Spain caused the murderers to be punished. Benzoni has probably confounded Von Speyer's death with some later bloody event.

to act as administrator *ad interim* at Coro. At the end of November, 1540, that prelate, who was a man of unusual ability, went thither with 150 men and 120 horses. He perceived at once that the colony, which had never been put upon an agricultural basis, could be restored to life only through a series of brilliant campaigns. The expeditions of Von Speyer and Federmann had defined the object of these further enterprises. He could not reckon upon Federmann, who would have been a valuable aid, because he was in Spain, whence, instead of returning, he was summoned to Germany by the house of Welser & Co. to answer for his equivocal conduct. He never came to America again. Federmann, however, had left a man in his place who was in no way inferior to him in vigor, recklessness, and energy, and had besides the extraordinary gift of making himself familiar with strange languages with great ease. This man, who had gained valuable experience in Federmann's following, was Pedro de Limpias.

We name this Spanish soldier especially because he was destined finally to play the part of an evil genius in the enterprises of the Germans. Fray Pedro Simon says that it was he who brought the legend of the *dorado* to Coro; but this is contradicted by the declaration of Gumilla. His knowledge and character nevertheless made him the soul of the contemplated campaign. An immediate occasion was offered for entering upon it. Georg von Speyer had sent on one of his officers, Lope de Montalvo, with a vanguard and the direction to wait for him "in the interior." "And nothing had been heard from this captain or from his men when the bishop arrived at Coro."* To seek for Montalvo and to find the way to the wealth supposed to exist in the south formed, therefore, the object which it was determined to pursue.

As leader of the expedition, the bishop, with wise regard for the Welsers, appointed the knight Philip von Hutten of Würtemberg, who had participated in Von Speyer's expedition as a lieutenant. He was still a young man, chivalrous, noble, and frank, the idol of his men, and in many respects the worthy successor of Georg von Speyer. Beside him, Pedro de Limpias acted as his adviser; Rodrigo de Ribera was *alcalde mayor;* and Bartholomäus Welser was one of the lieutenants. Few expeditions were organized in South America with better guarantees in the capacity and knowledge of their leaders. The bishop assured himself of the concurrence of the royal revenue officers in Coro, as well as of that of Welser's factor, Melchior Grubel, or Gruber, and thus combined the wishes and interests of both of the parties who were jealously watching one another.†

Thus enjoying every condition that could assure success, Philip von Hutten left Coro in August, 1541. He had a hundred horsemen. The route, which had been laid down in writing, was the same as that of Von Speyer, except that Von Hutten was to press

---

* Oviedo.

† It appears that Welser's agents were, besides, creditors of most of the soldiers who went in this campaign, so that their interests commanded them to give the men all possible assistance, in order that they might recover what was due them.

farther on. From Burburata, whither he went by boat, he marched rapidly through Barquicimeto to the plain of the Apure, wintered there in "La Fragua," and then advanced to the borders of Ecuador, in the vicinity of the mountain range of Timana, west of the cordillera of Suma Paz. Here, where he came upon the trail of the unfortunate expedition of Hernan Perez de Quesada, the Indians tried to induce him to go eastward by telling him of a powerful, wealthy tribe which inhabited a "city" in the plain called Macotoa. Von Hutten paid no attention to these deceptive stories, but followed the trail which Quesada had left; that is, he spent nearly a year of great privation, suffering, and toil, marching in a circle, and returned, at the beginning of 1543, to the same place, near the sources of the Caqueta or Japura, whence he had set out. The steadiness his men displayed during this terrible march speaks well for his capacity as well as for his character. Yet it is not impossible that Pedro de Limpias, then still true, contributed much, by his knowledge of the country and his iron tenacity, to the holding of the men together. He probably advised them to follow Quesada's trail, if for no other reason than because he was suspicious of the representations of the natives, and did the contrary of what they advised him.

When, however, he found himself back at his original starting-place with a small company of sickly men, Von Hutten recollected what the Indians had said about the gold-rich lands in the east, and determined to go forward in that direction, accompanied by Limpias, with forty horsemen. He proceeded to the Rio Guaviare, where the Uaupés received him in a friendly manner, assisted him in crossing the river, and furnished him with provisions. Their village contained about eight hundred inhabitants. They, however, advised Von Hutten not to go farther south, for his little company was much too weak to contend with the powerful tribe that dwelt in that region. They called this tribe the Omaguas.

Orellana had arrived at an Indian settlement, the chief of which he calls Aomaguas, on the 12th of May, 1541, at San Fernando de Machiparo at the junction of the Putumayo and the Amazon.* Fray Gaspar de Carvajal, in his report preserved by Oviedo,† speaks of "the tribe or settlement of Machiparo, of which we heard from Aparia '*el grande*,' as also of another kingdom called Homaga, which was in conflict with that of Machiparo." The analogy between Homaga and Omagua can hardly be disregarded; and as the account continues, "After the latter had withdrawn from the Machiparo to pursue us, we went on eight or ten leagues farther to an elevated village which we judged to be on the border of the settlements and of the kingdom of Homaga"—the supposition is therefore not improbable that the tribe of the Omaguas inhabited, in the middle of the sixteenth century, that extensive tract which is bounded on the north by the Guaviare, on the south by the Amazon, and may have had the Cassiquiare and Rio Negro (partly) on its eastern, the Rio Uaupés and the Japura on its western borders. Herrera's remark in his introductory "*Descripcion*" (of the year 1611) is

---

* Herrera, dec. vi. lib. ix. cap. iii.
† Lib. 1. cap. xxiv..

not without significance: that "south of the province of Venezuela are the Omaguas and Omigos, with the provinces of the *dorado*." At all events, the tribe seems to have inhabited a large tract, which included in the north extensive grassy plains, and in the south the thick woods of the shores of the Amazon. The Omaguas belonged in all probability to the linguistic family of the Tupi-Guarani, and therefore to the principal division of the Brazilian aborigines. Many words in their language are undoubtedly of the Tupi idiom. Indeed, Velasco said in 1789: "This people is scattered over an extent of more than fifteen hundred leagues in the interior of America, under the names of Omaguas, Aguas, Tupis, and Guaranis." According to the Jesuit Cristoval de Acuña,[*] who visited the Amazons in the Spanish service in 1639, their name means "Aguas," or Flatheads. The Portuguese called them "Cambebas," which has the same meaning in the Tupi language. Though unanimously pronounced, even as late as 1743, physically the handsomest Indians of the Amazon shores, their figures were deformed by the custom of pressing the heads of their infant children flat between two boards. The custom had been discontinued in 1777 when the Ouvidor Ribeira visited them at Olivenza at the mouth of the Rio Yavari, thirteen leagues below Tabatinga on the Amazon.

The Omaguas appear to have been at least half-sedentary Indians. They were probably divided into two groups, according to the character of the

[*] "*El Nuevo Descubrimiento del gran Rio de las Amazonas,*" Madrid, 1664.

country they occupied: a northern group, or the Omaguas of the plains; and a southern group, or the Omaguas of the wooded river-banks. The population cannot be supposed to have been dense; certain eligible points, usually in convenient proximity to the water, were the seats of villages, between which often lay uninhabited wildernesses several days' journey in breadth. No connection between the individual settlements and no kingdom of the Omaguas can be assumed.

The southern Omaguas are the best known to us. We have already referred to Orellana's chronicler, Padre Carvajal, as indicating the boundary where, according to his view, the territory of the tribe began. At all events, the Omaguas lived in the same region of the Amazon shore from 1639 to 1852, and we can therefore accept the Dominican's account as relating to that tribe. It appears further from his description that they lived in villages built of wood, usually on elevations on the shore. In one of these villages the Spaniards found two large idols made of palm-tree bark, which were set up in the great communal house (*galpon ó casa principal*). Much earthenware, very well worked, with dark colors and "glazed," was likewise found there, besides a copper axe, "such as the Indians in Peru use." These facts indicate some degree of skill in art, and therefore a settled abode and agriculture; and this is confirmed by the acquaintance of the people with natural products. The Portuguese first obtained caoutchouc from the Omaguas, and manioc meal, cassava, and maize were abundant in their houses. But fishing appears to have been their chief industrial occupation. They were very skilful in managing and steering the pirogue; and Velasco* calls them "the Phœnicians of the Amazon." Their weapons appear to have been javelins and the peculiar slings called *estolica*, and their warriors protected themselves with wooden shields. Concerning their organization, their religious rites and customs, the writers of the sixteenth century have left us no information. Later statements on the subject are scanty and indefinite, and are of a time when their rites had suffered notable changes through the memorable efforts of the Jesuits to introduce Christianity among them.

After the Spaniards of Quito had made several efforts, partly by force of arms, partly by spiritual means, to advance down the Amazon, Fray Gaspar Cuxia in the year 1645 founded "the mission to the Omaguas, who live on the islands of the Marañon and are excellent sailors. They have the fashion of lengthening their heads by compressing the skulls of their children in a kind of press of boards."

This effort of the Society of Jesus was based upon a grand plan, unique in its way, for connecting the aborigines of South America with one another through the gradual introduction of a general language, in order to prepare a spiritual kingdom which, though in this world, would not be for the world of that age, but should form in future centuries a point of support, or perhaps a place of refuge. Without dwelling on the particular features of this great religio-political missionary enterprise, we sim-

---

* "*Historia del reyno de Quito.*"

ply mention a Bohemian, Father Samuel Fritz, who gained the special title of "The Apostle of the Omaguas." He was born in Bohemia in 1650, and in 1687 founded seven mission stations among these Indians—San Joaquin, Nuestra Señora de Guadalupe, San Pablo, San Cristoval, San Francisco Xavier, Traguatua, and a seventh station which included twenty-seven small villages. Father Fritz spent fifty years on the forest-shores of the Amazon, shirking no danger, and died, one of the grandest figures in American missionary history, at the age of eighty years, among the Jeberos, in 1730. The constant attacks of the Portuguese hindered the prosperity of these colonies to an extraordinary degree. The suppression of the Society of Jesus at last terminated their existence, and the settled Indians went speedily to destruction. La Condamine visited the Omaguas at San Joaquin in 1743, and praised their industry and artistic skill. When Lieutenant Herndon visited them in 1852 there were only two hundred and thirty-two individuals left of the once numerous tribe.

Our knowledge of the northern group of the Omaguas is of the most indefinite character. All we have is derived from the reports of Philip von Hutten's expedition. We therefore take up again the thread of the story at the point where the German knight went on in the face of the warnings of the Uaupés, with only forty mounted men, in search of the Omaguas.

The little troop went southward in the best practicable order. They soon came to cultivated fields, in which natives were working. The Uaupés explained they were slaves, cultivating and taking care of the plantations of the Omaguas. They offered no resistance, and the white men hurried forward to surprise the "city" which was supposed to be in the vicinity. Looking down from the top of a hill, they observed a settlement of considerable extent, regularly laid out, with large dwellings, and a high structure amidst them. The view was a surprise. Convinced by it that this was the long-sought city and that the high building was the "palace" of the gilded chieftain, the Spaniards rode full speed down the hill; simultaneously the war drum sounded from out the village, and armed soldiers rushed into the streets and opposed the assailants with wild cries, letting fly a shower of missiles against them. Von Hutten at once saw that he could not accept battle on this ground. He therefore withdrew in good order to a level spot, hoping that he might find there compensation for his inferiority in numbers in the superior weight of his cavalry. Although pursued, he reached the position he sought without great difficulty. The sun had set, and the Omaguas remained quiet during the night. On the next morning they appeared again in great masses—fifteen thousand strong, Fray Pedro Simon asserts, and after him Gumilla; and their attack was so fierce as to occasion the most serious apprehensions. The contest was too unequal. One cavalry attack after another was repulsed, and Pedro de Limpias, who was in the lead everywhere, was wounded. At length the little troop struggled no longer for victory, but for life. With unexampled bravery a few leaders finally succeeded in forcing their way through, and with the remnant of their men reaching the settlements of the Uaupés, when the pursuit by the Omaguas ceased.

Although the unfortunate ending of the campaign against the Omaguas made further progress impracticable, the leaders of the expedition still believed they had obtained an important result. Their excited fancy discerned a great city in the large village of the Omaguas, and in the communal house that occupied the middle of the town the castle or palace of a powerful prince. Such illusions have often occurred in America, and the mere introduction of a European terminology into the domain of the ethnology of the new continent has occasioned a serious confusion which can only be gradually cleared up. In the eyes of Von Hutten and his companions that great settlement could only be the kingdom of the gilded chieftain, and they comforted themselves for their disaster in the fancy that they had at last found the seat of the long-sought *dorado*.

Philip von Hutten had received a serious wound in the battle, which necessitated a longer stay with the Uaupés. The examination of the wound was performed in a singular manner. An aged war prisoner of the Uaupés was dressed in the armor of the knight and set upon his horse. He was then wounded by an Indian in the same way as Von Hutten had been. The flesh was then cut about the wound, the course of which was thus determined upon the poor victim. The Uaupés inferred that Von Hutten's wound was of similar shape, and treated it upon that supposition.

In the meantime, and before Von Hutten could even begin the retreat, Pedro de Limpias, as the oldest captain, demanded the position of commander. It cannot be denied that in consideration of his experience and knowledge he was entitled to it. But Bartholomäus Welser, as a son of the family which had leased Venezuela, seems to have thought otherwise; and although we have no exact account of what took place, it is certain that a bitter quarrel arose between the old Spanish soldier and the young son of the German merchant. It is easily conceivable that Von Hutten would ultimately incline to the side of his German companion in arms. The little troop, nursing the germ of strife within itself, began, probably in 1544, the retreat, directly toward Coro. The usual difficulties attended their march, but the accustomed order does not seem to have prevailed. It soon became evident that the troop was divided. At last Pedro de Limpias abruptly took leave of it and hastened forward to the coast. His departure left Von Hutten without a captain. Bartholomäus Welser, it is true, commanded a small advance-guard, but he was little acquainted with the region. In the meantime, Limpias hurried on, occupied with thoughts of revenge: with the intention of going to Coro in order to bring about the downfall of the Germans and of their rule in Venezuela.

Philip von Hutten had now been absent four years from the settlement on the seacoast, and in that time events there had taken a turn very favorable to the plans of the revengeful Spaniard. After Von Hutten was sent to the south in the year 1541, and their main support was thereby taken from the Germans (even to the Factor), Bishop Bastidas returned to the Antilles. He left Diego de Boiça as his representative in Coro, who, however, was soon obliged to flee to Honduras on account of his misdemeanors. The chief court of justice (*Audiencia*) next appointed as *alcalde mayor* Enrique Remból, who, with a wasteful expenditure of the Welsers' property, brought a hundred men from Cubagua, and thus contributed somewhat to the encouragement of the settlement. The office was held after his death by Bernardino Manso and Juan de Bonilla, who both had, however, to seek safety in flight from the consequences of their misdeeds. Finally, in order to prevent the ruin of the colony, the licentiate Frias was in 1545 appointed controlling inquisitorial judge, and the licentiate Juan de Carvajal governor, of the Province of Venezuela. The latter appointment was significant of the intention of the Spaniards to terminate the contract with the Welsers. Frias remained on the island of Margarita, while Carvajal proceeded to Coro.

The new governor was a man of indubitable ability and vigor, but unprincipled and violent. His first important transaction was an act of formal disobedience. In the course of three months he by persuasion or intimidation induced the more active part of the population to leave Coro, and taking their property, to follow him across the country to New Granada, where he promised them wealth which the Venezuelan coast could not afford them. His adherents first plundered those who remained behind, and then, having collected their domestic animals, set forth on their migration. The route lay southward, along the plains, avoiding the woods.

Carvajal halted at Tocuyo, among the Cuybas Indians, in a pleasant and fertile region, favorable to agriculture and cattle-raising; and the fact that he began a settlement there speaks well for his judgment. He collected about two hundred well-armed men at Tocuyo, whose devotion to himself he assured by skilfully anticipating and gratifying their unrestrained passions and wants. The inquisitorial judge, Frias, proceeded to Coro to call the governor to account, but in the ruinous and plundered condition of the colony he had no means of making his authority felt. Carvajal therefore remained undisturbed in Tocuyo, stamped by his own acts as a rebel against the Spanish Crown, and the sworn enemy of the Welsers and their representatives.

Such was the man whom Pedro de Limpias met on his way as he was hastening to Coro, filled with hatred and thirsting for vengeance against the Germans. Limpias came into Tocuyo at night with six soldiers, called upon Juan de Villegas, one of Carvajal's officers, and represented himself to be a fugitive from the Germans, who were on the way to Coro to offer themselves to the judge there. This was sufficient to alarm all Tocuyo, for such a union of Von Hutten's tried soldiers with the inquisitorial judge's weak force would be highly dangerous to Carvajal. It seemed necessary to stop their march, to remove their leader by stratagem or force, and win over his men to their side.

Pedro de Limpias, at all events, gave his counsel in favor of the execution of this purpose. First, the advance-guard under Bartholomäus Welser must be captured. It had already reached Barquicimeto, north of

Tocuyo. Juan de Villegas met it there, and as Philip von Hutten had not come with it, two written messages were sent to him representing that Welser was waiting for him at Tocuyo. Thinking of nothing else than that his companion in arms was bringing him reënforcements, Von Hutten hurried on with his troop of sixty men to Barquicimeto. To his no little astonishment he was informed by Villegas that Governor Juan de Carvajal summoned him to appear at once before him, otherwise "he would come for him with fifty horse." The threatening tone of this message was clear enough, but Von Hutten was the weaker party and he thought it best to temporize and to submit, at least in appearance, to the "governor." Carvajal received him with a show of friendliness, prepared a feast for him, and tried to dissuade him from going to Coro. If he would stay with him he would show him a valley where much gold could be got, by the use of which reënforcements could be obtained from Cubagua and Margarita. The German knight did not directly refuse this invitation, but pleaded his duty to the emperor. If this required it he would stay where they were; but nothing could prevent him from defending himself before the imperial judge in Coro.

In the meantime the rest of the troops had arrived at Tocuyo. The two camps or parties had, as it were, coalesced. The moment seemed favorable for striking a decisive blow. On the second day of Von Hutten's presence Carvajal proclaimed orders early in the morning that all of the soldiers of the former should report themselves to him. The German knight, greatly astonished at this assumption, hurried to the house of the governor, whom he met at the door. He remonstrated with him and repeated his former declaration, that he was ready to account to "the king, the judge, and the Welsers" for what he had done. Carvajal had been waiting for the mention of the Welsers, and he used the occasion to call out aloud, "You are witnesses that he says this province belongs to the Welsers," hoping by this means to excite the animosity of the Spaniards against the Germans and provoke an immediate conflict. The passage of words between the leaders brought the soldiers to the spot. Carvajal ordered a notary (a necessary accompaniment of all Spanish expeditions) to draw up a warrant against Von Hutten. He protested, and both drawing their swords, appealed to the king. They were separated, but the men of the two leaders ranged themselves under their respective banners; two hostile camps ready for battle confronted one another—and Carvajal's plan to separate the leader from his soldiers had failed. In the conflict, Bartholomäus Welser rushed three times against Carvajal with upraised lance. His exhausted, famished horse failed him the third time, else, Herrera says, he would certainly have killed the "tyrant." He fled to his house, and the approach of night put an end to further action.

On the next morning Philip von Hutten escaped from the trap that had been set for him in Tocuyo, and collected his men on the llanos of Quiborc. Carvajal now tried negotiations. Priests and Welser's factor, Melchior Grubel, served as emissaries. It was finally agreed that Carvajal and his officers should swear peace and permit the Germans to go unmolested to Coro. With this assurance Von Hutten started thither, accompanied by his men.

It was often the case at that time, and in those wild, thinly inhabited regions, that two war parties could march one a short distance behind the other without knowing anything of each other. As soon as Von Hutten had started Carvajal followed upon his track, being probably guided by Limpias. The Germans went on in fancied security, not suspecting they had anything to fear, and apparently even neglecting the usual measures of precaution. Carvajal fell upon their sleeping camp on the night of the seventh day, and his officers, who had with him a little while before sworn peace with Von Hutten, seized the German knight in his bedroom. After the leaders had been captured the men surrendered without resistance.

By this act of perfidy Ulrich von Hutten and Bartholomäus Welser were now helpless prisoners. An old Spanish proverb says, "When the dog is dead the madness is over." Carvajal, therefore, did not wait long. He called a council of war at dawn to determine what the fate of the prisoners should be; they were promptly sentenced to death. Before the sun had set both the German knights were brought bound into the midst of the Spanish camp, and, together with two of their associates, were beheaded with a rusty *machete* that had been used a short time before for cutting wood.

Shortly after this tragical event the licentiate Juan Perez de Tolosa came to Coro as a representative of the weak inquisitorial judge Frias. He was an earnest, conscientious, inflexible, strict man. He collected the few soldiers that could be found on the coast, and fearlessly went with them in 1546 to meet Carvajal. He succeeded, notwithstanding the superiority of Carvajal's force, in arresting him without resistance, and in a few days Von Hutten's murderer was publicly beheaded at Tocuyo. Of the further fortunes of Pedro de Limpias we are not able to speak.

Although by this act of justice a kind of atonement was offered to the Germans, their rule in Venezuela wholly ceased from this time. It had lasted eighteen years, and had, it must be admitted, contributed very little to the development of the colonies. Robertson justly remarks that under the direction of such persons as the Welsers it might have been expected that a settlement would be founded on a plan different from that of the Spaniards, and more favorable to the advancement of those useful industries which commercial proprietors recognize as the most direct sources of prosperity and wealth. The failure to fulfil these expectations is ascribed by Robertson to the mistakes and misconduct of individual German leaders in Venezuela. His designation of these men as adventurers, who in their impatience thought of nothing but of snatching wealth, fits Ambrosius Dalfinger very well, and Federmann to a certain extent, although the latter was too prudent fully to come under it. But we cannot affix such a reproach to the grand and richly endowed nature of Georg von Speyer or the noble and knightly personality of Philip von Hutten. The cause of the lamentable failure lies in the nature of the transaction itself, in the way in which the possession of Venezuela was conveyed to the Welsers. They received the province from the Spanish Crown, not so much in the form of a leasehold as of a mortgage security for money loaned, and as commercial men their first object was to recover the advances they had made as quickly as possible from the revenues of the district. Whatever they might gain after that would be "good business." Their representatives acted in their interest as seen from this point of view.

The coast lands of Venezuela offered no hope of a profitable result; but golden reports came from the interior, and, clad in the alluring dress of the *dorado* legend, led the Germans on to those useless and destructive expeditions of which we have just described the last one. In pursuit of the gilded chieftain Dalfinger conducted his fatal campaign of desolation; after him Federmann pressed fruitlessly into New Granada; in the chase for the echo of the *dorado* in "Meta" Von Speyer sacrificed his fine troop and his own precious person; in the final effort to grasp the phantom were extinguished Von Hutten's young life and the last spark of the manhood and vigor of the colony. When we give close attention to the history of the German settlement in Venezuela, the importance of the part played in it by the *dorado* appears very clearly.

We have already shown that Von Hutten came back persuaded that he had really seen the home of the gilded chieftain in the country of the Omaguas. Henceforth, therefore, Omagua becomes nearly synonymous with the *dorado*, and the legend is localized near the Amazon, west of the Rio Negro and Cassiquiare. Oviedo had already placed it there at the time of the death of Philip von Hutten. Von Hutten's unhappy fate, the complete extinction of the settlement at Coro, the threatened depopulation of the Venezuelan peninsula, precluded any further thought of an expedition into the interior southward. The Brazilian coast, hardly touched at a few points by the Portuguese, was too far from the unknown interior, which was concealed in immense forests. The western coasts, particularly those of New Granada and of Peru, where the Amazon begins its course, not only lay geographically nearest to the region in question, but were also the seat of the strongest and richest settlements of the Spaniards in South America, the only ones from which any campaigns could now be undertaken.

But although the population had rapidly increased under the stimulus of the rich metallic treasures found in the country, events occurred, especially in Peru, which made further expeditions impossible for many years. The civil disturbances in Peru provoked in the extreme south by the conflict between Pizarro and Almagro concerning the limits of their respective jurisdictions culminated in bloodshed at Las Salinas near Cuzco, on the 26th of April, 1538. Hardly three months afterward, Almagro was strangled by Pizarro's command. An unbroken succession of betrayals and crimes, to which nearly all the conquistadors of importance fell victims (thereby expiating their own offences), marked the progress of the insurrection, till it reached such a height as to overshadow the whole west coast, like a dark cloud, from Chili to Popayan. And when, in consequence of the new laws and ordinances issued by the Spanish Crown for the protection of the aborigines, this cloud began to unload itself in a storm of open revolt against the mother-country; when Gonzalo Pizarro, urged by his lieutenant Carvajal,* refused obedience; when the viceroy Blasco Nuñez de Vela had fallen at Añaquito in Ecuador on the 18th of January, 1546, and the insurrectionists prevailed from Popayan to Atacamata—then the threatening storm loomed also over the southern horizon of New Granada, and the stunning reverberations of the thunders of revolt reached the heart of Cundinamarca. It was no time for daring expeditions into the mythical interior; every force had to be used for self-preservation. In this period a man came upon the stage of history in New Granada who was to be especially associated with the phantom of the gilded chieftain. He was Don Pedro de Ursua, a young knight from Pampluna, in the kingdom of Navarre. He was the nephew of the royal judge Miguel Diaz de Armendariz, and arrived with him in New Granada in the year 1545. Armendariz came to the "new kingdom" as inquisitorial judge, "*Juez de Residencia,*" and appointed his nephew his "lieutenant."

* The third of the able monsters of that name who lived in South America in the middle of the sixteenth century.

CHAPTER IV.

THE EXPEDITION OF URSUA AND AGUIRRE.

THE government of Bogotá and Santa Marta was lodged in 1542 in the hands of Alonzo de Lugo, a son of the former overseer of Gonzalo Ximenes de Quesada, the conqueror of Cundinamarca. With reckless greed Lugo had levied contributions on the province, plundered the original Spanish conquerors, and robbed the royal treasury. When he learned that a royal inquisitorial judge had been sent to Bogotá he hastily gathered up his spoil—300,000 ducats, according to Joaquin Acosta—and fled to Europe, where he died in Milan. Armendariz, having at first enough to do at Cartagena in hearing the numerous complaints against Lugo, despatched his nephew Pedro de Ursua into the interior. The latter established himself in Bogotá without opposition, and summarily arrested Lope Montalbo de Lugo, who had remained there as the deputy of the fugitive governor. Armendariz himself occupied the capital of New Granada in the year 1546, while Ursua became his military aid, although he was then only twenty years old.

The sedentary Indian tribe of Cundinamarca, the Muysca, had been completely subjugated, but numerous hordes of warlike, cannibal natives still roamed around their territory. These rovers by their constant attacks endangered the settlements of the

Muysca and the Spanish colony itself. Their subjugation was therefore a necessity for the prosperity of the "new kingdom," and seemed the more desirable because the gold which the Muysca possessed came from the regions inhabited by them. Already, under Lugo's wretched administration, the captain Vanegas had chastised the Panches in the west and conquered their country, but northwest of Bogotá the Musos still roamed in the extensive forest flats and grassy prairies, and their predatory attacks threatened to depopulate the district of Tunja. Ursua had led an expedition to the northeast in 1548 and founded the settlement of Pampluna. On his return to Bogotá from this expedition (which is commonly spoken of as a "*dorado* journey") the proposition was made to him, by the three royal judges who now ruled New Granada in place of his deposed uncle, to subjugate the Musos.

The knight, now twenty-three years old, advanced confidently into the enemy's territory with one hundred and fifty men. So rapid were his movements that he assailed a fortified camp in the middle of the region before the Musos could collect their forces. A bitter war of extermination followed. Unable to repel the well-armed Spaniards by direct attacks, the savages swarmed daily around their camp, and tried to starve them out by burning their own crops. Ursua held his position and finally forced the Musos to negotiate; but when a large number of chiefs had come to him to conclude the treaty, he induced them to go inside of his tent, where they were murdered to the last man. He hoped by an act of such surpassing terror to paralyze the force of the tribe; but the war only broke out again all the more furiously, and as soon as Ursua returned to Bogotá the Spaniards were expelled and the settlement of Tudela was laid in ashes by the natives. Notwithstanding the crime he had committed, Ursua obtained the position of chief-justice in Santa Marta. He subdued the Tayronas Indians in 1551 and 1552, but he did not remain long in New Granada, for his mind had been turned toward Peru, and he went to Panamá. He waited there till Don Andreas Hurtado de Mendoza, Marquis of Cañeta, viceroy of Peru, began his journey to Lima. The environs of Panamá and the Isthmus were then kept in a state of insecurity by bands of fugitive negroes (Cimarrones), and the perplexed municipality of the city were looking for a capable soldier who could deliver them from the plague. The story of Ursua's deeds was known to the viceroy, and he recommended him to the officers. Ursua exterminated the blacks in a two years' "bush war," and then, in 1558, followed the Marquis of Cañeta to Peru.

Ten years previous to this the licentiate Pedro de la Gasca had suppressed the great Peruvian insurrection. Two later uprisings—those of Sebastian de Castilla in 1552 and of Francesco Hernandez Giron in 1554—had been likewise suppressed by the adherents of the Crown; but quiet was not yet fully established. A considerable number of men were living in Peru, Bolivia, and Ecuador who witnessed the return of order with a dissatisfaction that was well founded, because their past would not bear an examination in the light of the law. The number of this "disorderly rabble" was so large that the new viceroy did not rely upon the mere exercise of force against them, but was considering upon the ways and means of removing the dangerous element from Peru by means of a campaign into distant regions.

The unknown lands east of the Andes offered the only objective point for such a campaign. Chili, New Granada, and the banks of the La Plata were already occupied by the Spaniards, and it was desirable to send the expedition only to some point where it could disturb no already existing colony, and whence the danger of its returning to Peru would be small. Then, very opportunely, by a curious accident, the legend of the *dorado* again rose in Peru.

Pedro de Cieza of Leon says in the seventy-eighth chapter of his "*Cronica del Peru*": "In the year of the Lord 1550 there came to the city of La Frontera . . . more than two hundred Indians. They said that since leaving their home a few years before they had wandered through great distances, and had lost most of their men in wars with the inhabitants of the country. As I have heard, they also told of large and thickly populated countries toward the rising sun, and said that some of them were rich in gold and silver." Cieza was in Peru from 1547 till 1550, and his statement is fully corroborated by a contemporary, Toribio de Ortiguera, who came to South America at the latest in 1561. It appears from the manuscript of the latter, entitled "*Jornada del Marañon*," that these Indians originally lived on the Brazilian coast, near the mouth of the Amazon. They had started between 2000 and 4000 strong, under the lead of a chief named Viraratu, accompanied by two Portuguese, and sailed into the Amazon and up that river, amid hard-fought battles with the shore-dwellers, to the borders of Peru. Their appearance aroused great interest amongst the Spaniards. Fray Pedro Simon says of the event: "Those Indians brought accounts from the province of the Omaguas, which Captain Francisco de Orellana mentioned when he went down the Marañon River. . . . In that province, of which the Indians told when they came into Peru, lived the gilded man."* Thus the idea of the *dorado* was awakened anew.

In the disordered condition of the country years passed before an expedition to the golden land of the Omaguas could be contemplated. The Marquis of Cañete readily perceived how favorable an occasion this story of the Brazilian visitors and the "*dorado* fever" it excited afforded him. After a personal interview with the Indians he proceeded energetically with preparations for an expedition to the shores of the Middle Amazon. Drafts were made upon the royal treasury for this object. The disorderly elements in the country seized the occasion with not less eagerness than the viceroy to secure for themselves an unmolested withdrawal; and thus the *dorado*, which had provoked the conquest of New Granada and had brought the colony of Venezuela to the verge of destruction, was this time the beneficent messenger of rest to Peru.

A campaign of this kind required a strong leader. The choice of the Marquis of Cañete fell upon Pedro

* "*Noticias historiales*," Part I., Noticia VI., cap. i.

de Ursua, who readily accepted the dangerous commission. Besides several other rewards he was to receive, in case of success, the title and all the rights of a governor of the countries expected to be conquered and settled.

A whole year passed before the preparations were completed, and it was not till the spring of 1560 that Ursua collected his men at Santa Cruz de Capacoba, on the Rio Llamas, a branch of the Huallaga, where he had had boats built for the voyage to the Amazon and upon it. It was really a "picked company" that met there. The scum of Peru formed the principal part of it; the majority, men accustomed to everything except order and morals; and with them were women.

To lead such a rabble with success in the face of uncertainties required an earnest and prudent, and at the same time a decided, character of moral worth. Ursua was frivolous and indolent, and often rashly bold. His preparations were incomplete. Much was still lacking when his money had all been spent, and his men were eager to embark. With the help of some officers—"all doughty champions with elastic consciences," says Simon—Ursua forced the priest of Santa Cruz to "lend" him all his ready money, some four or five thousand pesos. By this act he set the example of violence.

He likewise furnished an example of immorality from the beginning. He kept up a close relation with Iñez de Atienza of Pinira (near the coast), the young and beautiful widow of Pedro de Arcos. Without heeding the counsels of his friends, he took his mistress with him on this campaign in search of the *dorado*, and lived with her so intimately that the chronicler feels impelled to make the remark, in excuse, that "they all said, indeed, that he intended at some later time to marry Iñez de Atienza."

While the start was delayed, in consequence of the defects in Ursua's preparations, trouble was brewing in the camp. It culminated in crime—the murder of Ursua's lieutenant, Pedro Ramiro. Ursua's behavior in this affair (he drew the perpetrators of the murder from their hiding-places by promising them immunity and then in the face of his pledge had them arrested and hung) made him personal enemies. With the other elements of discontent among the men were now associated hatred and vindictiveness against their leader.

On the first day of July, 1560, Juan de Vargas was able to go forward with an advance guard in a brigantine to the mouth of the Rio Ucayali. The main body, increased by the colonists of Moyobamba with their goods, should have followed at once, but of all the fleet only three flatboats and one brigantine were seaworthy; the other vessels were unavailable. It was necessary to build rafts and canoes. The embarkation could not be effected till September 26th, when it took place in great confusion. The available space in the boats was unevenly allotted; only forty out of three hundred horses were taken; and all the cattle were left, without masters, on the shore. The flotilla at last moved slowly down along the thickly wooded shores of the Rio Huallaga. It sailed three hundred leagues, according to Pedro Simon (vi.), without passing in sight of a single Indian hut. Harmony among the men was not promoted by their getting under way. Every one appeared dissatisfied and envious of the others, while most of them censured Pedro de Ursua. At the mouth of the Ucayali they came upon the advance expedition under Juan de Vargas; the men were nearly famished in the midst of the richest vegetation. Their vessel had rotted, and it was necessary to distribute them among those who crowded the other already overloaded boats. Fresh discontent arose over this measure, and the dissatisfaction was increased by the fact that Ursua always claimed a full share of room for himself and Iñez de Atienza. At last settlements were reached above the mouth of the Rio Napo, in which were found maize, sweet potatoes, beans, and other vegetables. At one of these places the flotilla landed, and the boats were repaired and rebuilt. Some of the Brazilian Indians who had given the original motive to the expedition and who accompanied it as guides pointed farther eastward as the direction of the rich country of which they were in search. The Ticunas, indeed, on the southern side of the Amazon (between the Ucayali and the Yavari) possessed some gold, but the *dorado* lived north of that river. The fleet therefore sailed on, despite the murmurs of the men, who had become tired of the constant promises and deceptions.

Before Christmas of 1560 Ursua reached Machiparo, where he was near the country of the Omaguas. Encouraged by the extent of the Indian settlements he found there, and by the friendly demeanor of the inhabitants, he determined to make a longer sojourn at that place, for his crews were worn out by their labor, especially by rowing. The men were glad to resign themselves to rest on the shore, but their idleness also gave them leisure to consider and mature criminal plans. Besides their dissatisfaction with Ursua's leading, personal hatred, and many worse passions, thoughts of wider bearing lay at the bottom of their schemes.

Some of the members of the band had divined the secret thoughts of the viceroy of Peru, or had joined the expedition while realizing the improbability of the *dorado* legend, in order to use it for their own purposes. It is only certain that a conspiracy against Ursua was formed at Machiparo. He and his lieutenant were to be killed, and Fernando de Guzman, a young knight from Seville and the ensign of the campaign, was to be chosen commander in Ursua's place. Under his direction they would return to Peru and with armed hand conquer the country, expel the royal officers, and establish a new kingdom there. The soul of this conspiracy was the Biscayan Lope de Aguirre.

Born at Oñate in Biscay, Aguirre was then about fifty years old. He had spent twenty years in Peru, chiefly in the occupation of a horse-trainer. Involved in all kinds of violent and seditious acts, he had been several times condemned to death and then pardoned, and having become at last a fugitive from province to province, was glad of the opportunity to join Ursua's expedition. He is described as having been "small and spare in figure, ugly, . . . with black beard and an eagle eye, which he turned straight upon others, particularly when he was angry." Burning through and through with hatred against the Spanish Government, at home, at the same time, in all circles and ranks, endowed with remarkable shrewdness and great physical and mental force—a logical and impressive speaker, withal—with clearly defined purposes, he was in every respect a dangerous man. He was the most detestable character of the conquest.

Even before the beginning of the voyage earnest warnings against Aguirre had reached Ursua, but the indiscreet knight had disregarded them. The Biscayan had abundant leisure to intrigue with the men. Ursua was so blind as to allow the conspiracy to be organized under his eyes, without regarding the plainest evidences of it. On the 26th of December he embarked again and proceeded six or eight leagues farther to another village. Here a broad path led from the shore into the interior; a landing was effected, and a camp formed. "The path," it was said, "led to a large city and province;" the Spaniards had, in fact, entered the territory of the Omaguas. A strong detachment started out "to explore the new country"—by which the most faithful soldiers were removed from the camp, and the conspirators were given the opportunity they had been waiting for.

On the first day of January, 1561, two hours after sunset, a well-armed party, with Alonzo de Montoya and Cristóval de Chavez at its head, came into Ursua's quarters. He was lying in the hammock and speaking with a page. Surprised, he asked them, "What are you looking for here at so late an hour?" and was answered with a number of scattering shots. Before he could put himself on guard the whole band pressed in upon him, and with the cry, "*Confessio, confessio, miserere mei Deus!*" he fell to the ground and expired. The murderers hastened out, one of them crying aloud, "Liberty, liberty! Long live the king, the tyrant is dead!" The alarm brought Juan de Vargas, Ursua's lieutenant, to the place. He was immediately prostrated, and the conspirators returned to the hut that served as the quarters of Fernando de Guzman.

Dismay and terror prevailed in the camp. Those not in the conspiracy stood surprised and helpless before the numerous and well-armed murderers. These took advantage of the confusion to remove on the next morning a few other of Ursua's friends. A general meeting was then compulsorily assembled, in which Fernando de Guzman was without opposition proclaimed governor. New appointments of officers were made all around. Aguirre received the second highest place, with the rank of a *maestro del campo*.

The conspirators did not agree as to their further proceedings. The larger number, of whom Fernando de Guzman was the leader, would not give up the *dorado*. A second general meeting was called. Against the earnest opposition of Aguirre and Lorenzo de Salduendo, the view of the majority prevailed, and a continuance of the campaign was determined upon. A paper was drawn up in which Ursua's death was excused as being a necessity, and was signed by those present. Aguirre joined in the signature, and wrote with a firm hand, "Lope de Aguirre, the traitor." Murmurs were uttered audibly against this act, and Aguirre answered defiantly: "You have killed the representative of the king among us, the bearer of his power; do you think that this writing will exculpate you? Do you suppose that the king and his judges do not know what such papers are worth? We are all traitors and rebels, and even if the new country should be ten times as rich as Peru, more populous than New Spain, and more profitable to the king than the Indies, our heads are at the order of the first licentiate or pettifogger who comes among us with royal authority."

This speech was shrewdly calculated, and was based on known facts which were extremely unpleasant to most of the men. The meeting broke up in disorder; even the conspirators were now divided into two parties. Aguirre had on his side the active and determined mutineers. His unexampled audacity dazzled many and also made him many enemies, but he carried his point, for he was the only one among the reckless, disorderly adventurers who was seeking to execute a clearly defined purpose.

The first thing to be done was to divert the band from the pursuit of the *dorado*. When his powers of persuasion failed to be of effect in this attempt, Aguirre built upon the knowledge of the men. The reconnoitring party which Ursua had sent out came back with the report that the path which they followed led to some abandoned huts, and that the thick woods prevented further advance. The company then reimbarked and went on. The shores of the Amazon were solitary and deserted; for weeks they saw no signs of men. Food became scarce; the horses were killed and eaten, and thus all possibility of an advance overland was taken away. The spirit of license grew more and more rife under these toils and privations. Aguirre secretly made use of the demoralization to remove the most influential men under various pretexts, and to put in their places persons in whom he could perceive willing tools. Fernando de Guzman permitted these crimes, for he was himself only a tool in the Biscayan's hands, and was even so infatuated as to call the monster "father." When at length the Brazilian Indians confessed that they knew nothing of this country, and that it was not like the one they had previously passed through, Guzman concurred in Aguirre's plan to give up the *dorado* and invade Peru.

A halt of three months took place above the mouth of the Japura, and there it was determined at a general meeting to sail down the river to the sea. Margarita was to be secured by a sudden attack; thence Nombre de Dios and Panamá should be surprised; and once in possession of Panamá, the Europeans believed that the success of their scheme would be assured. This audacious plan was so attractively presented by Aguirre that a formal declaration of independence of Spain was drawn up, from which only three men ventured to withhold their signatures. Only one of these escaped death —the bachelor Francisco Vasquez, afterward historian of the campaign. Aguirre having thus succeeded in the first part of his design, it remained for him to acquire exclusive control of the expedition. A series of murders had relieved him of the officers most in his way, and the time had now come for Fernando de Guzman to fall. Knowing the ambitious character of the young Sevillan, he decided to exalt him to such a height that a fall should in any event be destructive. With absurd ceremonies Guzman was therefore proclaimed "Prince and King of the mainland and of Peru." The puppet-play did not fail of its anticipated effect. Guzman, naturally courteous and therefore beloved, after this became proud and imperious, and surrounded himself with a silly ceremonial, which was unpleasant to the men. They soon ceased to love him; he was disliked, avoided, and finally hated; and his fall became a question only of time and opportunity.

The three months' halt above the Japura was devoted to the building of two new brigantines of stronger construction for the contemplated sea voyage. When they were completed the company embarked upon them, and started, before Easter of 1561, down the river. Evidences of a numerous population were apparent on the right shore; and when the Indian guides said that wealthy tribes lived there, Aguirre, fearing that the thought of the *dorado* might be aroused again, contrived to change the course of the voyage. According to Simon,* he conducted the flotilla "through a bend into an arm of the river on the left side." Simon's account is based on the manuscript testimony of the eye-witness Vasquez, and he continues: "Therefore Aguirre determined to turn out of the direct way; and after they had gone three days and one night in a westerly direction, they came to some vacant huts." This took place above the mouth of the Rio Negro, and it indicates, as Mr. Clements R. Markham likewise

* Cap. xviii.

supposes, that the band left the continuous course of the Amazon and went through one of the numerous bayous that form a network of channels between the Japura and the Rio Negro, into the latter river. Von Humboldt and Southey are, on the other hand, of the opinion that Aguirre sailed down the Amazon to its mouth.

Yet that station of "some vacant huts" appears to have been situated, not on the main stream, but on a northern tributary.

The forsaken Indian town, surrounded by muddy water, in which the band found quarters while it consumed its scanty provisions, plagued day and night by clouds of mosquitoes, was a sorry stopping-place in which to spend the Easter season in idleness. Aguirre thought the place and the opportunity favorable for striking his last blow. Fernando de Guzman was ripe for his fall. Few of the men still adhered to him. But his death was to be preceded by those of two other persons whom Aguirre still feared. They were his former associate, Lorenzo de Salduendo, and Iñez de Atienza. This woman had soon forgotten her lover Ursua, and yielded herself without hesitation shortly after his death to the murderer Salduendo, with whom she afterward lived. Aguirre mortally hated her. A trifling contention about the division of the rooms gave the Biscayan a pretext for a quarrel with Salduendo. The result was that Aguirre killed his comrade in Guzman's presence. Then two hired murderers rushed into the lodging of Iñez de Atienza and took the life of the young woman in the most revolting manner.

Dr. Markham, on the strength of a few verses

of the licentiate Castellanos, calls Iñez de Atienza, after Madame Godin des Odonais, the heroine of the Amazon. The comparison is hardly admissible between Ursua's mistress, who shortly after his death became so readily the mistress of his murderer, and the faithful wife who, to seek her husband toiling in the service of science at Cayenne, bravely made her way through the wilderness of the Amazon shores almost alone. It is also painful to read Dr. Markham, in his defence of this woman, a concubine in station, calling the eye-witness Vasquez, who maintained his fidelity to the Crown through constant danger to his life, a "gold-seeking adventurer," and the noble Bishop Piedrahita, of Panamá, a "dirty friar."

Salduendo's death aroused Guzman from his dreams, but it was too late. Not able to accomplish anything openly against Aguirre, he determined to make an attack upon his life. Aguirre anticipated this, and speedily collected his adherents. The murderers pressed in the darkness of night into the quarters of the "prince of terra firma." The priest Henao was the first victim, six captains fell next, and lastly the simple-minded youth himself was shot. On the next morning, Aguirre, accompanied by eighty armed men, came into the midst of the camp and was without opposition proclaimed "General of the Marañon."

By this name, Marañon, Aguirre henceforth called the mutiny, of which he was now absolute commander, and it was so applied by the men themselves. Simon[*] says the word was derived from

[*] Cap. xxiii.

maraña (complication), and survived after Aguirre's campaign as a by-name for the Amazon. This is, however, not correct. Peter Martyr had already, in his "*De Orbe Novo,*" applied the name to the Amazon, of which Pinzon had seen the mouths; Oviedo, who died in 1557, describes the Amazon River as the Marañon; and Gomara, whose "*Historia general de las Indias*" was printed in 1552, applied the name in an indefinite way to the great South American river that empties into the Atlantic Ocean.

The Amazon is, however, also known as the Rio de Orellano; and in view of the extremely vague geographical ideas that prevailed in the sixteenth century, no conclusion can be drawn from the application of the term "Marañones" to Aguirre's men concerning the further course or route of the expedition. It is significant that Acosta * says, on the authority of a witness who was in the expedition of Ursua and Aguirre, and afterward went into the Order of Jesus, that the Amazon, Marañon, or Rio de Orellana, emptied into the sea opposite the islands of Margarita and Trinidad. In connection with this the statement of Cristoval de Acuña (1639), that Aguirre reached the sea through a side-mouth of the Amazon opposite Trinidad, is of considerable importance. Mr. Markham, therefore, does not seem to be wholly unjustified in supposing that the Marañones, having sailed up the Rio Negro, passed into the Orinoco through the Cassiquiare and thence through one of the mouths of the Orinoco, and not through the Amazon, into the Atlantic Ocean. In further confirmation of this view is the

* "*Hist. Nat. general de las Indias,*" lib. ii. cap. vi.

mention by Pedro Simon of Aguirre's having met a cannibal tribe, the Arnaquinas. In fact, the Arekainas, thorough-going cannibals, now dwell on the Upper Rio Negro. On the other side are the facts that the Falls of the Orinoco are not mentioned in the few meagre accounts we have of the further course of the expedition, and that the torrent at Atures and Maypures, and even below, was hardly navigable for the brigantines although, according to Simon, they were "as strongly built as ships of three hundred tons." But whether through the Orinoco or the Amazon, it seems to be certain that Aguirre with his two vessels reached the ocean on the first day of July, 1561.

With the murder of Guzman, Aguirre obtained supreme authority; and the compressed narrative of the voyage down the river to its mouth and into the ocean, which lasted not quite three months, gives us but little else than accounts of the Biscayan's behavior in the exercise of unlimited power. His whole course was intended to establish this power, and since he was burdened with guilt and crime, and guilt and crime alone bound his men to him, doubt and suspicion of his own people were his predominant feelings. At least eight of the Marañones fell victims to these feelings in the course of three months; and every new crime attached the rest, by the sense of common guilt, more closely to their leader, who, like an evil spirit, led them, with an iron will, to further crimes. No one dared to speak or hardly to think of the *dorado;* the men were permitted to entertain but one thought—that of the conquest of Peru.

The island of Margarita was to afford the first base for this enterprise. Aguirre reached it in seventeen days, sailing around Trinidad. The appearance of the two brigantines excited general astonishment. Aguirre knew how to appeal to the emotions of the inhabitants. The governor of the island and some of the other officers went down to the landing to see the new-comers. Aguirre seized and imprisoned the governor; his men then captured the fort; and before the people of Margarita came to their senses the island had passed without drawing a sword into the hands of the Marañones. The royal treasury was immediately seized, independence of Spain was proclaimed, and provisions and ammunition for the further prosecution of the campaign were energetically collected, by gentle means or forcible. Aguirre now needed larger and swifter vessels for the execution of his audacious plan, for Nombre de Dios and Panamá were to be surprised in the same manner as Margarita had been, before the news of the event could spread. A large vessel, which had brought the Dominican-Provincial Montesinos with his military escort to Venezuela, was anchored before Maracapanna (the present Piritú), on the coast of the mainland, opposite Margarita. Some of the Marañones were sent to seize the vessel. Instead of doing that, they took the opportunity to desert the standard of rebellion and surrender to the Provincial, to whom they also made a circumstantial confession of all the atrocities which Aguirre and his band had committed. Fray Francisco de Montesinos was shocked by the story, and at once sent messengers to all the settlements in Venezuela. The report of the impending danger spread so rapidly over the mainland that in a short time fifteen hundred men were under arms in New Granada. Venezuela had been so exhausted by the *dorado* expeditions of the previous period that it was only with extreme effort that it could supply two hundred and sixty poorly armed men.

Aguirre, who had in the meantime sunk both brigantines, confidently awaited the arrival of the expected ships at Margarita. In the excited and tense condition of his mind, delay was hardly possible without violent outbreaks occurring. Not only were Aguirre's own men exposed to his murderous caprices, but the defenceless people of the island stood in constant peril of death. Aguirre regarded their property as his legitimate spoil, and disposed of it arbitrarily for his own purposes. While the men of influence and means were robbed and murdered by him, the bad elements flocked to his party, and the reign of terror on the island increased as the Marañones gained accessions from the scum of the population. At last the Provincial's vessel came in sight, but flying the royal standard. Aguirre fell into a furious passion. Having caused the governor of Margarita and the principal officers to be slain, he proceeded hastily down to the port to prevent the vessel's landing. No battle ensued, however, for after an exchange of empty threats the Provincial set sail again in order to carry the alarm to the Antilles and the Isthmus.

Aguirre's plan for surprising Panamá having been thus defeated, he determined to invade Venezuela.

Before doing so he instigated a number of murders at Margarita. At length he succeeded in getting a vessel, on which he sailed "on the last Sunday of August, 1561," at the head of a well-armed band of criminals, for Burburata. The people of this place fled into the woods with their property as soon as they saw the vessel, which bore two blood-red swords, crossed, on its flag. Without halting at Burburata, Aguirre marched inland to Lake Tacarigua, on the shore of which the settlement of Valencia had existed since 1555. Some of his men deserted him in the tropical wilderness through which his road lay. Valencia had been abandoned, and the Marañones burned the vacant houses. Aguirre was ill, and therefore twice as irritable as usual, and gave himself up to the wildest cruelty, even toward his own men. In Valencia he composed a manifesto to the King of Spain, and sent it by a priest whom he had brought from Margarita as a hostage to the coast. The letter, which has been preserved by Vasquez and by Oviedo y Baños, begins, "To King Philip, a Spaniard, son of Charles the Invincible," and ends with the words, "and on account of this ingratitude, I remain till death a rebel against thee.—Lope de Aguirre, the Wanderer." The document is full of reasonable and unreasonable reproaches, contains the most glaring and absurd contradictions, and bears throughout the marks of insanity. From Valencia Aguirre went southwest toward Barquicimeto. The royal party was not prepared for resistance in the open field; but the number of the Marañones was perceptibly diminishing. Aguirre's daily recurring frenzies were continually costing the lives of some of the men; the scanty population, instead of joining his party as he had anticipated, fled from before him, and his people deserted him at every opportunity.

The end was approaching. Barquicimeto was deserted, but the military force on the side of the king now appeared before the place, under the lead of the *maestro del campo*, Diego de Paredes. While not strong enough to attack him, it prevented Aguirre from proceeding farther. Well mounted, the royalists passed around his camp daily, cut off all access to it, and by the judicious circulation of amnesty proclamations which Governor Collado sagaciously issued, they encouraged his men to desert. The number of these diminished every day, and Aguirre's mad spells of fury became steadily more impotent. At last Paredes decided to risk an attack on Barquicimeto. On the advance of the royal troops most of the Marañones threw away their arms and met their assailants with the cry, "Long live the king!" Aguirre found himself all at once entirely forsaken. Pale and trembling, he went into the chamber of his only child, a grown-up maiden, and with the words, "My child, God have mercy on your soul, for I am going to kill you, so that you shall not live in misery and shame the child of a traitor," stabbed her in the heart, and then weakly tottered toward the door which the royal soldiers were approaching. He suffered himself to be taken without resistance. The royal *maestro del campo* desired to spare his life, but the Marañones insisted on the instant death of their former leader, and he fell under the discharge of musketry. His head was cut off and was exhibited at Tocuyo in an iron cage. His memory survives to the present time in Venezuela as that of an evil spirit; and when at night the jack-o'-lanterns dance over the marshy plains, the solitary wanderer crosses himself and whispers, "The soul of the tyrant Aguirre."

With this closes the account of the series of expeditions which we undertook to describe in connection with the legend of the gilded man. The story justifies our comparison of the vision of the *dorado* after his real home had been conquered with a mirage, "enticing, deceiving, and leading men to destruction."

Notwithstanding the tragical consequences which the search for this phantom invariably entailed, it remained long fixed like an evil spell upon the northeastern half of the South American continent. Martin de Proveda tried and failed, in 1556, to reach Omagua and the "provinces of the *dorado*." Diego de Cerpa, in 1569, and Pedro Malaver de Silva, in 1574, met their deaths at the mouths of the Orinoco. There Antonio de Berreo, after he had fruitlessly marched through the whole interior of Venezuela, fell a prisoner into the hands of the English in 1582. The great expedition of Sir Walter Raleigh in 1595 only got as far as the Salto Caroni. In the meanwhile the locality of the legend, as Humboldt has remarked, kept shifting farther to the east, till it took final refuge in Guyana, "in the periodically overflowed plains between the rivers Rupununi, Essequibo, and Branco"—but shrunken at the same time to a purely geographical myth of Lake Parime.

As in the first half of the sixteenth century German soldiers were the earliest to pursue the gilded chieftain, the fact also appears like a curious fate that in the first half of the nineteenth century the German travellers Alexander von Humboldt and Schomburgk laid that phantom of the great lake, and with it terminated the last survival of the legend of the gilded man.

CIBOLA.

INTRODUCTION.

The most interesting period in the history of the discoveries on the American continent was in that part of the sixteenth century when the efforts of the Spanish people were directed to pushing from the already settled coast lands and isthmuses into the interior of both North and South America. I have already endeavored, in the preceding chapters, to project a brief view of the exploring expeditions of the Spaniards in northern South America. Since those sketches were composed, fortune has several times led me into those countries of southern North America which formed the scene of the most arduous efforts of the Spaniards in the sixteenth century to reach the north. I now purpose, as a contribution I owe to knowledge, to follow step by step the tracks of the earliest Spanish campaigns in the southwest of the present United States into the interior of Sonora.

The value of historical research on the American continent consists not only in the enrichment it affords to the fund of scientific knowledge, which has an indirect influence upon life, but also in the destruction it effects of deeply rooted errors, in which it acts immediately upon practical life. Accordingly as we represent to ourselves a people or a country when they first become known to us, so we shape our expectations of them when we go to establish our home among them. A correct notion of the past furnishes the basis for an intelligent forecasting of the future. I have tried to show in the history of the *dorado* what harm may result from incorrect views of history and misapprehensions of manners and customs.

The errors of this kind which arose in the southern half of the Western Continent were, fortunately, corrected at a comparatively early date. In North America similar errors have been reëchoed, with mischievous results, down to near the present time. Expectations awakened and cherished in the beginning of the sixteenth century, not fulfilled but never completely dispelled, have in past years prepared for the failure of many enterprises in the southwest of the United States. These expectations were built upon the basis of a misunderstood fact. The tradition of the "Seven Cities of Cibola" included a kernel of fact enveloped by a shell of exaggerated fancies and hopes. Much interest has been taken in recent times in inquiries respecting the "where" and the "how" of that kernel. While those questions were correctly answered by earnest and intelligent investigation thirty years ago, the practical seeker has been led by them into many unfortunate wanderings, and the settler looking for his future in the west has been lured into attempts that have forever buried his fortunes and those of his companions. The following pages have been prepared in the hope that, conveying the warnings of history, they may furnish the basis for the formation of more correct views.

CHAPTER I.

THE AMAZONS.

COLUMBUS had heard of the Amazons on his great voyage. He said, on the 4th of March, 1493, of the Caribs: "They are the same who have intercourse with the women on the first island which is found on the voyage from Spain to the Indies, on which no men live. These do not follow any womanly occupations, but use bows and arrows of cane, like those mentioned above, and cover and arm themselves with brazen plates, of which they have many." In the same letter the Admiral spoke of a part of the island of Cuba (Juana), "called Cibau, where the people come into the world with tails;" and of another island, "where, as they assured me, the men have no hair." In such a company, at that time, the Amazons also could not fail to be present.

The legend of the Amazons was unquestionably domiciled upon the American continent by the Spaniards, and was suggested by imperfectly understood accounts of distant tribes given by the natives, to whose words the Spaniards were not inattentive. Keeping pace with the efforts of the Spaniards to penetrate to the north, it appears first in the fourth letter of Cortés to the Emperor Charles V. (October 15, 1524): "And among the reports which he brought from that province [Colima] was an account of a very good harbor which was found on that coast; ... and also he told me of the lords of the province of Ciguatan, that many of them asserted there was an island inhabited only by women without any men, and that from time to time men went out to them from the mainland; ... when they bore daughters they kept them, but the sons were put away. This island is ten days distant from the province, and many persons have gone there from the province and seen them. I was also told that they were rich in pearls and in gold."

It was Gonzalo Sandoval, Cortés's most faithful lieutenant and friend, who brought this account. It was not allotted to Cortés himself to pursue the search for the Amazons' island, for the insurrection which another associate in his conquest of the Mexican tribes, Cristóbal de Olid, excited against him in Honduras forced him into the arduous campaign in that part of Central America, in which he only with great difficulty escaped death. Until that remarkable expedition, which penetrated southward from Mexico to the now hardly accessible interior regions of Chiapas and Yucatan, the Spaniards held the northern coast of the Mexican gulf to the present state of Tamaulipas, but on the western coast they had advanced but little beyond the twentieth degree of north latitude in the state of Jalisco. The subjugation of the tribes of the Rio Pánuco on the eastern coast brought about a conflict in the year 1523 between Cortés and the contemporary discoverer, Francisco de Garay, which ended in Garay's going to Mexico, where he espoused the natural daughter of Cortés, and then suddenly died. The behavior of Cortés had already aroused the distrust of the Spanish Government. There is no longer much doubt that, feeling his separation from the mother-country, and counting on the support of the natives, which he was beginning to cultivate systematically, he was working for the establishment of an independent kingdom in Mexico. He was therefore dangerous to all who stood near him in importance, and used every means to remove them. To this end he sent the most capable and most popular of his lieutenants, Pedro de Alvarado, to Guatemala, and Cristóbal de Olid to Honduras, while Sandoval, in whose frank and innocent character alone he could trust, was allowed to remain in Mexico. He had managed to get the first commissioner whom the Government sent to Mexico, Cristóbal de Tápia, out of the country; but Garay he permitted to come to Mexico—to die.

Cortés considered himself secure, and wrote a letter to the Spanish Crown, the language of which is little known, in which, while he insisted in the plainest manner upon his services and personal devotion, he in the most courtly terms denied allegiance, and declined any interference of the royal officers in the administration of the new colony. This letter, which bears the same date as the famous paper called the *Carta Cuarta* (October 15, 1524), was written when four officers of the Spanish Crown—the treasurer, Alonso de Estrada; the accountant and paymaster, Rodrigo de Albornoz; the factor, Gonzalo de Salazar; and the inspector, Peral Mendez Chirinos—had come to Mexico to take care of the financial interests of the monarch. The insurrection of Olid called away the conqueror of Mexico and took him to Honduras, else he would have carried out his ambitious plans at that time, when, it is hardly to be doubted, they would have been more successful than was afterward the struggle for independence of Gonzalo Pizarro in Peru.

After the departure of Cortés from Mexico, October 12, 1524, the administration of the province fell into the hands of the officers of the Crown. They soon quarrelled, and disastrous complications arose. Mexico itself was the scene of great disorder, while the Indians in the country rebelled. This interregnum lasted till the year 1525, and ended with the arrest of Salazar and Chirinos by the partisans of Cortés. Cortés, after restoring order in Honduras, returned to Mexico on June 20, 1526.

A brilliant reception was prepared for him there, but it had only a transient importance. The Spanish Government had perceived the magnitude of the danger with which it was threatened from the extraordinary but reckless conqueror, and had made the best of his absence. Cortés had indeed been honored with the title of "Adelantado" of New Spain, and with many personal privileges, but the most northern part of Mexico that had been discovered, from the mouth of the Pánuco River, was withdrawn from his dominion and placed under the administration of Nuño de Guzman. By this change he lost all the fruits of his agreement with Francisco de Garay and of Garay's premature death. A young jurist, Luis Ponce de Léon, was immediately sent to Mexico to make an impartial investigation on the spot of the complaints that were brought against Cortés. For this purpose he was privately given full power to arrest Cortés if necessary and send him to Spain, or in the other event to confirm him in his office.

Ponce de Léon arrived at the City of Mexico on July 2, 1526, and was received with pomp by Cortés, who placed himself wholly at his disposition; but the climate agreed no better with the new functionary than it had before agreed with Garay. He died in the same month after a short illness; and eight weeks afterward his successor in office, the Bachelor Márcos de Aguilar, also died. The process against Cortés dragged slowly along with many interruptions amid great disquiet in the country; for Alonso de Estrada had taken the reins of government, and had abridged the conqueror's prerogatives to the domain of military command and Indian administration. Shorn of all power, Cortés had to submit to the inevitable, and to suffer patiently a banishment from the City of Mexico, which Estrada imposed upon him in order to secure tranquillity.

Although further explorations in the north were temporarily interrupted by the disorders that prevailed in the country, Cortés found time to organize an expedition to the Molukkes on the western coast, and at least to open communication with them. The royal officers, on the contrary, could accomplish nothing, and in order to circumscribe their power, as well as that of the governor of Panamá, Pedro Arias Dávila, independent jurisdictions were created out of Honduras, Guatemala, and Yucatan. At the same time the Church assumed the control of Indian affairs, and finally, in order to terminate the arbitrary provisional system of government, the royal court of law, *Audiencia real*, was set up in the year 1527 as the chief authority in Mexico.

Nuño Beltrán de Guzman entered into possession of his government in Pánuco in the year 1528. He was young, vigorous, and energetic, but imperious, and his inconsiderate ambition was not capable of the wise patience that Cortés manifested. His first step was to stir up boundary disputes with the adjacent jurisdiction of New Spain or Mexico, and when no results accrued from them, he sent Sancho de Caniego to Madrid with a series of complaints against Hernando Cortés, which could not fail to excite earnest attention. Besides the charge of treason against the Crown already raised, Guzman accused the conqueror with having murdered Francisco de Garay and Luis Ponce de Léon. Cortés presented himself in Spain almost simultaneously with the charges, to defend himself personally against them. But an accusation of another more heinous offence had been more recently filed in secret against him at the court. His wife, Doña Catalina Xuarez, with whom he had not long shared the happiness of wedded life, having been separated from her a few years after their marriage by absence on his campaigns, had joined him again after the conquest of Mexico, and suddenly died three months later. He was therefore, although not openly, accused of murdering her. The Acts of the Process against Cortés included a "secret inquiry" (*pesquisa secreta*) into this terrible accusation. The Process resulted in an official acquittal; but the Acts themselves presented the death of Francisco de Garay in the most suspicious light, left the manner in which the death of Ponce de León occurred an open question, and made it certain that Cortés had with his own hands strangled in bed his first faithful wife, who had followed him to Mexico at his request. The Process did not detain Cortés later than till the year 1530. In the meantime the Spanish Crown, as soon as it was informed of the new accusations that had been brought against Cortés, appointed Nuño Beltrán de Guzman president of the court of law in Mexico, and thus elevated him to the highest official position in New Spain. The selection was an unwise one. Guzman proceeded to Mexico, where he arrived in 1529. His demeanor was very arrogant. The complaints against him soon became as loud, even on the side of the *Audiencia*, as they had been against Cortés. At last the King of Spain (the Emperor Charles V.) named a new *Audiencia*, and appointed as its president Sebastian Ramirez de Fuenléal, bishop of Santo Domingo. The president did not go directly to the mainland, but spent some time in his episcopal see, partly in order to observe quietly the course of affairs in Mexico, and partly to perfect his plans for the reorganization of the country.

Guzman's conduct was in the meantime intolerable. Directly in the face of the Spanish laws he pursued the natives in order to extort gold and slaves from them, and abused the former associates of Cortés. Even the *Audiencia* was glad when he left Mexico, on the 20th of December, 1529, at the head of a large Spanish squadron and more than eight thousand Indians, for the purpose of continuing the discoveries begun by Sandoval for Cortés in the northwest. The drafting of Indians to engage in this campaign was a transgression of the law, but he was personally supported in it by some of the members of the court. His march was directed first toward Michoacan, but its ultimate goal was the gold-rich and pearl-bearing island of the fabulous Amazons.

The Tarasca lived and still live in Michoacan. Although they spoke a different language from the Mexicans, their traditions pointed to an original connection with them, and they were in the same stage of civilization. The Tarasca were split up into a number of groups, which, like the other linguistic stocks or their subdivisions, of which Tlaxcala, Cholula, and the three large settlements of the Mexican Valley—Mexico, Tezcuco, and Tlacopan—were conspicuous examples, had a common leadership in war. The tribes of Michoacan had two such head war-chiefs, of whom commonly only one—like Montezuma in his day in Mexico—who is called Cazonci, is named. The Tarasca had voluntarily submitted to Cortés, and stood in friendly relations toward the Spaniards as long as the famous conqueror commanded in Mexico. Guzman, having arrived at Michoacan, in his rude way imposed considerable requisitions on the chiefs. As these could not be granted quickly enough, the principal leader, "Zinzicha," was tortured to death. Guzman then went northward, and this campaign constitutes the saddest page for the natives in the history of Mexico. The Indians there suffered generally only during two periods: first under the confusion which prevailed during the absence of Cortés, from 1524 to 1526; and, second, under the administration of

Nuño de Guzman, from 1529 to 1531. The rule of Cortés was wisely just and mild; and the later policy of the Spaniards was a paternal one, marked by a correct knowledge of the Indian character, its weaknesses and its capabilities.

Guzman has been often accused, by his contemporaries as well as by later writers, of having exercised deliberate cruelties on his march through the present states of Jalisco and Sinaloa, and his campaign has been described as one of devastation. Numerous acts of violence certainly occurred. The Indian tribes, divided, scattered, and living in constant war with one another, suffered much, but a careful examination of the authorities shows that it was more from fear than anything else; while no reliance can be placed upon the numerical statements concerning the so-called Spanish blood-baths, particularly none upon those of the bishop of Chiapas, Bartholomé de las Casas. The whole literature of that period should be read with the same reserves with which we receive the political "campaign literature" of the present; and the numerous official hearings of the Spanish civil officers furnish the most contradictory statements. Guzman was ambitious and avaricious; his outbreaks of cruelty were provoked by those passions. Where his interests demanded patience he could be gentle enough, but when excited by contradiction or negligence, he raged against his own Spaniards as well as against hostile Indians. Contrary to the orders of the Spanish Crown, he made slaves of a number of Indians in order that he might at least compensate himself for the disappointments he suffered in other respects; for the chief object of his search was gold in quantities, but he could only obtain it scantily. The civilization of the natives appeared to decline as he went toward the northwest; the houses of stone and plaster gave way to lighter structures of cane and wood, and shelters made of branches and foliage.

A bitter disappointment was awaiting him in Cihuatlan in the present state of Sinaloa. Sandoval had brought the story of the Amazons from there; but instead of the island on which he had placed the soldierly women, Guzman was shown only a few insignificant villages. He found them, however, exclusively inhabited by women and children, for the men had fled to the mountains. The legend of the Amazons was thus resolved into one of those mistakes which were sure to arise at that time on the first contact of Europeans with natives whose language they did not understand. No trace was found of gold, pearls, or treasures of any kind. The story of the Amazons ceases from this time to be of any significance in the history of discovery in the northern half of America. It plainly appears from the accounts of contemporaries that it was not a native legend in America, but was an importation from Europe, a survival from classical antiquity, which emigrated along with cultivated and uncultivated Europeans into what was called the New World.

Guzman, although unsuccessful as to his principal object, did not abandon the effort to press farther north. He reached Culiacan, and founded there a settlement under the name of San Miguel de Culiacan. His force, however, was exhausted and partially destroyed. His Indian guides especially had suffered much. He therefore despatched the Captain Chirinos toward the north, and the latter in turn sent his captains, Cebreros and Diego de Alcáraz, still farther in that direction. Guzman in the meantime started on his return. His direct work in this region ended with the foundation of the Spanish settlement in Culiacan. In the beginning of May, 1531, he left the young town and began a continuous march to the south. His kingdom had come to an end; Cortés had returned to Mexico and arrived at an understanding with the new *Audiencia*. Grave accusations were raised against Nuño de Guzman. All his orders concerning the Indians were revoked, and when at last the new president of the royal court of justice, Bishop Don Sebastian Ramirez de Fuenléal, came into Mexico, he took control of affairs with a firm hand, and banished his violent predecessor to the scene of his march on the western coast. In 1537 he was arrested by order of the Spanish Government and carried a prisoner to Spain, where, having been deprived of his property by confiscation, he died in poverty in 1544. When Guzman, even after he had become satisfied at Cihuatlan that he had been pursuing a phantom in the shape of the river of the Amazons, still endeavored to go farther north, he was moved by another story which excited his avarice and his imagination. Unable himself to follow this second phantom, he charged Captain Chirinos with the object. The latter went as far as the Rio de Petatlan, and thence sent out his subordinates, Cebreros and Alcáraz, to the Rio Mayo. The numerous though small towns which were found on the banks of this river were inhabited by the Mayo Indians, who now form a branch of the linguistic stock of the Yaqui, or Hyaquin. Cebreros crossed the Mayo, proceeded in 1532 into the present Sonora, and although he had hardly twenty men reached the Rio Yaqui. He did not venture to go farther than to the north bank of that river, but returned to Sinaloa. The Indians there were in active revolt, and the Spaniards had great difficulty in maintaining themselves in the weak settlement of San Miguel Culiacan. They had found on their northern excursions fertile intervales inhabited by warlike tribes. Beyond these tribes lived a people who built their houses of clay. Still farther north another wonder-story invited them, which promised more than the most fertile intervale, more than the most civilized Indian settlements. The account of Indians in Sonora who lived in large houses of clay was true, for it referred to the southern Pimas. But the story that attracted the Spaniards to the north was the legend of the "Seven Cities."

CHAPTER II.

THE SEVEN CITIES.

THE planisphere which Martin Dehaim constructed in the year 1492 for the Portuguese service contained, among other features, an island of Antilia west of the Cape de Verde group, with a note relating that at the time of the conquest of Spain by the Arabs a Portuguese archbishop and a number of Christians had fled to that island and founded seven cities upon it. The story is still more plainly marked on the map of Johannes Ruysch—*Universalior Cogniti Orbis Tabula*, A.D. 1508. The legend of the seven cities thus appears, like the myth of the Amazons, to have been known in Europe previous to the landing of Columbus. After the successive discoveries of the islands of the West Indian group in the last years of the fifteenth century "Antilia" (*ante insula*) ceased to designate a proper and special part of the land. The name of Antilles remained, and was applied to the whole chain of islands that separate the Gulf of Mexico and the Caribbean Sea from the Atlantic Ocean. The seven cities also passed into complete oblivion till they were brought again into a kind of indefinite recollection about the year 1530 by the expedition of Nuño de Guzman. It is uncertain when, how, or where Guzman heard of the "*siete cibdadis.*" The anonymous author of the "*Primua Relacion*" speaks of them in connection with that campaign as if he had already heard the story in Mexico; while other contemporary writers say nothing of them, but mention a large river that emptied into the Southern Sea, which the inhabitants had barred with an iron chain. Neither the seven cities nor the broad river with its barrier chain were found by Cebreros and Alcáraz.

It is proper, therefore, to inquire whether, or to what extent, a story concerning the seven cities existed among the natives of Mexico before the arrival of the Europeans. But such an inquiry should be prefaced by this statement of general fact: Wherever it is possible to follow the development of popular legends in groups of men not acquainted with writing, but who have been taught to transmit these stories by verbal tradition from generation to generation, we are surprised at finding that the legend has been preserved with careful fidelity through centuries, and that any novelty or change which has been introduced into it must always be ascribed to foreign influence. Such influence is not necessarily to be attributed to an extra-continental contact; but where such a contact takes place—and where, as everywhere in America, one group of the human race is suddenly caused to live with another of whom it is so far in advance in established historical foundations and knowledge, and in the means of perpetuating the remembrance of them, as the Europeans of the sixteenth century were then in advance of the American aborigines all over the continent without exception; and where this living in contact is at the same time combined with the exercise of a religious influence by the superior race on the other—then a reconstruction of the legends is inevitable. It is expressed first in efforts to adapt the mythology of the inferior people to that of the higher; and as mythology and history are closely interwoven, a partial insinuation of the sagas, stories, and legends of the superior people into those of the others can hardly be avoided.

Great care is therefore necessary to extract the real kernel of the Indian traditions, in Mexico for instance, from the investing shell of the legends of the sixteenth century. The subject has been treated till now not only with little critical care as to this point, but for the most part without any critical sense. Everything has been accepted as pure coin which, since the subjection of the Mexican tribes by Cortés, has been called Indian historical tradition. Only superficial consideration has been given to the time, place, and manner of the origin of the Indian paintings and other documents. It has not been considered, in using them as historical authorities, that the Codex Mendocino, the Codex Vaticanus, and the Codex Telleriano Ramensis were painted by Indians in the middle and second half of the sixteenth century, by order of the Spanish viceroy and Don Martin Enriquez, as illustrations of the local traditions which were collected at the time by a commission in the name of the Crown. No inquiry has been made into the extent to which those paintings agree with the earliest declarations of the natives, which were made and recorded not more than ten years after the institution of Spanish rule. The Church also, as well as the Spanish Government, made earnest efforts a short time after the conquest to collect the historical legends and stories of the

Indians. About the middle of the sixteenth century a statement was introduced into the publications concerning these traditions, that the Nahuatl tribes of Mexico believed that they had originated out of seven caves. The Codex Mendocino had nothing about this, and it was not composed much before 1549. Later writers made seven tribes out of the seven caves, and finally seven towns or cities. We have already seen that Nuño de Guzman had heard or knew of the story of the seven cities about 1530; and the supposition therefore seems not unauthorized that the seven caves of the Mexican tradition, as they were conceived and represented after the discovery of New Mexico, were an interpolation of the European legend into the Indian recollections of their history.

In 1531 the bishop of San Domingo assumed control of the government in Mexico as president of the Royal Law Court. No further advance of importance was made in the discoveries in the northwest, and the settlement of San Miguel de Culiacan in Sinaloa was held as the extreme post in that direction whence occasional excursions to the north were attempted. In the meantime Nuño de Guzman was removed from the scene and called to answer for his misdemeanors before the Spanish courts. Melchior Diaz commanded in Culiacan as *capitan* and *alcalde mayor*, and Diego de Alcáraz was at the head of an advanced post which was pushed out between Culiacan and the borders of the present Sonora. Some of the men of this reconnoitring party, when about eighty miles north of Culiacan, met in the last days of March, 1536, a strange spectacle. A man, nearly naked, with long tangled hair and beard, accompanied by eleven Indians and a negro, came to them, and spoke to them in Spanish, with warm emotion, expressing great joy that after eight years of wandering he had at last been permitted to meet white men, and Spanish countrymen. He bore the outer traces of great physical suffering, and spoke in so excited a manner that the other Spaniards at first regarded him and listened to him with suspicion. He gave his name as Alvar Nuñez Cabeza de Vaca, and that of the negro who was with him was Estévanico. Two other Spaniards, Alonzo del Castillo Maldonado and Andrés Dorantes, were a day's journey back, in company with a number of Indians who had followed them from the north.

When the Spaniards had recovered from their surprise, they took the new-comers to Diego de Alcáraz, who immediately sent three of his men with fifty Indians to search for the other Spaniards. His purpose, however, was not so much to deliver his countrymen as to find provisions and gold. For this object he kept back the Indians who had come with Maldonado and Dorantes, removed the latter from them, and finally put the four, including Cabeza de Vaca and the negro, under arrest. The Indians escaped by flight; and the prisoners, after having been abused in various ways, were delivered on May 1st to the commander, Melchior Diaz, at Culiacan, who gave them an honorable reception, and to whom they were permitted to relate the wonderful history of their adventures.

This story of the wanderings of Cabeza de Vaca and his companions is indeed a wonder-tale, and is hardly matched in thrilling incident by anything of the kind of the sixteenth century. De Vaca has himself written it out in the book "*Naufragios de Alvar Nuñez Cabeza de Vaca y Relacion de la Jornada que hizo á la Florida con el Adelantado Pámfilo de Narvaez*," which was printed at Valladolid in 1555. Having been composed from recollection and not on the basis of notes of any kind, the book is obscure in its geographical data. Many of the details are erroneously set forth, and the glowing fancies excited by the contemplation of the author's terrible sufferings and privations are in many cases obviously detrimental to historical truth. The substance of the story is true, and gives a vivid picture of the fortunes of Cabeza de Vaca and his companions.

An expedition was organized in 1527 under the command of Pámfilo de Narvaez, the former rival of Cortés, whom he had attacked and captured in 1520 at Cempohual, to explore the peninsula of Florida, concerning the wealth of which extremely vague and therefore exaggerated accounts were in circulation. Five vessels, with six hundred men, left San Lúcar de Barrameda in Spain on June 17th. Cabeza de Vaca was treasurer of the enterprise. Rarely has any campaign of conquest met with such a series of consecutive disasters as befell this unhappy expedition of the "Armada of Pámfilo de Narvaez." One of the vessels went down in a squall during the stay of the fleet at the island of Cuba. The flotilla could not leave Havana till February, 1528, and it was so hindered by storms and head-winds that it did not reach the coast of Florida till Maundy-Thursday of that year. It anchored in a bay on the shore of which was an Indian village. The men were landed, and it was decided, against the advice of Cabeza de Vaca, to leave the ships and march inland. The unfortunate march began on May 1, 1528, with three hundred men and forty horses.* Amidst great difficulties, without provisions, they went northward through marshy woods and morasses, and across broad rivers, at no very great distance from the seashore. Till the 17th of June they found only a single Indian village (on May 16th). Then some Indians met them from whom they learned that they were near the settlement of Apalache, of which they were in search, concerning the wealth of which fabulous reports had found their way to the Spanish Antilles. They suffered a bitter disappointment when, on June 24th, they came in sight of the desired place. Forty Indian huts constituted the whole village. They were now in northern Florida, on the Suwanee River. At Apalache serious hostilities began with the natives, who daily harassed the weary and famishing Spaniards and killed some of their men. After a halt there of twenty-five days, Narvaez decided to go westward.

It is not necessary to go further into the melancholy details of the march of this expedition. Once in the swamps and bayous that extended along the coast of Alabama, and perhaps Louisiana, no escape was to be hoped for. An attempt to build rafts and sail upon them across the gulf to the Mexican coast resulted in the drowning of a part of the men. The rest, cast back upon the shore with-

---

* The Bay of Santa Cruz, in the present State of Florida, appears to have been the point where Narvaez landed.

out food and without water, fell victims to the hostility of the natives, to hunger, and to the winter, which came upon them. Only four survived, viz., Cabeza de Vaca, Castillo Maldonado, Dorantes, and the negro Estévanico. The vessels which had been left in the Bay of Santa Cruz, Florida, went to pieces in the storm, and their crews perished.

The subsequent adventures of the four survivors may be described very briefly. Buffeted from one Indian tribe to another, often cruelly treated, participating in the privations to which their savage masters were exposed by their miserable way of living, they arrived in northwestern Mexico, as we have already seen, in the year 1536.

Two facts are officially and indubitably established: that Cabeza de Vaca and his companions were members of the expedition of Pámfilo de Narvaez, which went from Spain in 1527 to Cuba, and in the following year from Cuba to Florida and there vanished; and that they appeared again in the year 1536, in a naked and almost savage condition, in the company of Indians, in the present state of Sinaloa. It is therefore evident that they had wandered during an interval of eight years across the North American continent from east to west, from the peninsula of Florida to the Gulf of California.

It is almost impossible to determine the course they took, or probably took. They remained for a long time with the tribes which periodically inhabited the marshy regions of the Mississippi Delta, and were then conducted westward. The fact is of importance that the *tuna*, or fruit of the great leaf-cactus (*opuntia*), constituted a principal food resource during the whole time. This indicates that the first year was mostly spent in the southern parts of the present United States; and the description of the country, as well as the fact that the mesquite tree is mentioned, are evidence that they passed through the present State of Texas. Their course was generally westward, and it may be very clearly inferred from that that they at all events crossed the Rio Grande.

At a considerable distance beyond that river they found permanent dwellings, the inhabitants of which planted beans, melons, and maize. In this part of their wanderings they heard of an animal which Cabeza de Vaca called a cow. It has been concluded from this that the wanderers entered New Mexico and saw there the American bison or buffalo. I cannot agree with this opinion. The *casas de asiento* were much too far west to be identified with the pueblos. The Pimas of southern Sonora, their northern neighbors the Opatas, and several tribes of the Sierra Madre, lived in permanent houses of clay and stone; and if Cabeza de Vaca and his companions had seen the large, many-storied houses of New Mexico they would not have omitted to describe their remarkable stairlike structure. The dress of the inhabitants of these "permanent dwellings" also agrees rather with the costume of Sonora and Chihuahua than with the recognized dress of the Pueblo Indians. By the word "cow" Cabeza de Vaca probably meant to speak of the hides he saw rather than to describe the animal itself. The untanned hide of the large brown deer (*cervus canadensis*) is but little smaller than that of a cow; and a description of the striking figure of the bison would not have been wanting in the "*Naufragios*" if Cabeza de Vaca had actually seen the "hump-backed cow," as the older Spanish writers called it. It is possible that he heard of the buffalo and perhaps saw some of the robes, but it is not certain; for, in the verbal explanations which he gave at Madrid in 1547 to the historian Gonzalo Fernandez de Oviedo y Valdés, he spoke only of "three kinds of deer, one of which was as large as an ox," but said nothing of "cows."

The fact that the Spaniards constantly wandered toward the "setting sun," and that from Texas, and that they did not cross the great waterless plains of that state, excludes the supposition that they entered New Mexico and that the "permanent dwellings" meant the pueblos of the Rio Grande. Further decisive is the declaration that the inhabitants of those permanent houses obtained green stones (turquoise or calcite) in exchange for parrot feathers. There are no species of parrots in New Mexico and Arizona, but the Sierra Madre is the habitat of the large green sittich, the feathers of which I have often seen in the possession of the Pueblo Indians, who had bought them in Sonora. The southern Pimas and the Opatas of Sonora used parrot feathers as decorations in their dances till the middle of the last century; and I have surveyed numerous ruins of the clay and stone houses of the Opatas in the Sierra Madre which, now a solemn, silent wilderness, is covered with lofty pine woods in which the loquacious green sittich flit in the early morning from limb to limb. The Indians of whom Cabeza de Vaca speaks bought the turquoises far in the north, and they told of many great houses in which the people there lived. These statements may refer to New Mexico and Arizona; for turquoises are found in the neighborhood of Santa Fé, where they are called "cerillos," as well as not far from Zuñi, and in southern New Mexico, at no great distance from the present Silver City.

With the stories of permanent settlements, of natives clothed in cotton, and of turquoises found in the far north, which Cabeza de Vaca and his companions told their countrymen, were associated speculations concerning great metallic riches in the northern regions. The wanderers brought no definite statements on this subject, nor could they present visible evidence in the shape of mineral specimens of the existence of the metals; but the thirst for the precious metals was quite as intense in the sixteenth century as in the nineteenth, and the credulity of the gold-seekers of that time was not less ready than that of the "prospectors" of to-day. It could, however, have hardly been greater. As soon, therefore, as Melchior Diaz heard the marvellous story of the new-comers, he sent an account of it, not to Guzman, but to Mexico, to Don Antonio de Mendoza, who had arrived there in the year 1554 as the first viceroy of New Spain, and had superseded the provisional government of the bishop of Santo Domingo. Cabeza de Vaca and his companions were invited to Mexico, were well received there, and with the exception of the negro and Maldonado, who remained in Mexico, were sent to Spain. The subsequent fortunes of Cabeza de Vaca are of no further interest in connection with the purpose of this sketch, and we need only say that his adventurous career did not terminate with his wanderings in North America, but that other sufferings as great but of different character awaited him in South America and in Spain, and misfortune pursued him till the end of his life.

Stories like those which came to Mexico through Cabeza de Vaca could not fail to direct the attention of the government to the northwest. Nuño de Guzman was succeeded as provisional governor of New Galicia* by the licentiate Diego Perez de la Torre, and when he died, in 1538, his place was taken by a young noble of Salamanca, Francisco Vasquez Coronado, who had married the daughter of the former treasurer, Alonzo de Estrada. As royal visitador he had already travelled over a large part of Mexico, and enjoyed in a high degree the confidence of the viceroy. Young and energetic, disposed, according to the fashion of the time, toward a knight's career, he was a most suitable person to direct the further progress of the exploration of the northwest.

The stories of Cabeza de Vaca appear still to have been received with some distrust. Without wholly rejecting them, people hesitated to follow the first impulse, which would prompt them to send an expedition to the north at once. Antonio de Mendoza was a sagacious, quiet, careful statesman, and he preferred to reconnoitre before taking decisive steps. In his reconnoissance he received the assistance of the Church.

Among the Franciscan monks in Mexico was a

---

* This province comprised the undefined northwest of Mexico, while New Biscay included the northeast, on the coast of the Mexican gulf.

Sardinian brother named Marcus, who, having been born in Nice, was known as Fray Marcos de Nizza. As he figures in history under this designation, I shall continue to call him Fray Marcos. His real name and the date of his birth are still unknown. He came to America in the year 1531 in the service of his order and went to Peru, whence he proceeded with Pedro de Alvarado to Guatemala, and finally to Mexico. He had distinguished himself by his intelligence, capacity, and devotion, and was respected by the brethren of his order. Fray Antonio de Ciudad Rodrigo, father provincial in Mexico, proposed in the interest of the mission to detail one or more Franciscan monks on the contemplated reconnoissance. It is not improbable that Fray Marcos voluntarily offered himself for the service. His long experience among the natives especially fitted him for the work; and, whether by his own free will or out of obedience and a sense of duty to his order, he undertook the arduous and dangerous task.

A few historians, among whom are Torquemada and Arricivita, suppose that a preliminary expedition was sent out in 1538, in which, according to some, Fray Marcos did, according to others did not, take part. We have no official reports of such an expedition, and it is possible that these accounts originated in a mistake. The instructions which Don Antonio de Mendoza sent to Fray Marcos, and the receipt of which he acknowledged from New Galicia on November 25, 1538, do not agree with the supposition of such a preliminary reconnoissance. In those instructions the monk is advised to insist upon good treatment of the Indians by the Spaniards of Sinaloa, to protect them against every attempt to reduce them to slavery, and to promise them all support and help in the name of the Crown. He was then ordered to proceed into the interior with all possible precautions, carefully to observe land and people, to avoid all personal danger, and should he find himself on the coast of the "Southern Sea"* he was to bury written reports at the foot of a tree distinguished by its size, and to cut a cross in the bark of the tree, so that in case a ship was sent along the coast, its crew might know how to identify it by that mark. Finally Estévanico, the negro who had made the perilous journey with Cabeza de Vaca from Florida to the coast of the Pacific Ocean, was assigned to him as leader and attendant; and in case any of the Indians who had come with those men and their companions to Sinaloa could be of use to him, Francisco Vasquez Coronado, the new governor of Culiacan, was instructed to engage them to accompany Fray Marcos and the negro. The negro was to be subordinate to the monk in every point.

The zealous Franciscan left San Miguel de Culiacan on Friday, March 7, 1539. Besides Estévanico and several Indians, a brother of the order, Fray Onorato, accompanied him. Their route was northward, toward the present state of Sonora. The Indians who went with them belonged to the southern branch of the great Pima tribe. They had, as we have already said, followed Cabeza de Vaca, Castillo,

* *Mar del Sur*, the Pacific Ocean, in distinction from *Mar del Norte*, the Northern Sea, the name by which the Atlantic Ocean was known in the sixteenth century.

Maldonado, and Dorantes from central and southern Sonora to Sinaloa, and a part of them had remained there and founded a village on the Rio Petatlan. Probably in this village, certainly on that river, Fray Onorato became so ill that it was necessary, after three days' delay, to leave him. The party kept as nearly as possible to the coast of the Pacific Ocean, leaving the villages on the Yaqui to their right. A halt was made at Bacapa, and the monk sent the negro forward, with directions to go fifty or sixty leagues (from 135 to 162 miles) north, and send him from time to time news of whatever he saw and heard. The more favorable the reports the larger should be the cross on the piece of white wood which the negro was to send with each despatch of an Indian messenger.

Bacapa appears on the map that Father Joseph Stöcklein, S. J., published in the *Neuen Weltblatt* in 1728, which is based on the journey of the famous Jesuit missionary P. Eusebius Kühne (Eusebio Kino), as St. Ludovicus de Bacapa, and is located in Arizona, west of Tucson—Fray Marcos himself gives the distance from the coast as forty leagues, or 108 miles. He arrived there before Easter of 1539. Bacapa could not therefore have lain so far north as Father Kühne's map represents it, but must at farthest have been in the northern part of the southern half of Sonora, near the present Matape. In this case it was probably a Pima settlement, as the name denotes.* Four days after the negro de-

---

* Particularly the first syllable, *Bac*, a corruption of *Bat Ki*—old house—as it often appears in the names of places in Arizona, e.g., *San Xavier del Bac*, *Tubac*, etc.

parted the monk received a first message from him through Indians, who brought a cross the height of a man. The Indians told "such wonderful things of his discoveries," Fray Marcos says, "that I would not believe them unless I saw the things myself. . . . The Indian told me that it was thirty days' journey from the place where Estévanico was to the first city of the country, which was called Cibola. . . . He affirmed and maintained that this first province contained seven very large cities which were all subject to one lord. In them were large houses of stone and mortar, the smallest of which were one story high with a terrace, and there were besides two- and three-storied buildings. The chief's house was of four stories. There were many decorations at the entrance of the principal houses, and turquoises, which were very plentiful in the country. The people of these cities were very well clothed." Notwithstanding these reports, Fray Marcos was in no hurry to go away from Bacapa. He seems not to have placed an absolute trust in the negro, and waited for the return of the Indians who had gone by his command to the coast (of the Gulf of California). They came back bringing with them natives of the seashore. These belonged, no doubt, to the Seris, a wild tribe who still live on the islands of the Gulf of California. On the same day men came into Bacapa from the east, Indians whose faces, breasts, and arms were painted. They confirmed the stories that the negro's messengers had brought. Fray Marcos de Nizza hesitated no longer. He started away two days after Easter, following the track of his dark-skinned guide, in search of the "seven cities of Cibola."

The name of Cibola was thus known away in the interior of Sonora. Whence was it derived? From what Indian language was it borrowed? These are questions with which till recently only my eminent friend F. H. Cushing, and, to a small extent, I myself have been engaged. How far our investigations are of definite value can hardly be determined as yet, for the languages of Sonora are still very little known. They are reduced, if we exclude the Apache idiom, to three large groups. In the south is the Cahita or Yaqui language, which includes the Mayo; in the west the Seri; and in the centre, north, and east the Pima-Opata, which is divided into two principal branches—the Pima and the Joyl-raua or Opata. The Eudeve and Jova appear to be dialects of the Opata. At Bacapa Fray Marcos was among the Pimas; Estévanico, a few days' journey north, was either among the Pimas, the Seris, or the Opatas, for those three tribes met in the vicinity of Ures. The word Cibola might therefore belong to one of the languages or dialects of northern Sonora and the districts north and northeast of it. Its home need not be sought south of there.

Both the Pima and the Opata languages have names of places which somewhat resemble the word Cibola. East of the little village of Huachinera, at the western foot of the Sierra Madre, the Yaqui River emerges from a dark gorge and turns thence to the northwest, to irrigate the narrow, fertile valley of Bascrac and Babispe. At the place where the river leaves the gorge, to turn a little later upon its northern course, lie some ruins of former villages of the Opatas, concerning the fate of which definite traditions exist. Not far from the mouth of the gorge is Batesopa; farther west are Baquigopa, then Cobora, and lastly Quitamac. When in April, 1884, I passed through this wilderness with my intelligent guide, Spiridion Lucero, to explore the ruins, exposed to constant danger of our lives from the swarms of Apaches around us, we came, after twice fording the Yaqui, to a rock around which led an extremely perilous, dizzy path, fully a hundred feet above the raging stream. The Opata Indians call this critical spot "Ci-vo-ná-ro-co," or the rock which one goes around. A distant resemblance can be recognized between this name and Cibola, or, as it was sometimes written in the sixteenth century, "Cevola" and "Civona"; and the ruins of Batesopa opposite the dangerous cliff, as well as those of Baquigopa west of it, point to the former existence of villages of considerable extent.*

The language of the Pimas is divided into several dialects. Besides the southern and northern Pima, there are the Pápago and the now extinct Sobaypuri dialects. In the idiom of the northern Pimas, the ruins on the southern bank of the Rio Gila in Arizona, generally known as Casa Grande (in distinction from Casas Grandes in Chihuahua), are called "Civano-qi," the house of the Civano. The traditions as I heard them on the spot relate that in the times before the coming of the Spaniards the Pimas lived

* The large former settlement of the Opatas at Casas Grandes, at the western foot of the Sierra Madre in Chihuahua, cannot be considered in connection with this discussion, for it was called "Hue-hueri-gi-ta," and was already deserted in the sixteenth century.

on the banks of the middle Gila, between Riverside and Phenix, in Arizona, in permanent houses, which were grouped into small villages. No common bond connected the different villages, except in those cases where small settlements gathered around a larger neighboring one. Such tribe centers existed at Florence, Casa Grande, Zacaton, and Casa Blanca on the Gila, and at Mesa City and Tempe on the lower Rio Salada. The best known of these is the ruin of Casa Grande.

Thirty days' journey north of Ures carries the pedestrian to the other side of the Gila River. In ten days he can easily reach the present southern boundary of Arizona, and following the course of the little Rio San Pedro, he can in five or six days more be at San Carlos on the Gila. But the old Pima villages around Casa Grande lie a hundred miles in a straight line west of San Carlos, and it would be hard to keep in this straight line, for the mountains south of the Gila as far as Riverside are high, wild, broken, and poorly watered. The estimate of thirty days' journey might therefore possibly fit Casa Grande. The first description of Cibola which Estévanico's Indians gave the monk is, however, more important. It does not apply to the stairlike style of building of the pueblos, but to such architecture as I found at Casa Grande, and everywhere in the ruins on the Gila, Salado, and Rio Verde. The principal building at Casa Grande, still standing, is indeed not of stone, but of coarse adobe; but three stories are still plainly visible, while smaller, one-storied houses are scattered around it. The supposition is therefore not to be absolutely rejected, that the accounts concerning Cibola current in Sinaloa were a recollection of the former Pima settlement of Civano-qi, eighty miles northwest of Tucson, on the Gila River, the ruins of which are now known by the name of Casa Grande—the great house.

Settlements of similar architectural character existed in Sonora in the sixteenth and seventeenth centuries, and belonged likewise to the Pima, or, as it was sometimes called, the Névome tribe. The Jesuit missionary Padre Andrés Pérez de Ribas wrote of them in 1645: "Their houses were better and more solidly built than those of the other nations, for the walls consisted of large air-dried brick of clay, with flat roofs and balconies. They built some [of these houses] much larger, and with loop-holes, in order to take refuge in them as in a fortress in case of a hostile attack, and to defend themselves with bows and arrows." The principal building of Casa Grande seems to have been a place of refuge of this kind.

Whilst it appears probable and even certain that these "permanent houses" of the Pimas in Sonora, and not the great communal structures of the New Mexican pueblos, were what Cabeza de Vaca had seen in his wanderings, it is still doubtful to what extent an indefinite recollection of their former settlement of Civano-qi may have made the southern Pimas the originators of the story of Cibola. It is to be remarked, however, that according to the reports which Estévanico sent to the priest, Cibola designated a still existing Indian settlement, and not a ruin, as Casa Grande undoubtedly was at that time. I have taken much pains to determine on the spot which of the numerous settlements of the Opatas, Sobaypuris, and Pimas, of which the ruins are still visible, may have been inhabited and relatively prosperous in the sixteenth century, and have found that (except the villages of the southern Pimas already mentioned, which are not, however, in question here) not one of these so-called pueblos corresponds to what is known to us of Cibola. It therefore seems useless to look for Cibola anywhere south of the Rio Gila or on that stream; but only north of it, either in the present Arizona or the present New Mexico, can we expect to find such a clue in language and tradition as shall lead with any certainty to a definite locality.

There is no doubt that the whole extensive region between the course of the Gila in the south, its sources in the east and the present San Carlos in the west, with the northern half of New Mexico and Arizona, was controlled in the sixteenth century by a single linguistic stock—that of what are called the "Apaches." I say controlled, for the Apaches had no fixed abodes then more than they have now, and they roamed through the whole wild chaos of mountains, by their incursions excluding other tribes from the country. Most of their little huts of branches, sometimes plastered with mud, were set up along the streams, but they only stayed in one place so long as no occasion, however frivolous, prompted them to move their camp to some safer or more favorable place. The Apaches therefore furnish nothing to support us in localizing Cibola among them, and I know of no place-name in their language that can be connected with it. Farther east, along the course of the Rio Grande in New Mexico, are the pueblos of the Piros; these, too, aside from their distant situation, give no clue. The region, clothed with magnificent fir-trees, between the Gila and the Rio Colorado Chiquito (the Little Colorado) in western Arizona, the noble mountain landscape of the Sierra Blanca, the wild and precipitous rocks of the Escudilla and Sierra del Dátil, the still sparsely populated hunting-grounds between the Rio Grande and the Rito Quemado—were uninhabited, and only the Apaches and their northern relatives, the present Navajos, swept through them from time to time on hunting and predatory expeditions.

An undulating, often bare, highland begins in the northern part of the Escudilla, the average height of which is 6000 feet above the sea. One may wander for days at a time on the mesas, as if in a large garden of low, spreading junipers. At rare intervals a valley cuts through the uniform level, the borders of which sometimes present picturesque rocks of inconsiderable height. This region is bounded on the north by the valley of the western Rio Puerco. In the east it passes through the continental watershed of what is called the "Atlantic and Pacific Divide" into the more broken heights of San Estévan de Acoma to the Cerros Mohinos, not far from the Rio Grande. In the west it flattens out, without losing in height, into the treeless district of the Little Colorado. This desert country, visited by the summer's heat and the winter's cold, situated in New Mexico and on the borders of Arizona, is penetrated by a small river which rises in the Atlantic and Pacific Divide, flows generally from east to west, and unites in Arizona with the Rio Puerco. This stream flows at first through a narrow and exceedingly fertile valley. About thirty miles from the borders of Arizona it widens into a sandy and treeless but productive intervale. This intervale, which is hardly fifteen miles long and nowhere more than twelve miles wide, is watered only by the muddy brook. An isolated table-mountain rises on the southeast side over the edge of the intervale to a perpendicular height of 1026 feet above its level. The rocks everywhere hang wall-like over the valley, or swell out at the foot over the river; and only a few dizzy paths lead to the summit. Similar colossal rocks tower upon the north side, far above the rest of the valley's edge. This plain, with the little sand-burdened river that bears its name, is the plain of Zuñi.

I can never forget my first view of this plain from a distance, nor the entrance into it. I had left the provisional station of Bennett's late in the morning, alone, on foot, without arms, to go thirty miles to Zuñi on a strange road through a wholly uninhabited country, which was only occasionally traversed by Navajo Indians. Till four o'clock in the afternoon I passed through the apparently endless plateau, on which the sandy trail was visible only from one juniper bush to another, and seemed to lead around each one. From the few elevations only the next rise could be seen; no mountain ranges enlivened the horizon, for thick clouds covered the sky; it was in February, and a snow-storm might come on at any moment. About four o'clock in the afternoon I reached an ascent on the summit of which rested a little light. In the southeast rose gigantic masses of red sandstone menacingly high above the dark-green wood. These were the mesas of Zuñi. The sun broke out of the clouds and its beams in a little while changed the distant colossi into glowing pillars of fire; the sky was then covered again, and instead of the dreaded snow-storm there came on a shower, with distant thunder in the west. Beyond the light pine woods encompassed me; the eatable piñon (*Pinus edulis*) overshadowed the dwarf forms of the junipers. It began to grow dark, and the frequent thunder-claps were sounding nearer. When I came out of the wood the plain of Zuñi lay before me in a sombre half-light; sand-whirls were driving through it and veiled the lofty mesa; I stood at the foot of the northern table-mountain, which rose sheer a full thousand feet. A flash of lightning ran through the sky and struck the rocks below, and an icy gust brought a shower of hailstones. The lightning flashes were numerously repeated and always struck the same peak—a phenomenon with which the Indians are well acquainted, and which occurs in every thunder-storm. A shower of hail followed without rain, and then it became calm and dark. Distant lightning reminded us of the storm that had passed, but the sky was still clouded and extreme darkness covered the plain. I could not see the way. Then the eastern horizon brightened up with the light of the rising moon without the clouds breaking, and I could perceive the outlines of the rock mass in front of me, in the direction of which the village of Zuñi lay. At last the moon came out, and the stars shone in the zenith. A procession of clouds was floating in front of me, over the top of a dark, low hill. That hill was Zuñi, where I afterward spent weeks of instructive research in the house and the company of Mr. Cushing.

The name of Zuñi does not belong to the language of the tribe that bears it, but to the Queres idiom of the valley of the Rio Grande. The pueblo is named "Halona," and the Zuñi Indians call themselves "A-shiui."* They call the land they occupy "Shiuano," a name the analogy of which with Cibola should not be overlooked.† It is therefore not strange that the general direction in which Estévanico went, and in which the monk followed at a regular distance behind him, was north. Unfortunately

---

* The application by the whites of foreign names to Indian tribes is very frequent in America.

† We may remark further that interchanges of *b* and *v* were common with the early Spanish writers, and that Fray Marcos de Nizza was a Piedmontese, who, writing in the Italian style, wrote *Ci* for the English *Chi;* thus the similarity between Shiuano and Chivola becomes greater, and the difference limits itself to such a confusion of sounds and such exchanges of letters arising from it as are often and strikingly exemplified in the Indian names of places in New Mexico; for example, in the Tehua language, *Ta-ui* into *Taos;* in the Queres, *Pa-go* or *Pa-yo-qo-na* into *Pecos, Hamish* into *Jemez, Qo-tyi-ti* into *Cochiti;* the Tigua word *Tuth-la-nay* into *Tutahaco, Saray* into *Xalay, Na-si-ap* into *Napeya;* the Zuñi names *Mu-gua* into *Moqui, Hacuqua* into *Acuco.* It is therefore not unreasonable to suppose that the name Cibola, as the Italian monk heard and pronounced it, was strikingly similar to the word in the Zuñi language that denotes the Zuñi country; therefore this first linguistic clue suggests that the "seven cities of Cibola" may be sought in the region of Zuñi.

the single report which Fray Marcos, the only scribe in his party, wrote is unsatisfactory, or deficient in geographical data. No conclusions can be drawn from it in respect to the character of the country or to the number of rivers, the volume of water in them or their course. Equally indefinite are his statements concerning the inhabitants. The zealous Franciscan seems to have been animated by only one thought— that of finding the seven cities of Cibola. The farther he advanced, the more he heard of them, and the more definite were the accounts. Besides the Indians of Sonora, probably Pimas, by whom he was accompanied, men of the northern tribes joined him as he proceeded on his journey. It is still, however, possible that he continued entirely within the territory of the Pimas; for the Indians of Bacapa, who belong to the southern Pima tribe, served him everywhere as interpreters.* Only short distances separated them from their tribal relatives, who were known under the name of the Pápagos (Pápap Ootam), and then † formed the lowest, the most miserable, branch of the great linguistic group. Fray Marcos crossed the southeast corner of the "Papaguerćá" and turned toward the northeast, where he successively met the Sobaypuris and, on the Gila, the Ootam (men) or northern Pimas. He was everywhere received in a friendly manner. Estévanico kept sending back the cross signs, as had been agreed upon, and thus fortified the zeal of the enthusiastic monk. The stories of the natives set forth the glories of Cibola in ever more brilliant

---

* They are also known in Sonora as Névomé.
† As they still did at the beginning of this century.

colors. Then he heard names of places suggestive of grandeur: they spoke, for instance, of the "province" of Totonteac; of a "city" of Ahacus, which was one of the seven cities; of a "kingdom" of Hacus in the vicinity of Cibola, and of another "kingdom" called Marata. They told of green stones that adorned the doorposts of the houses of Cibola, of houses several stories high, of skins that came from a large animal of the cow-kind with curly hair. And the negro sent him back not only crosses for his encouragement, but also verbal accounts that confirmed all that the Indians had given the Franciscan to understand by signs and words.

The negro also travelled in company. During his wanderings with Cabeza de Vaca he had obtained a clapper or gourd-rattle, like those which are used by most of the Indian tribes in their religious rites and in working their cures. He carried this with him, and thereby acquired for himself the dignity and fame of a medicine-man. But Estévanico seems to have made an unwise use of the advantage which this prestige gave him. Besides requiring from the natives more provisions than he needed, he sought greedily for precious metals and green stones, and abused the superstitious Indians because they had not enough of them to satisfy his avarice. He seems also to have made requisitions upon the highest and most precious possession of the people, their women. Yet he obtained leaders and guides everywhere, and when Fray Marcos had reached the interior of Arizona, the black was far ahead of him with a numerous retinue.

All that can be definitely gathered from the scanty ethnographic information which the monk has left is, that even tribes that spoke the same language were separated from one another by uninhabited tracts. When he had crossed the Gila there lay before him a wide, depopulated district which he calls a desert (*desierto*). This word should be understood, however, not in the sense of a dry, barren region, but simply of a country without inhabitants. On the other side of this land, forsaken or neglected by men, far in the north, lay Cibola. The missionary entered upon the passage of that desert region with a numerous company, and it was midsummer when the Indians of his retinue at last assured him that only a few days' journey separated him from the long-sought spot. Then natives met him who flocked around him trembling and distressed, with all the evidences of great trouble. Their scanty clothing was torn, and they appeared to be starved and exhausted by long flight. They were men who had been with Estévanico, and brought bad news.

The negro had arrived at Cibola a little before, and had behaved there in his peculiar reckless manner. So much, and no more, was disclosed in the confused expressions which Fray Marcos obtained from his agitated and frightened informants. Some of them had soon perceived that their presence was not welcome to the inhabitants of the place, and had concealed themselves in the vicinity. Others remained with the black. Trustworthy details of what occurred afterward are wanting, for the catastrophe appears to have taken place in the interior of the village, or, as the story has it, "the city." The fugitives, who were still in hiding, one day saw a number of persons coming out of the place. They recognized those of their company who had remained behind, as fleeing, and pursued by the people. The negro Estévanico, however, was not among them; the people of Cibola had killed him, notwithstanding his medicine rattle. The fugitives succeeded in escaping, and eventually in finding the hiding-place of their companions. Then they all took to flight, for the people were searching the vicinity for them. They now implored the priest not to make any further effort to approach Cibola. Estévanico had been killed, and the inhabitants were in great excitement. Only rapid flight could deliver them all, for the braves of Cibola were already on their track.

After nearly reaching his aim, having come almost to the threshold of the place so long sought with so much toil and anticipation, Fray Marcos de Nizza could now feel the force of the warning,

> Back, thou canst serve thy friend no more.
> Then save thine own life.

The trial was a severe one to Fray Marcos. Yet suddenly and unexpectedly as it had come, he came as quickly to a decision. His object was to reconnoiter; the instructions enjoined him to learn as much as he could, but in doing so to expose himself as little to danger as possible. He questioned the fugitives searchingly concerning what they had seen in Cibola, and they confirmed all that he had previously heard of it. They told him that the place where Estévanico was killed was only one of the seven cities of Cibola, and was not the most populous one. The priest concluded from their accounts and expressions that even to go to the place would be attended with great risk to life. He would have to give up his missionary work temporarily, for a martyr's death would under such circumstances be fruitless. Yet it seemed possible to him to steal carefully into the vicinity and cast a glance from some favorable point into the region of his hopes and desires, in order to be satisfied by seeing for himself, even if it were only from a distance, of the truth or untruth of the accounts that had been brought to him. By this method he hoped properly to perform his duty to the Spanish authorities, and at the same time, if he succeeded in executing the attempt without harm, to gain some knowledge of the land and be prepared to carry out the work of conversion if he should return at some later time and with better opportunity.

Attempts have been made in later times to fasten a charge of cowardice upon Fray Marcos because he did not give himself blindly up to death by taking the risk of going among the excited people of Cibola. Catholic missionaries have set examples of heroic devotion in many other places, and have with their blood fertilized the earth, to the securing in later times of rich spiritual harvests to the Church. The reproach is in this case undeserved and unjust. As the instructions of Don Antonio de Mendoza show, the Franciscan's position was ambiguous, and his purpose was rather to prepare than to complete. Obviously nothing was to be gained by a heroic sacrifice of his life, while everything, the whole object of his journey, might have been defeated by it. If this object was to be secured, he must before everything else spare his life in order to return to Mexico and make new attempts thence.

The censure is especially unfair in view of the effort which the priest resolved to make before he began his retreat to Mexico. That the attempt to steal up into the vicinity of Cibola was attended with great difficulties and considerable danger is attested by the opposition of the men of his company, otherwise so obedient, when he asked them to assist him. He eventually succeeded in persuading a few to go with him, but the majority held back. The party went upon the precarious way with extreme caution, and at last reached a hill whence they looked down into a valley in which lay several villages, the houses of which were unusually large, of several stories, and apparently built of clay and stone. The village nearest to them was pointed out as the one in which the negro had been killed. It seemed to be "as large as the City of Mexico," and men could be clearly seen in it who appeared to be dressed in cotton. Rejoicing in these discoveries, and at now being able to make a report to the viceroy of what he had observed, Fray Marcos started on his return. He first, however, set up a wooden cross on the spot from which he had seen Cibola. It was intended to be an evidence to the natives of his having been there without their knowledge, and at the same time a notice that he would at some time return.

The retreat during the first few days naturally

took the character of a carefully guarded flight. But the fugitives soon felt safe, and with less caution, and accordingly greater speed, they went toward the south without meeting any further obstacles. The monk arrived at Culiacan on September 2, 1539, and shortly afterward sent the viceroy the report to which we are indebted for our knowledge of his journey and for the first authentic account of New Mexico.

Few documents of Spanish origin concerning America have been exposed to a sharper and more severe criticism than the *"Descubrimiento de las siete Ciudades"* of Fray Marcos de Nizza. It has been condemned for defectiveness and superficiality, and charges of exaggeration and untruth have been made against it. A one-sided and inadequate investigation has also caused doubt to be cast upon the declaration that he saw Cibola. The fact has not been without effect in the inquiry that no one has ever succeeded in finding among the Indian tribes of New Mexico a tradition, myth, or story, even in a distorted form, containing a reminiscence of the march, presence, or fate of the negro Estévanico or of the Franciscan. Both, the black and the monk, were prominent figures, well fitted to leave deep traces in the memories of the natives. This total disappearance of all recollections of these two personages has also, perhaps unawares, moved other more meritorious inquirers to look for Cibola in the ruins of long extinct pueblos.

In the year 1880 Frank Hamilton Cushing, commissioned by the Bureau of Ethnology at Washington, went to the pueblo of Zuñi, in order, for the first time in the annals of science, to subject a tribe of men who stood on a lower plane of civilization than ours to a thorough study by completely identifying himself temporarily with their condition. The distinguished young student was even more successful than he had hoped to be in accomplishing his difficult and somewhat dangerous task. Through becoming a Zuñi by all the forms of their law he made himself thoroughly acquainted with the past and present of the tribe, and has, by his discovery of the esoteric bond among the Indians for religious purposes, made the most important contribution of recent times to our knowledge of primitive peoples, as well as to the history of polytheism.

In the course of his laborious researches, which occupied him and his devoted wife and prevented their permanent return to civilization till 1884, Mr. Cushing collected a valuable store of historical legends and folk-stories. Most unselfishly he permitted me to draw from his collection, and whatever these sketches contain of linguistic explanations, traditions, customs, and usages from the circle of the Zuñi is of his acquisition; and I more gladly use it because it gives me the opportunity to acknowledge with hearty thanks the eminent merit of their collector.

There are associated with the whole region of Zuñi a mass of tales and household stories of a religious and historical nature and of a more or less contemplative character. Many of these stories, transmitted through the esoteric union with exact fidelity during hundreds of years, reflect the influence which the surroundings have imperceptibly exercised in a powerful degree upon human thought and feeling. The treeless, sandy plains, the low heights of the borders covered with junipers, stand in impressive contrast to the few isolated table-mountains which rise perpendicularly here and there like gigantic towers. Many of the tales rest upon historical foundations, and the history is clothed as with the drapery of a wonderful landscape. The high mesa of Zuñi, called in the language of the tribe "To-yo-a-la-na," or Thunder-mountain, is four miles at the northern end, six miles at the southern end, from the pueblo; then it bends around to the east and turns back to the north. The red sandstone rocks rise nearly everywhere perpendicularly from the plain. The summit is a plateau, overgrown with junipers, piñons, and cactus, and with scanty grass. On it are the ruins of six small pueblos. This group of ruins has been christened "Old Zuñi," but erroneously, for the aggregated villages were built after 1680 and deserted about 1705, when the tribe of Zuñi, which had fled to the rocks before the Navajos and from fear of the Spaniards, returned of its own accord to the valley where its pueblo now stands. But several ruins of old towns lie at the foot of the mesa, concerning which very definite historical traditions still exist. "Ma-tza-ki," once an important place, is in the northwest, and "O'aquima" in the south. The rocks there form a niche which is filled to the height of about one hundred and fifty feet with steep, partly barren heaps of *débris*. Imposing cliffs menacingly overlook these hills, but the rock-wall in the background of the niche rises less perpendicularly, although inaccessibly smooth, to the plateau of the summit. At the foot of the hill is permanent water, to which extend the scattered individual fields of the Zuñi Indians.

On the crests of these hills, imbedded as it were in the niche, stand the ruins of "Heshota O'aquima," a former village of the Zuñi. It was a pueblo of moderate importance in 1599, but was wholly deserted after the insurrection of 1680, and fell into ruins. The population may be estimated, from the appearance of the ruins, to have been equal to about half that of Zuñi, which was 1608 in 1880. Difficult to assail, easily defended against an enemy who had no artillery or long-range guns, provided with water and a fertile soil, O'aquima had an exceptionally protected situation. The village could be seen only from the southern, southwestern, and southeastern sides; on every other side it was enclosed and hidden by the rocks.

The Zuñis definitely informed Mr. Cushing, after he had become an adept by initiation into the esoteric fraternity of warriors, that a "black Mexican" had once come to O'aquima and had been hospitably received there. He, however, very soon incurred mortal hatred by his rude behavior toward the women and girls of the pueblo, on account of which the men at last killed him. A short time after that the first white Mexicans, as the Indians call all white men whose mother-tongue is Spanish, came to the country and overcame the natives in war. This tale is of indubitable authenticity, and of evident significance. It proves what I have only intimated above, that Cibola represented the present country and tribe of Zuñi. It is also of great importance in its bearing upon the truth of the statements of Fray Marcos. The hill from which he, coming from the southwest, looked at Cibola, could have been nowhere but on the southern border of the plain of Zuñi; and it is only from that side that the pueblo of O'aquima can be seen, while it is possible to approach it thence unremarked to within two miles, and to observe everything plainly. There, too, the remains of a wooden cross were visible till a few years ago. It has been supposed that this was the cross which the monk erected; considering the dry atmosphere of the region, the supposition, even if it is not probable, is not to be wholly rejected.

The charge of exaggeration and distortion which has been made against the *"Descubrimiento de las siete Ciudades"* is based chiefly upon two points—on the comparison of Cibola or O'aquima with the City of Mexico, and on the statement that the people of Cibola were accustomed to adorn their houses with green stones, or turquoises.

Besides the fact that every New Mexican pueblo appears larger and more imposing from a distance than it really is on account of the peculiar structure of its houses, we should bear in mind that the priest's comparison was not with the earlier Indian pueblo of Tenochtitlan that was destroyed by Cortés, or, still less, with the present City of Mexico, but with the new Spanish town as Fray Marcos knew it in the year 1539. It is very doubtful whether it had a thousand inhabitants then, and the houses they lived in were all grouped, for the sake of security, in the vicinity of the present Zócalo. The comparison, therefore, instead of being exaggerated, seems to have been fitting and correct. As to the decoration of the doorposts with turquoises, Mr. Cushing has found that a custom formerly prevailed, in Zuñi at least, of decorating the openings in the roof through which the inmates of the house went down into the rooms and chambers with green stones, among which kalaite, or turquoise, carbonate of copper, or malachite, and phosphate of copper, etc., were occasionally introduced. The monk was therefore correctly informed concerning this matter, and repeated truly what had been told him.

Efforts have been made for a long time in vain to localize the names which Fray Marcos heard of what were styled "kingdoms," "provinces," and "cities" in the vicinity of Cibola. Mr. Cushing has succeeded in explaining the names of "Marata" and "Totonteac." Although they are distorted, they both belong to the language of the Zuñi, and denote directions, rather than particular regions. "Ahacus," on the other hand, is one of the seven cities— Ha-ui-cu or Aguas calientes—situated fifteen miles southwest of Zuñi, and deserted since the year 1679. "Hacus," finally, which Fray Marcos called a kingdom in distinction from the others, is a tribe independent of Zuñi, that of Acoma, the real name of which is A-co, and which the Zuñi, according to Cushing, call Ha-cu-quü.

The return of the priest, his remarkable experiences, and the stories which he brought from the far north attracted the highest degree of attention from the officers and people of Mexico. Nobody doubted the truth of the statements of Fray Marcos. He had not found gold and silver, but he had discovered settled tribes and a fertile country. The notion of great wealth in metals readily associated itself with these two elements, and it was not difficult to obtain help in men and means for the organization of a campaign on a larger scale into those regions. Don Antonio de Mendoza therefore did not hesitate, after the discovery had been made and the way pointed out, to proceed to conquest. For this he found a ready and willing instrument in Francisco Vasquez Coronado.

CHAPTER III.

FRANCISCO VASQUEZ CORONADO.

ALTHOUGH still young, Coronado had filled offices of no little importance in Mexico. He was born in Salamanca, Spain, and had married the daughter of Alonzo de Estrada, royal treasurer in Mexico. Nuño de Guzman had persecuted and imprisoned Estrada because he would not connive at the robbery of the royal chest of 9000 pesos. After the inquisitorial judge, Diego Perez de la Torre, who had put Guzman in prison, died in 1538 at Guadalajara, Cristóbal de Oñate, father of the future conqueror of New Mexico, succeeded him as governor in New Galicia, and Coronado was appointed by a royal decree of April 15, 1539, to conduct the usual examination of the administration of the deceased. He exchanged this position of *juez de residencia* in the same year for the higher one of governor of the province, with which Oñate had been only provisionally invested. When Fray Marcos returned to the City of Mexico Coronado was there. He asked of the viceroy Mendoza the privilege of attempting at his own expense the conquest and colonization of the newly discovered lands in the north. The viceroy had always regarded and treated Coronado as a favorite and readily accepted his offer, which would save him all material expenditure, and as readily agreed to another condition: to the preparation of an expedition by sea from Natividad, in the present state of Guadalajara, to explore the coast toward the north and the interior of the Gulf of California,* but principally to keep along the coast in touch with Coronado's land expedition. A comrade of Coronado's, Pedro Casteñeda, writes of the object of this cruise: "When the soldiers had all left Mexico, the viceroy ordered Don Pedro de Alarcon to sail with two ships from Natividad to the coast of the Southern Sea and proceed to Jalisco, in order to take on board the things which the soldiers could not carry. He was then to sail along the coast, following the march of the army, for it was believed, according to the reports, that it would not be far away, and could easily keep in communication with the ships by means of the rivers. But matters turned out differently, as we shall see further along, and the effects were lost, at least [Casteñeda grimly adds] to those to whom they belonged."

The cost of the fitting out of these two expeditions amounted, according to Herrera, to 60,000 ducats, a sum at that time equivalent to more than a quarter of a million dollars of our currency. Coronado was therefore deeply in debt, when he, on February 1, 1540, left Compostella, whither the viceroy had accompanied him, to march with his land "army" toward the north. The force consisted, according to Casteñeda, of 300 Spaniards and 800 Indians. Mota-Padilla says definitely that Coronado

---

* Then called *Mar Vermejo*, the Red Sea. It was navigated for the first time by Francisco de Ulloa, in 1539.

had 260 horse and 60 foot, with more than a thousand Indians, and that he took with him six swivel-guns, more than a thousand spare horses and other horses carrying freight and ammunition. According to Herrera, the train was accompanied by large numbers of live sheep and swine. The Spaniards were divided into eight companies, which were commanded by the captains Diego de Guzman, Rodrigo Maldonado, and other officers. Lopez de Samaniego was master of the ordnance (*maestro de campo*) and Pedro de Tobar ensign. Four priests of the Franciscan order went along with the battalion: Fray Marcos (who had in the meantime become provincial), Fray Juan de Padilla, Fray Juan de la Cruz, and Fray Luis de Ubeda. Another priest and a lay brother seem to have afterward joined the force. Don Antonio de Mendoza took so much part in the expedition as to choose and appoint the higher officers. Pablo de Melgosa commanded the infantry and Hernando de Alvarado the small artillery force. Nothing was forgotten that could give the expedition splendor of equipment, the most effective leaders, and the largest provision. Coronado himself enjoyed general confidence, but he left behind him, says his morose subaltern Casteñeda, "great wealth and a young, noble, and lovely wife."

The viceroy, while setting in operation the preparations for this miniature massing of forces, had made a farther step toward the exploration of the north. With the caution that attended every important transaction of the Spanish officers, he had already taken measures to test upon the spot the trustworthiness of the representations of Fray Marcos. Not so much from suspicion as from prudence, based on a knowledge of the honest weaknesses of human nature, Don Antonio de Mendoza had ordered Captain Melchior Diaz to follow from Culiacan the route of the Franciscan toward the north, and approach as near Cibola as possible. Diaz started out with fifteen horsemen on November 17, 1539. On the 20th of March, 1540, the viceroy received a letter from him from Culiacan, whither he had returned with his task so far unaccomplished that he had not succeeded in getting farther north than "Chichiltic-calli." Beyond that point lay an uninhabited region at the end of which was Cibola. "When one has passed the great desert,"* wrote Diaz, "he will find seven cities which are about a day's journey from one another. All together are called Civola." Diaz received this information and a description of the houses of Cibola which was extraordinarily accurate from the Indians between Chichiltic-calli and Culiacan. There was much snow in the former region and the country began to be again mountainous there. He consequently returned, convinced that he could not go farther with his small means.

The name "Chichiltic-calli" is derived from the Nahuatl language of Central Mexico, and means literally "red house." It therefore probably came from the Indians who went with Fray Marcos on his first journey, among whom were some who spoke the Nahuatl language. The word has now disappeared as the name of a place. The position of Chichiltic-calli is thus an object of careful search,

* Properly, uninhabited region—"*desierto.*"

the more so because the determination of its location will afford an important aid in the identification of Cibola.

General Simpson and several writers following him have expressed the opinion that the ruins of "Casa Grande," which the Pimas call Civano-qi, on the southern bank of the Gila River and about eighty-five miles northwest of Tucson in Arizona, represent Chichiltic-calli. Mr. Lewis H. Morgan has very pertinently objected to this supposition that no single ruin on the Rio Gila corresponds with the description which Coronado's contemporaries have left us of the "red house." At the risk of anticipating the course of historical events, I shall examine this question more closely.

Casteñeda says definitely that Chichiltic-calli was 220 leagues, or about 550 English miles, north or northeast of Culiacan, and 80 leagues, or 216 miles, south or southwest of Cibola. The distance and direction point to southeastern Arizona, near the western line of New Mexico, and not to the region of Casa Grande, which is situated rather west of north from Culiacan. Although the measurements as well as the statements of direction of the itineraries of the sixteenth century cannot be implicitly relied upon, still the fact that the companions of Coronado—Casteñeda, Diaz, and Juan Jaramillo—agree in respect to the direction is important. Of still more decisive significance are the descriptions of the country, the account of the building at Chichiltic-calli, and the itinerary itself.

Melchior Diaz, who first saw the "red house," does not mention the ruins. Juan Jaramillo, without speaking of the building, mentions a chain of mountains that was called Chichiltic-calli. Casteñeda, on the other hand, is very circumstantial. He says first, explicitly, that the unpopulated region begins there, and that "the land ceases to be covered with thorny trees and the aspect of the country changes. The Gulf [of California] terminates there, the coast turns, the mountains follow the same direction, and one has to climb over them to get into the plains again. . . . The soil of this region is red. . . . The rest of the country is uninhabited, and is covered with forests of fir, the fruits of which tree are found in abundance. . . . There is a kind of oak there, the acorns of which . . . are as sweet as sugar. Watercresses are found in the springs, rosebushes, *pulegium*, and marjoram." In the vicinity he saw flocks of wild sheep, very large, with long horns and long hair. Finally, he describes the inhabitants as belonging to the wildest tribe which they had met in that country. They dwelt in isolated huts and lived solely by hunting. The ruin was roofless, extensive, and had been built of red earth.

A later writer, Matias de la Mota-Padilla, who was born at Guadalajara in 1688 and died there in 1766, gives a very detailed description of Chichiltic-calli. It is not probable that he had access to the manuscript of Casteñeda, for he was never away from Spanish America.* He borrows nothing either in his account of the "red house" from Herrera, who copied Jaramillo. His statements are, then, derived

* Casteñeda's work was not printed till 1838, and then in a French translation.

from some still unknown source, and are therefore doubly interesting. He says: "They went through a narrow defile (*portezuela*) which was named Chichiltic-calli (which means 'red house,' because there was a house there plastered on the outside with red earth, called *almagre*). There they found fir-trees with fir-cones full of good meat. On the top of a rock lay skulls of rams with large horns, and some said they had seen three or four of these sheep, which were very swift-footed."

Not one of these descriptions corresponds with the Casa Grande of Arizona, and still less do they fit the Casas Grandes in Chihuahua. The latter is even quite out of the question. The former is situated a mile and a half south of the bank of the Gila, in a wide waterless plain of dazzling grayish-white sand and marl. The plain stretches out of sight in the south, but the horizon is bounded in the distant west by the low range of the Maricopa hills, while in the east the Sierra Tortilla is visible in the distance. On the north bank of the Gila the foot-hills of the Superstition Mountains rise precipitously, and back of them that range unfolds itself like a broken wall, overlooked by the Sierra Masásar in the northwest, while in the northeast the Sierra Pinal lifts itself up, the only range crowned with fir-trees. All the near mountains are marked by an awful wildness, frightful steepness, and terrible cliffs and gorges, while the vegetation is sparse and exclusively thorny. There are found the beautiful red-flowered ocotilla (*Fouquiera splendens*), the creosote-plant (*Larrea gigantea*), and quantities of mezcal-agaves. Every plant pricks and the leaves are gray. A lowly vegetation grows on the white sand flats and gravel hills and clings to the bare rocks. Only when showers fall the ravines are filled in a short time with wild torrents, which overflow and irrigate the plain; for while in June, July, and August the clouds discharge daily upon the mountains, a whole year has often passed at Casa Grande, sometimes eighteen months, without its raining. The thermometer rises every day in summer to above 100° in the shade, and snow-falls are almost unknown. It is a hot, arid region, covered with desert plants, to which the coarser forms of the lower animal life, the disgusting bird-spider (*Mygale heintzii*), the great millipede (*Scolopendra heros*), the scorpion (*Scorpio boreus* and *Telyphonus excubitor*), the rattlesnake (*Caudisono molossus*), and the large warty lizard, appropriately called the Gila monster (*Heloderma horridum*), are eminently adapted. The mountain sheep (*Ovis montana*) formerly roamed in the mountains. The region has for many centuries been inhabited exclusively by the Pima Indians, who have always been a more or less settled, agricultural people, like the Pueblos of New Mexico, living in villages composed of round huts, and acquainted with the art of irrigation by canals.

I have already mentioned that the Pimas claimed to be descendants of the inhabitants and builders of the Casa Grande. Casteñeda says that the "red house" was destroyed by the people who lived there at the time of his arrival, and describes them as completely savage.

The ruin of Casa Grande is composed of a whitish-gray calcareous marl, is three stories high, and has no floor or roof. The roof was probably destroyed by fire, kindled by the Apaches. It is not certain but is possible that the building was once covered on the outside with a red plaster, as it still is on the inside, so as to make it look from without like a red house; and in this possibility consists the only analogy that can be discovered between Casa Grande and Chichiltic-calli. In all other points there is not the slightest resemblance.

It is useless to look for the "red house" farther west, or between Florence and Fort Yuma. The ruins cease at Gila Bena, and the country beyond is almost a clear desert. East of Florence, between Riverside and San Carlos, the mountains are too wild and ragged. Within New Mexico there is no place affording any ground for identification with it in the latitude corresponding with the head of the Gulf of California. Chichiltic-calli, therefore, was situated in the southeastern corner of Arizona, and within a quadrangle which is bounded on the east by New Mexico, on the west by the Rio San Pedro, on the south by Sonora, and on the north by the Gila River. As the ruin does not stand upon any stream, it is impossible to fix the exact place; yet I was disposed at first to look for it in the vicinity of the new Fort Grant, or south of Mount Graham, where the fir woods really begin. The height above the sea of this station, where there are considerable ruins, is 4753 feet, while the mountains rise to 10,516 feet, and snow-storms are not only regular every winter, but considerable. If this site should not be found to answer, then the ruins at Eagle Creek, west of Clifton, might be considered. But they lie north of the Rio Gila, and that stream has a considerable breadth and a notable supply of water even in summer. The fact that the mountains north of the banks of the Gila for a short day's journey toward Mount Turnbull, Mount Graham, the Sierra Bonita, and the Peloncillo, are still bare or covered with thorny plants, as at Casa Grande, is against seeking for Chichiltic-calli at Fort Grant. There are also more substantial reasons, as I shall proceed to show, for not looking for it on Eagle Creek.

The march of the troops from Compostella to Culiacan was not free from hindrances. The horses were too highly fed for hard work, and the soldiers did not know how to arrange the loads upon them. Much of the baggage was therefore lost, and the provisions began to fail at Chiametla. The Indians were hostile, and *Maestro de Campo* Samaniego lost his life in a skirmish with them. On Easter Monday, 1540, the little army arrived at Culiacan, where it was received with much enthusiasm and military pomp. Hermandarias de Saavedra was appointed to the place of the slain officer.

Discontent had already broken out among the men in Chiametla. Diaz had met them there on his return, and although his reports were kept secret, stories of misfortune became current, and the storm broke out against Fray Marcos, who was now accused of having purposely exaggerated. We do not know what the Franciscan had said, but what he wrote is fully confirmed by the report of Diaz. The morose Casteñeda says that the priest and Coronado especially had told the men stories about mountains of gold. We have nothing in writing on the subject except Casteñeda's own testimony. It is curious that while he raised such complaints, he at the same time quarrelled with Coronado because he would not stay in New Mexico.

After Coronado had tarried two weeks in Culiacan, he started somewhat hurriedly with fifty horsemen to hasten forward to Cibola in advance of the main body. Ten foot-soldiers and the priests went with him. Cristobal de Oñate remained as representative of the Governor in Sinaloa, and Tristan de Arellano was given the chief command over the main body, with instructions to follow on in fourteen days. The departure of Coronado probably took place at the end of April. The campaign was thus divided into three parts: the advance under Coronado, the rear under Arellano, and the expedition by sea under Alarcon. The last contributed so little to the result that I prefer to tell its story briefly at once.

Hernando Alarcon sailed with the ships "San Pedro" and "Santa Catarina" on May 9th and kept along the coast; encountered the usual storms, terrors, and shoals; added a third ship, the "San Gabriel," to his fleet at "Aguaiaval"; and arrived on August 26th at the mouth of a large river, the current of which was so rapid that the vessels could hardly make way against it. He launched two boats and embarked in them with a few men and light artillery to ascend the stream. The shores were inhabited, and the houses were round, made of limbs of trees, and plastered and covered with earth, like those of the present Pimas. Several families lived in the same building. Not much reliance is to be placed on the reports of the Indians which he repeats in his *Relacion*, for great mistakes were unavoidable in the absence of interpreters. For that reason the statement which would otherwise be valuable, that the Indians showed him a village of stone houses on a height in the distance, is doubtful. Alarcon thus went up and down the river twice, and asserts that he sailed 85 leagues, or 230 miles, upon it. Finally he heard of Cibola, of the arrival of the Spaniards there, and of the death of the negro. The distance at which he was from Cibola is variously given by him at thirty, forty, and ten days' journey. In despair of meeting Coronado, he returned to the Mexican coast at the end of the year 1540, with the purpose of his voyage unaccomplished.

Although the main object of this voyage, coöperation with Coronado, was not gained, it contributed much to geographical knowledge, for it determined the form of the Gulf of California and elicited the first information concerning the lower course of the largest river on the western coast of America—the Rio Colorado; for this is the river which Alarcon ascended with his boats. The map in the *Ptolomæus* of Messer Pietro Andreas Mattiolo, of the year 1548, already represented Lower California in its true shape as a peninsula.

Postponing for the present the story of the efforts which were made by the land expedition to establish communication with Alarcon, I return to Coronado, who left Culiacan and marched northward with sixty men, five priests, one lay brother, and a few Indians who were more bold than discreet. He first met the Yaqui Indians in the territory of Sonora, and north of that, 12 leagues, or 32 miles, from Sonora, he met the southern Pimas in the "Valley of Hearts" (*Valle de los Corazones*). On the third day after his departure from Culiacan, a mishap befell the expedition: a priest, Fray Antonio Victoria, broke his thigh and had to be sent back. The Valley of Hearts is south of Batuco, and Coronado therefore probably reached the Rio Sonora in the vicinity of Babiácora, or about 160 miles south of the Mexican border of Arizona. Forty leagues, or 108 miles, farther on, he founded a Spanish colony in the Valley of Suya, to which he gave the name of San Hierónymo. As the Valley of Suya lay on the Sonora River, San Hierónymo should be looked for north of Bacuachi. The place was situated on the bank of "a small river." Although there are names of places that likewise end in Sonora west of the Sonora Valley, in the country between Magdalena and Altar, once controlled by the Pimas, there is no doubt that Coronado entered the real Sonora Valley. Casteñeda gives names of places that are only to be found there. "Guagarispa," called "Ispa" by Jaramillo, is unmistakably "Huc-aritz-pa," the present "Arispe."

Few valleys have so small a breadth for so great a length as the valley of the Sonora River. From Babiácora to Sinoquipe, a distance of forty-five miles, the fertile intervale widens out at only one place, Banámichi, to three miles; elsewhere it is seldom more than half a mile wide. Large gravel dunes with thorny bushes of mesquite, *choya, pitahaya, agovin,* and *palo-blanco* form a base of greater or less breadth on both sides, from which mountains rise abruptly with wild, picturesque profile, forming on the eastern side a continuous chain which is crossed by only a few extremely difficult paths. The defile which Jaramillo mentions as leading from the south to the Sonora River can only be that one which enters the valley at Babiácora and comes down from Batuco. The Rio Sonora turns thence toward the southwest, and runs through the dark gorge of Ures to the present city of Hermosillo and the Gulf of California. When the first Jesuit missionaries visited the region in the year 1638, they found its inhabitants numerous and more peaceful and better civilized than the other peoples of the country. These inhabitants are now known by the name of "Opata"; they call themselves "Joyl-ra-ua," or village people. The name "Opata" belongs to the Pima language; it arose toward the end of the seventeenth century and is analyzed into "Oop," enemies, and "Ootam," men. The Pimas designate themselves by the latter word. Opata is therefore equivalent to "men hostile to the Pima tribe." The languages of the two tribes are very closely related.

Few tribes in Spanish America have so readily and completely assimilated with the whites as the Opatas of Sonora. I am convinced, after a slow journey of three months through their whole country, that there are hardly two dozen of them who can and will speak their own language. The dress of the Opatas is white, customary in all Mexico, with the palm-leaf hat. Their houses are like the habitations of the Mexicans. They wear sandals or moccasins indifferently, although the latter are more common on account of the great roughness of the mountains. They are generally ashamed of their mother tongue, desire to be *castellano* or *ladino*, and speak only Spanish with their children. Hardly more than recollections and a few dances that have been converted into church festivals are left of their former customs. Four of these were danced a hundred years ago, but only the "daninamaca" and the "pascola" are still in use. The "mariachi," a dance which is similar to our round dances, has been abandoned on account of its obscenity, but the "majo dani," the stag dance, still exists in the recollections of the people.

The present organization of the Opatas has been conformed since the reform legislation of 1857 to the North American pattern—that is, one in which the old and the new are partly combined. The original community of goods of the Indians, which the Crown accorded to them in the seventeenth and eighteenth centuries, still subsists. Hence, since the Indians live alongside of the Spanish families, there is a double administration, which is plainly apparent at some places in the Sonora Valley.

The easy and voluntary, even eager, denationalization of the Opatas cannot be ascribed to the influence of the Jesuits alone, although they exercised an almost theocratic rule over the tribe for one hundred and thirty-eight years. The Pimas were under the same influence for a like period, yet even the Pápagos of Tucson tenaciously hold to the language and partly to the religion of their fathers.

There was an element of greater docility in the nature of the Opatas, which the fathers of the Society of Jesus encouraged, and vigilantly guarded against all interference of the officers and colonists. Then the necessity of defence against a common formidable enemy, the Apaches, attached the sedentary Opatas closely to Spanish civilization and customs for more than two hundred years. The awful desolation which this hereditary enemy inflicted upon the Opatas after the conspiracy formed at Casas Grandes in Chihuahua in 1684 drove them all to the large towns, and compelled them to seek the better protection which the adoption of the Spanish-Mexican arrangement of houses and manner of living afforded them. Those who did not adapt themselves to this condition and remained outside of the pueblos soon fell victims* in the Sierra Madre, the sierra of Texas, to the Janos and Jócomes, and afterward to the Apaches, which gradually absorbed these tribes.

The chroniclers of the campaign which is the object of this study spoke of the Opatas as being "numerous and intelligent." Their habitations in the Sonora Valley were, however, not so large as those of the southern Pimas, and their villages were less populous. I have surveyed seventeen ruins between Los Fresnos and Babiácora, and have visited many other sites of ruins, but have found no village there that contained a hundred huts. But Batesopa, at the foot of the Sierra Huachinera (a branch of the Sierra Madre), may have had two hundred houses. The houses there are also more durably

* The earliest documentary data on the subject are of 1655.

built of clay and stone, or their posts rest on square or rectangular foundations of stone, while the walls are made of intertwined reeds and the roofs of palm leaves or yucca blades, for it is cold in the Sonora Valley. A fan palm is growing in Arispe which has a height of twenty-five feet; and the artistically woven roofing of the leaves of this species, which I have admired in Oaxaca, is an adequate protection against the heavy rains of summer. The little villages were always on elevations near the water, and the rainfall flowed away safely to the lower land. I found no settlement fortified, but places of refuge are numerous in the interior of the Sierra Madre. They are very significantly called fort-hills (*Cerros de Trincheras*). They are natural heights, often very steep, along the brows of which and bending to their sinuosities rude bulwarks of stone have been raised. The hill could thus be converted in the simplest way into a fortification, and where it is conical, as at Terrenate, Ymúrez, and Toni-vavi, near Nacori, the walls naturally assume a spiral form. The Indians thus adapted their constructions to the irregularities of the slopes. The people of several villages could take refuge in one of these fortified heights. These primitive fortifications have attracted the attention of travellers in recent years, and have given rise to exaggerated newspaper reports concerning a gigantic artificial pyramid in the vicinity of Magdalena.

Division into many small tribes was the original constitution and social order of the Opatas. The people of Opasura attacked them on the Sonora

River at Banámichi, and the river-side tribes made war upon one another. The Opatas had slings, stone axes, clubs, and arrows without stone heads, but burnt hard and strongly poisoned. Their clothing was of cotton and skins, and their decorations were of colored feathers.

Our information respecting their religious rites is very scanty, but I have succeeded in collecting some of their folk tales, which permit a glimpse into their earlier forms of belief as well as into their history. They affirm that they came from the north and moved gradually southward. The New Mexican Pueblo Indians recognize the Opatas, as well as the Pimas and the Yaquis, as allied to them, although they are of different linguistic affinities.

Coronado's movements in the valley of the Sonora River appear to have been rapid. He could not possibly have reached Arispe in about a day's journey from Babiácora, as Jaramillo asserts, for the distance is seventy miles; and though a single horseman might accomplish it in case of emergency, a troop composed of horse and foot could not. His relations with the natives seem to have been friendly—Coronado was always very much liked personally by the Indians—and they recognized Fray Marcos and welcomed him. The advance to Sinoquipe in the months of May and June, or before the rainy season begins, is attended with no difficulties. The river is really shrunken to a brook, as Jaramillo describes it, and there are only occasional very low dunes to climb. But the thickets of river poplar, elder, willow, and cane which bordered the course of the Sonora may have presented impediments then, for the paths from village to village wind up and down over the dunes. At Sinoquipe the Spaniards would come upon the series of deep ravines which extend uninterruptedly to Arispe, and thence with slight intermissions to near Bacuachi, and often force the traveller to take to the bed of the river. In the whole distance of one hundred and forty miles between Babiácora and the source of the Sonora the traveller leaves the river bank only once for a short time, while he crosses the narrow stream two hundred and fifty times. It is one of the most charming and at the same time least difficult routes which the North American continent offers to a horseman. A steadily mild climate enhances the traveller's pleasure.

The "Cajon," more than twenty miles in length, through which one passes in going from Sinoquipe to Arispe, is rich in the magnificent development of the most diversified rock-forms. When the "Cabezon de San Benito," a massive, bell-shaped peak, has sunk behind the ever-increasing heights north of Sinoquipe, and these gather thickly around the river's course, there also disappears in the east the rudely notched mountain of the *nueve Minas*, and the inviting cove of Tetuachi reposes on the right bank, surrounded by mighty mountains. Narrow tongues of rock jut forward into the peaceful valley, fall perpendicularly to the ground, and imitate artificial masonry in their resemblance to squared stones piled up in regular symmetry. The rocks that overhang them, rising thousands of feet, are clothed with the peculiar vegetation of the country, which lends a tint of green to even the highest crests.

Through this grand valley as a door one goes into the Cajon proper. The river is bordered with thick foliage, and gigantic cliffs rise like coulisses, one behind another, away up, in the most varied colors of the quaternary rock, alternating with lava. The pillar-shaped *Pitabaya* fastens itself in the clefts of the steepest, even vertical cliffs. Rarely wider than half a mile, yet affording by its numerous bendings a constant change of view, never bare, but unceasingly grand and wild, the ravine appears to go along with the traveller, till the solitary palm-tree at the entrance to the half-ruined city of Arispe introduces him to a new and entirely different landscape: a hollow verdant with fields and with poplars; in the east the Sierra Arispe rises bare and forbidding; the west bank descends steeply to the river's edge, and to it clings a group of adobe dwellings with many ruins of stone buildings and a large, bare church. This is the former capital of Sonora, the population of which has diminished by two thirds in half a century—a melancholy place of decay in the lead region. Here the Rio de Bacanuchi empties into the Sonora from the north, and the Sonora turns; between Bacuachi and Arispe it flows from northeast to southwest. I have already observed that Guagarispa most probably stood on the site of the present Arispe. No ruins of it are visible; they have been built over; but stone axes, mortars, and grinding stones (*metates*) are unearthed here and there. A ravine like that between this place and Sinoquipe begins on the Sonora River farther north, and at "Ti-ji-só-ri-chi" stand above the river the ruins of an ancient pueblo. The country becomes more level at "Chinapa"* and a short distance farther along shapes itself into the sides of the wild Cajon, in the bottom of which one rides beside the foaming Sonora to near Bacuachi. Here the country becomes open, the depression of the chain of the "Manzanal" permits a glimpse in the west of the pillar-shaped Picacho; on the eastern side the dunes extend like a low table-land ten miles toward the east, where a majestic cordillera of picturesque shape and covered with fir-trees stretches from northwest to south. There are a succession of high chains—the Sierra de Bacuachi, the Sierra Púrica, and, in the farthest southeast, the mountains of Oposura or the Sierra Grande.

If Coronado steadily followed the course of the Sonora, Suya should be looked for in the valley of Bacuachi. But if he followed the Bacuachi River, going therefore directly north, he would have approached the Cananía, and consequently the sources of the Rio Santa Cruz. The accounts on these points are unusually indefinite, the same writer often contradicting himself several times. I am inclined to the opinion that he followed the Rio Sonora all the time, and that San Hierónymo should therefore be sought near the ruins of Mututicâchi. Juan Jaramillo says that the Spaniards marched from "Sonora" for four days through an uninhabited region, and then came to a brook which he calls "Nexpa"; followed down this brook for two days to a chain of mountains, along which they continued for two days. This chain of mountains was

* A former mission, which the Apaches burned in 1836, and in the place of which stands a miserable hamlet.

pointed out to him as "Chichiltic-calli." The itinerary of this writer, who marched with Coronado while Casteñeda probably followed the main body, deserves to be reproduced literally.

"After we had crossed these mountains, we came to a deep brook with steep banks, where we found water and grass for our horses. Leaving this brook, which is the other side of the Nexpa of which I have spoken, we took the direction toward the northeast (as it seemed to me), and came in three days, so far as I can remember, to a river which we named *San Juan*, because we arrived there on the day of that saint. Leaving this stream, we passed through a very mountainous country, and turning more to the north, we came to another stream which we named *de las Balsas*, because, it being very high, we had to cross it on rafts. I believe we were two days in going from one river to the other. . . . Hence we went to another brook, which we called *de la Barranca* (of the ravine). The distance from one to the other may be estimated at two short days' journey. The direction is northeast. We then came to a river, after one day's march, which we called *Rio Frio*, on account of the coldness of its water. Thence we passed through fir woods, at the end of which we found cool brooks. . . . In two days we came to another brook, called *Vermejo*—always in the same direction, namely, toward the northeast." There they met Indians from Cibola, and two days afterward they reached the last pueblo. Casteñeda mentions striking a "river" which "flowed" in a deep ravine three days after they entered the "wilderness" north of Chichiltic-calli. He says that the "Rio Vermejo," the waters of which were muddy and red, was eight leagues from Cibola.

I believe that we may without mistake regard Cibola as identical with the country of Zuñi. In view of the extreme indistinctness that rules in all the statements of the participants in the expedition through Sonora, it is impossible to identify its route following it from the south alone. I think I may properly, taking the reverse course, make Zuñi the starting-point of the investigation and pick up the threads of the itinerary thence southward.

Eight leagues, or 22 miles, southwest of Zuñi flows the river of the same name, a muddy, red stream. Two days' journey from Zuñi toward the southwest brings us to the Rio Colorado Chiquito at San Juan, Arizona. This river is as turbid, muddy, and red as the Zuñi. The Rio Vermejo of Jaramillo is therefore the one called the Little Colorado. Casteñeda, who did not go with Coronado, saw the likewise muddy Rio de Zuñi, and confounded the two.

As Coronado reached the Rio San Juan on St. John's day, June 24th, the date of his arrival at Cibola may be fixed as about July 12th. He did not go to Hâ-ui-cu (*Aguas calientes*), fifteen miles southwest of Zuñi, the village nearest to him, but to "Oa-quima," because the negro was killed there. The inhabitants of Oa-quima had been warned by some of their people that the Spaniards had come in sight of the Colorado River. The pueblo stood, as the ruins now show, on a hill. It could not turn out more than two hundred men of war, but the whole male population of all the villages, seven in number, which constituted the tribe of Zuñi, had come to its assistance and were awaiting the Spaniards on the little plain separating Oa-quima from the mesa south of it. The peaceful message sent to them by Coronado was answered with threatening gestures. The horsemen then dashed at them, and the Indians speedily fled from the sight of the strange, rushing figures. The capture of the pueblo proved to be a difficult task, for the steep, rugged precipices were exposed to a hail of stones, which rattled down upon the Spaniards. The assault was made on foot; and in it Coronado narrowly escaped death by a stone. The village was, however, captured in an hour, and the whole tribe submitted soon afterward. The tradition of this event, according to Mr. Cushing, is still living among the Zuñi Indians.

I cannot forbear giving here a final and irrefragable proof of the fact that Zuñi is really Cibola. The French translation of Casteñeda says that the largest pueblo of Cibola was called "Muzaque." In the original manuscript, which is in the Lenox Library in New York, this word is written several times plainly and clearly "Maçaqui." "Matzaqui" is the ruin of a large village situated three miles east of the present pueblo of Zuñi near the foot of the great mesa, and some four or five miles north-northwest of Oa-quima. The Indians say that this village was once the largest of the tribe. The ruins are very much decayed now, but they indicate a considerable settlement. The testimony of the original text of Casteñeda thus lifts the identity of Cibola with Zuñi above all doubt. The possibility that

Matzaqui was not the village of which Casteñeda speaks is quite removed by later documents: first, by the definite affirmation by Espejo in the year 1583 that Zuñi was Cibola, which is confirmed by an act of the year 1601; and second, by the enumeration in the act of submission and pardon of the Zuñi Indians of 1591 of Maçaqui as one of the pueblos of that tribe; and finally, by the language of Fray Augustin de Betancurt, who wrote in the year 1689: "Four-and-twenty leagues from Acoma is the pueblo of Alona, with its Church of the Purification of the Virgin, with two hamlets belonging to the diocese, each with its little church, called Mazaquia, at the entrance to the province of Zuni, Moqui, and Caquima, two leagues from Alona."

The immediate object of the expedition was therefore attained with little trouble in comparison with the labor with which the preparations had been made. A fifth part of the force had already succeeded in conquering the "seven cities of Cibola," yet, if faith is to be given to Casteñeda's expressions, this result was not at all pleasing to those who had won it rather with sweat than with blood. They were bitterly disappointed. As soon as the men saw Cibola, they "broke out in curses against Fray Marcos." The historian afterward adds, "For his account was found to be false in every respect."

I have already said that I believe these accusations cannot be substantiated. The written account of the priest is absolutely true, not at all exaggerated, and agrees fully with those of Melchior Diaz, Juan Jaramillo, and especially with the representations of Casteñeda himself. But this account was in a very short time repeated on many tongues, and it shared the usual fate of stories transmitted verbally in being added to, exaggerated, and colored in the imaginations of those through whom it successively passed. The original account, by which all these falsifications might have been corrected, was not given to the public, and the officers, using Coronado as their instrument, suffered only the most flattering parts of it to be put forward. What Fray Marcos said of gold was from hearsay, and was so represented by him. It, moreover, did not relate to Cibola, but to a region much farther south. His accounts also agree with those which Alarcon received concerning Cibola from the Indians on the Colorado River.

As is always the case when the passion of the multitude turns against a single man, no regard was paid in this instance to the voice of reason. Fray Marcos was no longer sure of his life in Zuñi; the Spaniards, who had deceived themselves, made him responsible for their mistake, and concern was felt for his safety. Coronado had a report of his success to send to the viceroy. Juan Gallego was commissioned to carry it, and the Franciscan went with him. He was even then Padre Provinzial of the order in and for Mexico. He died in the capital on March 25, 1558. The sufferings which the cool climate of New Mexico and the innumerable hardships of his journeys caused him had culminated in paralysis in Cibola, and it is not improbable that it was this and not fear of violence from those around him that moved him to return to Mexico.

Gallego and the priest on their return met in the Sonora Valley the main body of the army, as it was called, which Coronado had left in Culiacan. It had been started fourteen days after the departure of the commander, but the cavalry "went on foot, with lances on their shoulders, and carrying provisions; all the horses were loaded." Having arrived in the Sonora district, Arellano, who was in command, sent Rodrigo Maldonado down the river toward the sea, in order if possible to establish communication with the marine expedition. He appears to have reached the mouth of the Rio Sonora, but he found no trace of Alarcon. It was the first time that the places where Hermosillo, the chief city of Sonora, and Guaymas, the principal port of the Gulf of California, stand were visited by white men. The Spaniards consequently came in contact with the still savage tribe of the Serès. Coronado had founded the settlement of San Hierónymo at Suya, and Melchior Diaz was left with eighty men to hold it. The main body of the command was reduced by this measure to one hundred and seventy Spaniards, so that when it arrived at Cibola in the winter of 1540–41 Coronado could not count upon more than two hundred and twenty-five men. He performed all his later acts in New Mexico with this small force.

Although Melchior Diaz had particular orders to guard the new settlement, he could not remain idle. Attempting further explorations of the regions west, he left Diego de Alcáraz* at San Hierónymo, and

* The same who in his time had so inhospitably received Cabeza de Vaca and his companions.

started out with only twenty-six men—Casteñeda says to the southwest, but this is probably a mistake for northwest; for after wandering 150 leagues, or 405 miles, Diaz seems, according to the account, to have reached the great Colorado River of the west, where he found letters from Alarcon buried at the foot of a marked tree, which contained news of his having reached that place and then gone back to New Spain. Diaz followed up the eastern bank of the river for several days' journey; but I have not been able to learn anything concerning the conclusion of his campaign. During his absence* the Indians attacked the settlement at Suya and destroyed it, depriving Coronado of an important link of communication between his isolated position in the north and the Spanish advanced posts in the south.

The campaign of Diaz was probably begun in the winter of 1540–41, for the main part of Coronado's expedition was still in Sonora in October, 1540. The destruction of Suya (by the Opatas) probably took place about the end of 1542 or in 1543. The chronology of the whole expedition is obscure and extremely confused. Pedro de Sotomayor went with it with the purpose of describing its events, but not a line of his writings is known. Even Herrera, who had all the sources of that kind at his command, appears to have consulted Jaramillo almost exclusively, with, perhaps, Coronado's letters and the anonymous "*Relaciones*," which cast light upon single parts of later events. Possibly these

---

* It appears that he did not return to Sonora.

"*Relaciones*" were fragments of Sotomayor's account.

The history of the discovery and conquest of the "seven cities" closes with the capture of Cibola, and the union of the whole force under Coronado's command. The geographical and ethnographical problem has been solved. Connected with this solution are a number of practical consequences which are of greater importance than the mere satisfaction of the promptings of an adventurous curiosity. Even when this satisfaction is obtained, there lies in it the germ of further inquiry.

In the situation in which Coronado was placed continued effort was a condition of existence. He saw that his highly strained anticipations were not fulfilled in Zuñi-Cibola, and that his campaign to that place had been a material failure. The force which he commanded was still more bitterly disappointed, for their expectations had been of a more immediate character. A plundering expedition meant mutiny and destruction. Coronado learned, however, that Zuñi (as I shall henceforth call Cibola) was not the only tribe that possessed a superior rank among village Indians, and that farther on in the country, in the west and especially in the east, were similar groups or pueblos. The stories told him awakened hopes that there were perhaps better regions and mountains richer in metals in those directions. His men agreed in his conjecture, and it grew during the cold winter in Zuñi to a probability. Soldiers and leader therefore awaited with impatience the mild weather, when they could go forward into the great unknown region on the edge of which they were. Their eyes were turned predominantly toward the east, and thus the conquest of the "seven cities of Cibola" was the starting-point for the exploration and opening of New Mexico.

CHAPTER IV.

THE NEW MEXICAN PUEBLOS.

Residence in a pueblo is not without a charm for single persons in winter. It is, indeed, rather smoky and damp than warm in the many-storied houses, the inner rooms of which, where the sunshine never penetrates, are used only for storerooms. The outside rooms now possess the luxury of real windows, with panes of mica or gypsum, of which a number are fixed together in a wooden sash. These gypsum windows are of Spanish introduction; in their primitive condition the Pueblo Indians were acquainted only with holes for air and light. The fireplace of adobe or stone warms the long room in which large and small, in sweet innocence, eat and talk and sleep. This fireplace is one of the original possessions of the Indians, which they had before the time of the Spaniards. If it is stormy without, the fire will be smoking within, and staying there becomes unendurable. Yet winter is to me a very pleasant season to be in the pueblos. Everybody is at home then, and conversation is lively; and the men gather at night and often sit till daybreak, smoking their cornstalk cigarettes and talking of the old times. This is the season when the treasury of their legends and household tales is opened to those who gain the confidence of these simple men; it is also the favorite season for their public dances. A week rarely passes that the drum is not heard sounding some noon, with the shrill notes of the long reed-pipe, and the rhythmical minor song of the exclusively male chorus. The dancers come marching into the plaza in pairs, a man and a woman, the former always with bare chest and shoulders, and the latter "modestly" half-clothed. All are elaborately painted, often disfigured in the most fearful manner with rainbow-colored stripes on their faces and bodies. They wear, according to the occasion, rude colored masks, or feather ornaments only, or animals' heads, or colored head-dresses of wood. And thus they dance and sing and drum and play till the sun sets, even though the weather be freezing or stormy. They return dripping with perspiration to the house, and place themselves right before the blazing fire unclothed. Colds, coughs, and catarrhs follow, but the next week they go again to the laborious ball, for it is a matter of duty, and, then, the new colds they catch are supposed to drive away the old ones—*Similia similibus curantur*.

I once attended between the 22d of February and the 8th of March four different dances in Zuñi amongst the descendants of those Indians of Cibola whom Coronado visited. Yet the chroniclers of his campaign have not a word to say of these festivals and ceremonies which are so curious to the whites. The silence is easily accounted for. The dances, which are now as many curious survivals of a condition that formerly extended over all America, were then customary among all the Indians of all Mexico, as they now are in the pueblos alone, and were therefore well known to the Spaniards. The historians were less likely to describe local differences in costume, songs, or dance-figures, because they, or at least Casteñeda and Jaramillo, did not write their accounts for a number of years after the occurrence of the events. It is also probable that the erection of the Spanish quarters in the Valley of Zuñi indisposed its people from performing their dances, the meaning of which is wholly symbolical, and which have in their eyes the significance of a religious act. The "cachinas" in the pueblos of the Rio Grande are for the most part strictly private; entrance into these not always decent ceremonies is permitted only to the initiated, and under vows of complete secrecy. I am convinced that, although neither Coronado nor Casteñeda and Jaramillo mention the dances, they were still zealously performed in the winter of 1540–41 in the seven pueblos of Zuñi; not participated in by the people as a whole, but that the secret fraternities of the priests, the medicine-men, the soldiers and hunters, each fraternity by itself, performed its festive dances and invocations in its smoke-filled *estufa*, before the altars on which stood the colored images of the sun-father, "Ya-to-kia-Tâtschu"; the mother, "Yao-na-kia Isita"; the divine hero-brothers, "Maitza-la-ima" and "Ahuiuta"; and the terrible god "Achi-a-lâ-topâ."

The picture which this life in the plain of Zuñi afforded was a peculiar one. Over the white covering of snow projected the pueblos of Matzaqui, Halona, and Pinana like little hills of clay, with thin clouds of smoke rising from them. Villages were visible at once from the southern edge of the basin, and at the foot of the colossal mesa, which stood up clear red out of the snow-field, could be seen the niche in which Oa-quima was concealed. There lived the Spaniards, going about in rusty helmets, battered cuirasses, ragged doublets, and worn-out boots, but with good weapons, amongst the Indians, who wrapped themselves in thick coverings made of rabbit-skins. There were heard the neighing of horses, the bleating of sheep, and every morning the sound of the mass bells and the songs of the church, together with the call of the crier, announcing his day's duties to every one in the village. While in the other pueblos the monotony of life was interrupted only by the dances, Oa-quima was turned into a miniature Babel, for there could be heard there at the same time Spanish, Latin, the Zuñi language, the Mexican Nahuatl, and the sonorous Pima and Yaqui. Conversation could not be very lively, and mistakes were frequent but innocent. In consequence of this, and of the cold, everything went on quietly.

The information which the Spaniards obtained concerning the regions still unknown to them was necessarily not very definite, and the names of places were unavoidably incorrectly understood by them, and erroneously recorded. An example is afforded by the word "Marata," than which no other occurs more frequently in the chronicles of Coronado's campaigns. Fray Marcos says of it only, that southeast of Zuñi was a group of pueblos called Marata, which had been brought to the verge of ruin by constant wars with the Zuñi. Mr. Cushing has learned that "Matyà-ta" in the Zuñi language means the south, or rather a region in the south, in the vicinity of the salt lake or "Carrizo." Large, well-preserved ruins still exist there. Melchior Diaz says of it that in his time the Zuñi Indians drew their supply of salt thence, as they do now, but he says nothing of the pueblo. The statement of Fray Marcos, therefore, rests on a mistake so far as it refers to a previous destruction of the village on the Carrizo. The Zuñi declare besides that that village belonged to a branch of their tribe.

A similar instance is found in the name "Totonteac," which is likewise mentioned by Fray Marcos, and later by Melchior Diaz. By it a group of pueblos was meant, situated west or northwest of Zuñi, the description of which exactly fits the Moqui villages.* Coronado heard of this tribe in the summer of 1540, but under the name of "Tusayan." He immediately sent Pedro de Tobar thither, with about twenty men and one priest. The distance (five days' journey) and the direction (northwest) are correctly given by Jaramillo. A brief conflict took place, probably at the now deserted pueblo of Ahuâ-tu, after which the Moquis immediately surrendered. There were seven villages, of which two are now deserted, but fugitives of the Tehua tribe have formed a new settlement, which bears their name. Tobar heard a large river spoken of among the Moquis as situated in the west, the other side of a desert, at whose mouth lived a tribe the men of which were of unusual stature. He considered it his duty to return immediately to Zuñi in order to communicate this story to Coronado. Garcia Lopez de Cárdenas started with only twelve men to go and search for this river. He was hos-

* The Zuñi call them Mu-qua, whence the word Moqui is derived.

pitably received by the Moquis, who supplied him with guides and provisions, and after twenty days' journey through a perfectly desolate region, he came to the vicinity of the stream he was seeking.

I say purposely near and in sight of it, but not on its shore, for "its banks were so high that they seemed to be raised three or four leagues into the air. The country is covered with little stunted fir-trees, is exposed to the north, and is so cold that although it was summer we could hardly bear it. The Spaniards followed these mountains for three days in the hope of finding a passage down to the river, which, appearing from above not more than a fathom in width, had, according to the Indians, a breadth of half a league. But it was impossible. Two or three days later they believed they had found a place where the descent seemed easier, and Captain Melgosa, Juan Galera, and a soldier . . . determined to make the effort. They went so far that they were lost from sight. Toward four o'clock in the afternoon they returned." They had been obliged to give up the attempt after they had climbed down about a third of the depth; but the river appeared very large to them, and "some rocks, which seemed from above to be hardly the size of a man, really exceeded in height the tower of the Cathedral of Seville." Finding that the banks of the river were destitute of water, the Spaniards gave up further efforts in that direction. They returned to Zuñi, and neither the Moqui nor the countries farther west of there were visited again by them while Coronado and his men continued in New Mexico.

In this description of Casteñeda's it is easy to

recognize the upper course of the great Rio Colorado. The Spaniards also explicitly declare that it was the Rio del Tizon, by which name Melchior Diaz designated the Colorado. In the course of less than six months the Spanish reconnoitring corps had thus three times touched the largest river of western America, had explored its shores with tolerable accuracy for a considerable length of its course, and had also travelled in two directions through parts of Arizona, which have only in a very recent time again attracted attention. Coronado had even followed the New Mexican boundary northward through two thirds of the length of the territory, and the documents relative to his campaign give correct accounts of the Gila River, and excellent descriptions of the Sierra Blanca region and the Little Colorado. Diaz had crossed southwestern Arizona. Alarcon had, besides, explored and correctly described the mouth and the lower course of the Rio Colorado. Lastly, Cárdenas had traversed the whole of Arizona from east to west. The accomplishment of such enterprises with small means deserves admiration; and when we consider that official reports were made of these matters by eye-witnesses—reports the great accuracy of which as regards the country and people only more recent researches have made it possible to demonstrate—we cannot refuse to pay these men, so long decried as "Spanish adventurers," "cruel freebooters," etc., all honor for their achievements. The Spanish government also deserves high praise for the carefulness and far-sightedness with which it permitted such enterprises, and preserved the written records of them.

While the reconnoitring operations toward the west were thus discontinued, the eyes of the Spaniards were turned from Zuñi more earnestly toward the east. Coronado had given the people of the Zuñi tribe to understand that they must spread the news of his coming and of his intention to stay in the country as widely as possible. The command was unnecessary, for reports of that kind spread very rapidly among the Indians without any postal system. A certain kind of peaceful intercourse is constantly going on, even between hostile tribes, and news passes from one tribe to another through numerous channels, though distorted in many ways, to great distances. I cite the accounts of Cibola, which were carried to the middle of Sonora. Thus there existed, and still exists, a close bond among the Village Indians, or Pueblos, especially, which connects the far distant Pecos and Moqui with the Opatas, and the most northern Taos with the most southern Piros. Their scattered position among nomadic tribes made them sensible of the need of a connection, and the equal condition of their civilization confirmed the feeling. Neighboring Pueblos often made war upon one another, and would still do so were it not for the whites, but visits were made between the more remote ones for trade and for purposes connected with religion. There are fetishes and incantations which, when they have been discontinued in one pueblo, can only be recovered from some other one, often far distant.

In these and similar ways had the story of the coming of the Spaniards reached Moqui, and their horses had been represented there as man-eating creatures.

THE NEW MEXICAN PUEBLOS. 201

There came also to Zuñi Indians from the extreme east of the Pueblo region, from a village called Cicuyé. This village was situated "seventy leagues toward the east." The arrival of Coronado was already known there. The men brought buffalo robes with them, and invited the Spanish commander to visit their place, presenting him with skins and shields and "helmets" of buffalo leather.* With the reports from Cibola, the Spaniards had also received in the south accounts of the existence of "wild cows," confirming what Cabeza de Vaca had previously related. The Indians of the shores of the extreme lower Colorado had likewise told Alarcon of these animals. Now the Spaniards were in contact with people whose home was near the buffalo, and who hunted it.† A very welcome occasion was thus presented to them for making themselves acquainted with these new animal forms, and an excellent opportunity to advance with good leaders farther into the interior. Coronado therefore sent Hernando de Alvarado with twenty men to go with the people of Cicuyé on their return to their home, and to report to the chief in command in eighty days concerning what he had seen and done. The main corps remained in the meanwhile at Zuñi, whither Alvarado was to return after completing his tour. His campaign took place in August, 1540.

* These helmets, or, rather, leather caps, are still in use among the Pueblos. They belong to the aboriginal equipment for war.
† It is doubtful whether the Zuñis at that time took part in the periodical buffalo-hunts which the Pueblo Indians farther east still engaged in as late as 1881.

14

The word "Cicuyé" is "Tshi-quité," the aboriginal name of the Pecos Indians. I will here mention that Casteñeda says that Pecos is the last village to the east, and that the great plains are only thirty leagues, or eighty miles, distant from it. I have already shown in my earlier work, "A Visit to the Aboriginal Ruins in the Valley of the Rio Pecos,"* that Cicuyé is identical with Pecos. It is not necessary to repeat the demonstration here.

Alvarado and his company reached the first village in five days. It was built on a rock, and was called "Acuco." This is the "Ha-cu-qua" of the Zuñi, the pueblo of Acoma, so famous for its situation. Casteñeda very appropriately describes it as being upon "a perpendicular rock . . . so high that a bullet could hardly reach the top"; but with less accuracy he speaks of a "stairway" of three hundred steps hewn in the rock as being the only way to the highest story. Acoma is indeed situated on a rock, the shape of which resembles that of a spider. The walls of the rock fall perpendicularly down for nearly three hundred feet, while four winding paths lead to the pueblo, none of which has been cut out by human hands. Slight improvements in the shape of implanted posts and notches for the hands and feet have been made in a very few places. At the summit is the pueblo, with its great church of adobe and stone, and the churchyard, the soil of which has all been brought up on the backs of the inhabitants. Not a foot of other loose ground can be found on the gigantic cliff; the ten houses stand on the bare rock,

* Vol. i. of the "Papers of the Archæological Institute of America," 1883.

whence the view down into the yawning depth is awful. The six hundred inhabitants draw their supply of water the year round from the accumulations of rain and snow in two deep natural cisterns. The cultivated fields are fourteen miles away.

I hope I may be pardoned if I repeat here a few impressions which were deeply marked upon me during a long sojourn in Acoma, and in words which I have already published in "A Letter from Acoma" in the German journal *Das Ausland* (1884, No. XIII.). These impressions have been renewed on two visits to the place, when the same feelings were daily awakened.

"When the visitor stands upon the rocks which immediately surround the water-pool, he looks down from them into the valley upon the great mesas that surround them, and beyond these upon the massive pyramid of Mount Taylor, or the Sierra de San Matéo. . . . As evening approaches the shadows lie deep upon the ground, and as they climb up the rock-walls, as cliff after cliff is swallowed up in darkness, his heart is oppressed with the feeling that all intercourse with the outer world is henceforth cut off. This feeling has crept upon me every evening at sunset; for escape from Acoma in the night would be impossible to any one who had not lived there a long time. When the last ray of the sun has taken leave of the lofty sierra, one feels absolutely alone, forsaken, helplessly floating in the darkness of night. But this feeling soon passes away; for a clear, although monotonous, singing sounds from the pueblo, fires blaze on the roofs, and when one has returned to the houses laughing voices greet him, and joyous groups are moving around and above him. The oppressive feeling of desertion changes into one of pleasure in being the plain guest of a simple people."

The population of Acoma has not changed much in three hundred and forty years, for Casteñeda speaks of two hundred braves. The people prepared to defend themselves against the Spaniards, but no battle took place, the fear of the horses inducing a speedy peace. It seems, however, that Alvarado did not stay in Acoma, and he was quite right in not trusting to the peaceful disposition of the people, for once on the rock the same fate might easily have met him that, fifty-eight years later, overtook the *Maestro de Campo* Zaldivar and his men at that place. Three days' journey from Acoma brought him to Tiguex, where he met a friendly reception. Tiguex (pronounced Tiguesh), according to Casteñeda, was a group of twelve smaller pueblos situated on a large river, in a valley about two leagues, or five miles, wide. From that place Alvarado sent a messenger to Coronado with the advice to remove his winter quarters there.

Tiguex has been looked for at various places in New Mexico: on the eastern Rio Puerco, at the site of the present Santa Fé, and at other points. I have marked as the situation of this pueblo group the banks of the Rio Grande near Bernalillo, or rather between Algodones and Albuquerque. The very name points thither, for the Tiguas Indians call themselves Tiguex, and they formerly lived in a chain of larger and smaller pueblos along the Rio Grande. They were divided into two groups: a northern group, of which I know of twelve ruins between the "Mesa del Cangelon" in the north and "Los Corrales" in the south, and of which the present pueblo of Sandía is the only one left; and a southern branch now concentrated at the large village of Isleta, but which was still, about 1630, scattered in several small places. I have no doubt that the Tiguex of Coronado denotes the northern group of the Tiguas, for it lay north of Acoma and on a large river. This river east of Zuñi could only have been the Rio Grande del Norte, for the Puerco is in that latitude in parts of its course filled up with sand, and in other parts reduced to an insignificant, muddy rill. An expression of Casteñeda's, likewise applying to Cicuyé-Pecos, is decisive on this point. "Tiguex," he says, "is the middle point," and "from Cibola to Cicuyé, which is the last village, we count seventy leagues." The villages of Tiguex were not, like Zuñi and Acoma, built of stone and mortar, but of adobe; and that is also the structure of the pueblos the ruins of which I have examined around Bernalillo. I mention still another piece of documentary evidence, although it is derived from an account written at a later period. At Tiguex Coronado stormed and destroyed a pueblo—the only case of the destruction of a village in New Mexico during his campaign. In the year 1583 the "Tiguas" told Antonio de Espejo, on his arrival among them, that his countrymen on their first coming had burnt one of their towns in the vicinity of the present Bernalillo. This fixes the locality of Tiguex, as I have attempted to show in an earlier publication, beyond all doubt.

Five days' journey brought Alvarado from the Rio Grande to Cicuyé, where a friendly reception was also given him. Of this village Casteñeda writes: "The village of Cicuyé can furnish about five hundred men of war. . . . It is built on a rock, and the middle is occupied by an open place in which are the estufas. The houses are four stories high, with terrace roofs, all of the same height, on which one can go around the whole village without stepping into a street. The first two stories have passages resembling balconies, on which one can go round the whole village, and where he can be under shelter. The houses have no doors below; one goes up to the balconies which are within the village by means of a ladder. All the doors open upon the balcony, which serves the purpose of a street. The village is surrounded on the outside by a low stone wall. There is also a spring there, which could be diverted. . . . Cicuyé lies in a narrow valley, in the midst of fir-clad mountains. A small river, in which very fine trout are caught, flows through the valley. Very large otters, bears, and good falcons are found there."

It is not necessary to compare this description with that of the Valley of Pecos and the present ruins of the former pueblo. Casteñeda describes this pueblo so well and truly that when, after completing the measurement of the ruins in September, 1880, I restored the plans and afterward wrote them out, I perceived with astonishment that they exactly repeated the picture which the Spanish soldier had sketched three hundred years before. He was but little wrong even in his estimate of the population of Pecos-Cicuyé. Five hundred warriors represent among the Village Indians eighteen hundred inhabitants of all ages and both sexes. In the year

1630 Pecos contained "over a thousand souls," in 1689 about two thousand. The latter number might easily, according to the plans, have been accommodated within the village, for it was the largest pueblo that New Mexico contained in the sixteenth century, or afterward.

The tribe of Pecos has not yet died out. When the inhabitants in 1840, reduced by a hundred years' hostilities with the Comanches and by illness to five families, fled to their tribe-relatives at Jemez, their immediate extinction was considered inevitable. Instead of that they have increased, and numbered twenty-eight persons in 1885. They live with their kindred, and participate equally with them in the governmental affairs of Jemez. They also speak the same language.

Alvarado was received by the Pecos with drums and flutes. The native flute might rather be called a clarinet, for it has a mouth of painted gourd-shell, and is blown from the end and not from the side. Many cotton cloths and turquoises were presented to him. Such a reception indicated that the Pecos Indians were somewhat doubtful concerning the human origin of their guest. He also met here a strange Indian who lived with the Pecos,* and whom the Spaniards called a "Turk" on account of his appearance. He was a native of the Mississippi Valley, and belonged to one of the tribes of that region.

---

* Casteñeda says he was a slave, but that is not correct. He did not belong to the tribe, and had attached himself to a family, but he was not and could not be a slave, according to the custom of the Pueblos. Every Indian has a right to be a permanent guest with them.

He informed the Spaniards that gold-bearing and thickly populated districts lay toward the east. Such information was extremely welcome; he was taken as a guide for the visit to the buffalo herds of the plains that was to be made in pursuance of Coronado's directions; but this was not continued long, for Alvarado hastened back, in order to communicate to his commander what he regarded as important news. He returned speedily to Tiguex or Bernalillo, where Garcia Lopez de Cárdenas had in the meantime arrived, Coronado having despatched him to prepare quarters for the whole army, which was to spend the rest of the winter there.

"The Turk" (*el Turco*) was to play so important a part henceforth in the fortunes of Coronado's expedition, that I think it right to give the charge of deliberate deception which the Spaniards have made against him a closer examination. The charge has perhaps some foundation. The Indian was unquestionably a native of the plains, and had been carried to Pecos by war or the incidents of hunting expeditions. It was a custom among the Pueblo Indians (and it ceased only a few years ago) to make at least one expedition a year to these plains for the purpose of providing themselves with buffalo meat, and more particularly with buffalo skins, which they used in armor, for shoes, and for many other of their needs. The plains were not constantly inhabited; even the Apaches, who regularly roamed through a part of them, did not live there, for they are without water, and are a long distance from it, and the buffaloes resort to them only at certain seasons. As the tribes of the southwest made their regular hunts on the plains, those of the east likewise resorted to them, from Kansas, Arkansas, and the present Indian Territory, in similar expeditions, and they met. Trade or war was the result; often both; and thus these deserts were the market in which the novelties of either half of the North American continent were exchanged. "The Turk" there fell into the hands of the Pecos Indians, and they did not kill him. He tried now to make the Spaniards understand whence he had come, and what was the character of the country there, and as his language was not sufficient for the purpose, he was obliged to employ gestures. Conversation in this way was very inconvenient, and mistakes were inevitable. He is said to have told the Spaniards of houses like those of the pueblos, but larger. If he did this, he intentionally falsified, as the result showed. But while the Spaniards were thinking of houses, he may have had something quite different in his mind, and may have mentioned the pueblos only for comparison. He spoke, they said, of gold. Did he know what gold was? I am satisfied that he did not know the difference between gold, yellow mica, bright pyrites, and copper pyrites, of which there is much in the Mississippi Valley. That he should prefer his native land, where vegetation was apparently more luxuriant than in New Mexico, and where animal life was consequently more abundant, to the more barren southwest was natural, and so it was, too, that he should extol it to the Spaniards, for he had reason to suppose that he might possibly, with the aid of these strangers, be restored to his people. It is also probable that "the Turk" eventually led the Spaniards wofully astray, but this, too, was possibly as much the result of mistakes as of wilful deception on his part; for it was not possible to reach an adequate mutual understanding under the circumstances.

Alvarado's return to Tiguex was marked by an event that places that officer's character in a most unfavorable light. To provide quarters for his few men he forced the evacuation of a whole pueblo, and would not permit the inhabitants to take away anything but their clothing. The pueblo cannot have been of great size, for those communities were generally not large previous to the advent of the Spaniards. The villages were smaller but more numerous than they have been since; for the Franciscan monks combined them into larger settlements, both for purposes of defence, and in order to attach the Indians more closely to the churches and to the schools connected with them. It may be readily conceived that the forced occupation of this pueblo created an unpleasant feeling in the whole region of the present Bernalillo. It was the introduction to subsequent difficulties and dangerous contentions.

Coronado had in the meantime gone away from Zuñi with a small number of his men, leaving the larger number behind under the command of Arellano, who was to follow him after twenty days to the Rio Grande. The route he took led him to that river, about thirty miles south of Bernalillo, in the vicinity of the present Isleta. He recognized that the people there belonged to the same tribe as those of Tiguex. Their houses were likewise of adobe. Casteñeda calls this region "Tutahaco," while Jaramillo applies that name to Acoma. The latter is right to the extent that the name is "Tutahaio," a corruption of the word "Tuthea-uây," by which the Tiguas call the rocks of Acoma. As the Spaniards came from there the name of the place was confounded with that of Isleta. The Spaniards asked for the latter, and the Indians gave the name of the other place, a confusion such as I have often encountered among the natives.

Casteñeda mentions eight villages in the vicinity of Isleta, but adds that they were situated "down the river." The ruins of hardly more than four are to be seen between Albuquerque and Los Lunas, nine miles south of Isleta. The statements of Jaramillo, who gives the Tiguas of the Rio Grande fifteen villages in twenty leagues, or fifty-four miles, are on the other hand correct. It is forty-six miles from Algodones to Los Lunas, and fifteen or sixteen Tigua villages were inhabited in the year 1627. The four or five villages farther south, which Casteñeda counts besides these, were those of the Piros. They began in the vicinity of Tomé and Los Lentes, and extended to San Marcial and Fort Craig. Casteñeda was acquainted only with the most northern of them, for there were fourteen in all.

Marching up the Rio Grande to Tiguex, Coronado arrived there when the quarrels among his subordinates had just broken out. He found that his men had "the Turk" with them, and were rejoicing over the pretended information which he gave them. This Indian's conduct became more suspicious, and he appears to have harbored a resentment against the people of Pecos. He complained that they were keeping a golden arm-band of his. The knave had never had such a thing, or it may have been a copper ring; but the Spaniards understood it to be gold, and Alvarado went to Pecos to recover it for him. When he was assured there that "the Turk" had never worn an ornament of the kind, he seized the cacique and another chief of the place by treacherous means, and carried them prisoners to the Tiguas. The Tiguas were very angry at this act, for, the two tribes not being adjacent, peace prevailed between them and the Pecos.

Since Cortés had in 1520 made a prisoner of the "war captain" (*capitan de la guerra*) of the Mexican tribe, whom later historical description transformed into the monarch Montezuma, the Spaniards had tried many times to secure other similar hostages. They had forgotten, or rather had never comprehended, that the importance of a chief among the Indians is very relative, and in no way comparable with the significance which the head of the state in a civilized commonwealth possesses. The fall of a valiant leader may decide the issue of a battle, but the capture by craft of the same chief in time of peace is of no greater moment than a similar treachery exercised upon a common Indian. Offices are never hereditary among these Indians, but are and were always elective. Only in the case of a leader in the mystic service, a medicine-man, or shaman, being taken away, or of one of those whose function it is to work for the good of the tribe by mortification or sacrifice, would that tribe be moved to offer a ransom for his recovery. For while an administrative officer, even a warrior, can be easily replaced, the importance of the other one lies in his knowledge of the secret arts; if he is lost, the connecting link with the beings of a higher order is removed, and the pueblo is, according to its own striking expression, "made an orphan." The successor of the medicine-man is elected only in cases when he is taken away by sudden death; otherwise the candidate is carefully selected and slowly trained by the incumbent, and cannot enter upon the practice of his art till one or more years after the death of his predecessor. At the present time the functionary whose duty it is to suffer on all occasions for the good of the pueblo is called the "cacique," or, by the Zuñis, "Châcui Môsona."

Coronado not only supported the attempt of his officers, but proceeded to still further and more offensive acts of violence. He required the Tiguas to furnish a considerable quantity of cotton goods for his soldiers. They certainly were in great need of covering, for it was bitterly cold, and snow-falls were frequent, but the manner in which the articles were demanded and obtained deserves the severest reprobation. The pueblos on both sides of the river were ravaged and plundered, and outrages were committed against the women. The Tiguas would not endure this long; the whole tribe rose against the strangers and seized some of their horses. Coronado was obliged to take the field against them, even before his main force could join him. A bloody war arose, that lasted fifteen days, in which the Spaniards lost several officers and a number of men. Two pueblos were captured after a long siege, the taking of the first of which was followed by an atrocious massacre of prisoners. Coronado and his company behaved on this occasion with a cruelty that fixes an indelible stain on their memory, and which demanded in requital in later days the sacrifice of innocent persons. The Tiguas did not submit, but fled to the mountains, and notwithstanding Coronado's efforts to pacify them and recover their confidence, did not return to the Rio Grande so long as the Spaniards remained in the country.

It is true that this was the only instance during the whole continuance of the expedition in New Mexico in which the Spaniards behaved barbarously and cruelly, but their treatment of the Tiguas is not easier to explain on that account. I can find no ground of excuse for it; and the behavior of Coronado is in so complete contradiction with his previous and subsequent course that I cannot easily understand it, unless it be that necessity drove him to the first summary measures, and the severe cold (the Rio Grande was frozen) and the scarcity of provisions then provoked his soldiers to wild excesses. Yet single events occurred during the war with the Tiguas that indicated that cruelties were perpetrated in cold blood. First among them was the slaughter of the prisoners who surrendered in the first pueblo. Let it be said in behalf of Coronado that he was not privy to this atrocity, which was ordered by Garcia Lopez de Cárdenas, at the time in command in his stead. He was in quarters, and had just received the army which had come from Zuñi under Arellano, when the blood-stained conqueror returned. "It was snowing heavily, and the weather was bad for two months," says Casteñeda. Intense cold and a few heavy snow-storms occur every winter on the Rio Grande, but I have never known of continued severe weather there of so long duration. The first months of the year 1541 were unusually cold in New Mexico, for it is said that one could cross the Rio Grande on the ice during four months. I very much doubt the correctness of the statement as to the length of time.

Coronado did not hesitate, however, to extend the exploration of the country even while the hostilities against the Tiguas were still in full progress. He was impelled to it, not only by the desire to become acquainted with the region, but also by the fear of a general rising of all the natives, which would have been fatal for him and his company. The Pecos had first to be pacified, and with that object he went to the pueblo and gave up to the people, who met him with demonstrations of a peaceful character, their captured officers. By this measure the former friendly relation was restored. After his return to the Rio Grande, he formed connections with a village called "Cia," situated four leagues, or eleven miles, west of the river; and six Spaniards visited and quieted the Indians of "Quirix," a group of seven pueblos joining the Tiguas on the north and partly scattered along the great river. Cia, properly Tzia, is not more than twenty miles in a straight line from the Rio Grande. Still nearer, and situated on the same branch (the Rio de Jemez), was the pueblo of Santa Ana (Tâ-ma-ya). The same language is spoken in both, and they are in frequent communication. They belong to the numerous group of the "Queres," with which the Quirix of Coronado are identical.

It is easy to identify the eight pueblos which Casteñeda mentions. Following the eastern shore of the Rio Grande, we meet first "Oâ-tish-tye" (San

Felipe, now, and since 1630, on the west side) and "Gui-pu-i" (Santo Domingo, now called "Tihua," and formerly situated a mile northeast). On the western shore lies, six miles north of Santo Domingo, "Oô-tyi-ti" (Cachiti). On the Jemez River, six miles from San Felipe, stands "Tâ-ma-ya" (Santa Ana), and farther up Tzia, or Cia. The other three villages may be sought for in the vicinity of Cia, where their ruins are still standing.

Cia is now going down into decay, after having been, till 1688, one of the largest Indian villages in New Mexico. Its inhabitants speak a dialect of the Queres tongue, somewhat like that of Acoma. All the pueblos of the Queres formed, and still form, like the other groups, autonomous communities. The common language does not prevent hostilities between neighboring villages, but should an enemy from without threaten one of them, it has the right to call the others to its aid, and in that case the war-chief of the threatened village, the "Tzyâ-u-yu-qiu," or *capitan de la guerra*, takes the chief command. The Queres held a passive attitude toward the Spaniards until the insurrection of 1680, in which they were very active.

I have followed Casteñeda's statements exclusively in these last researches. Jaramillo says that Cia, Uraba, and Ciquique were situated on the same river, a stream which flowed into the Rio Grande from the northwest. This river is undoubtedly the Jemez. He goes on to speak of the "Rio Cicuique" as another stream, situated northeast of the former one, and seven days' journey distant from it. He is, as he concedes, very confused in his narrative, and is therefore not to be relied upon on these points. Mota-Padilla calls Cicuyé "Coquite." Herrera copies Jaramillo. Only Casteñeda is clear and consistent, and his statements agree perfectly with the country and with the relics left by its former inhabitants.

Coronado, with an energy to which due recognition cannot be refused, notwithstanding the outrages that attended his proceedings at Bernalillo, thus in a short time brought Central New Mexico within the compass of his knowledge, and obtained the first correct information of the Village Indians of six linguistic stocks; but his attention was still chiefly directed toward the east, of the great wealth of which "the Turk" continued to talk to him and the Spaniards. What he had so far seen of New Mexico did not appear sufficiently favorable for him to be satisfied to devote himself to its settlement. The Valley of the Rio Grande is, indeed, not very inviting in winter, especially in so severe a winter as that of 1540–41 seems to have been. The clearer the sunshine and the deeper the blue of the arch of the sky, the more dreary in their barrenness are the dunes that border alternately both sides of the river, and the more welcome is the sight of the black mesas and of the peaks of volcanic stone which in groups and singly interrupt the monotonous profile. Still more gloomy is the waterless plateau which extends from the eastern edge of the river valley to the foot of the Sierra de Sandía, and farther south to the Sierra de Manzano and the Puerto de Abó—a gray flat, twenty miles wide and fifty miles long from north to south, without brook, spring, or pond. The Sandía Mountain towers over it like a gigantic wall, with awful clefts and cliffs rising perpendicularly 5000 feet above the river. The chain of the Manzano, less steep but treeless, is still 2000 feet higher. The river valley itself, seldom more than two miles wide, passes in summer like a green band among the dunes, which are then tinged with green, but in winter the fields are barren and the trees are leafless, and stand on the heights like white skeletons on a vast, bare waste.

When it is stormy on the Rio Grande, the dark-blue sky and the dazzling light vanish, the clouds sink low down to the foot of the high mountain range, and it is gloomy, cold, and oppressive. Sand whirls chase one another along the stream, break up and dash whistling upon the gravel hills. Dust and sand add to the darkness of the atmosphere, and one is relieved to see the snow begin to fall thick and then thicker, while the roaring of the wind is lulled to a mournful sigh. When the snow has ceased and the clouds have disappeared from the slopes of the mountain, a thin white sheet covers the ground, which at night glows in the starlight with phosphorescence. The snow does not stay long, for the sandy ground soon absorbs all moisture.

This sandy soil in the Valley of the Rio Grande is fruitful, extraordinarily productive. When it can be watered it rewards, and that always bountifully, even the feeble efforts which Indian agriculture puts forth. No doubt the Spaniards were not specially attracted by the view of an agriculture which did not, with more labor and in a more difficult because colder climate, afford them all the products of the tropical climate they had left, and into which they would have to introduce the grains and fruits of the temperate zone. Cattle and sheep raising might have appeared more promising to them, but a long time would have to pass before they could establish those industries and a safe, accessible market could be built up for their stock. This could certainly not be expected in the first generation, while every one wanted first of all to be rich himself.

Only productive mining could be profitable in a short time, but the Spaniards, who lacked neither desire for the metals nor practical skill in discovering them, did not suffer themselves to be misled by the traces, universally present, of malachite and carbonate of copper. They indeed recognized the existence of silver ore in the rocks, but shrewdly doubted as to the paying quality of the mineral. The Indians did not possess, nor were they acquainted with, gold, silver, copper, or iron. Green stones, kalaite * and malachite,† colored flints and obsidian, gypsum for whitewashing, iron-ochre for painting pots, faces, and feathers, were their mineral treasures. Coronado soon perceived that New Mexico was a poor country, which could not be developed in the immediate future, a land fit only for commonplace work and minor industries. The Spaniards had not made the long, dangerous journey from the sunny south for such a purpose as that. To compensate them for their pains they must find more.

The representations of "the Turk," on the contrary, sounded very differently. He talked of a river two leagues wide containing fish as large as a horse, on

* Blue turquois is rare.

† Available only as a pigment on account of the difficulty of working it.

which canoes sailed with forty rowers, their bows richly adorned with gold. He declared that the vessels in that country were made of silver and gold. With keen craftiness he had watched the Spaniards, and had discovered that they esteemed gold more than copper, and had learned to appreciate the difference between the two metals even in weight. Gold, he intimated, was abundant at "Arche" or "Arahei," but "Quivira" was the place to which he would take the Spaniards before all others, and where he promised them the precious metal in profusion.

The Rio Grande Valley was quiet, and Coronado set about beginning the march to Quivira. The whole army followed him, while Pedro de Tobar was in the meantime to come up with reinforcements from Sonora; for written orders had been left for him with the Indians of Zuñi to follow Coronado, guiding himself by the wooden crosses which he would erect from time to time. The Spaniards left Bernalillo May 5th, and entered Pecos on the 9th. The tribe received and entertained them gladly.

I have in the preceding pages referred to six linguistic stocks with which Coronado had so far come in contact in New Mexico. Only five of them have been named to this point, viz., those of Zuñi, Tigua, Piro, Pecos or Jemez, and Queres. The sixth is never designated with a name, but is inferred from the scanty account of the route from Bernalillo to Pecos.

This route is not hard to follow. Coronado could reach Pecos from the Rio Grande only by going up that river to the vicinity of San Felipe, and then turning in toward the pueblo of "Tunque." There Alvarado had probably already come in contact with the Queres. In passing the Cañon del Infierno, the Spaniards would have become acquainted with Chilili, Tajique, Manzano, and with the remarkable salt basin beyond, of which they say nothing, and they would, moreover, be near the buffaloes, without touching Pecos. They also probably went by the "Paso de Tijeras" (the Scissors Pass) to San Pedro, where they found the pueblo of "Pä-qu"; from San Pedro to "Golden" (Real de San Francisco), where the pueblo of "Kaapô" (El Tuerto) stood, already almost deserted; and then past the pueblo of "Hî-shi" (*Pueblo largo*), south of Galisteó, to the Pecos Valley. They thereby avoided all the northern villages; and Casteñeda says, "They count seven other villages between this route and the Snowy Mountains (la Sierra Nevada)."

The Sierra Nevada is that wild, picturesque mountain system south of Santa Fé which parts into the three groups: the "Sierra del Real de Dolores," the Sierra de San Francisco, and the Sierra de San Pedro. They lie east of the Sandía Mountain and parallel to it. These grand masses are often covered with snow early in the fall. The Sierra de Santa Fé, which contains the highest peak in New Mexico, is covered with snow nearly the whole year, and towers majestically over the other side of the basin of Galisteó. The seven pueblos which Casteñeda mentions were "Pânt-hâm-ba" (San Cristobal), "Tage-unge" or "Glisteó" (Galisteó), "I-pe-re" (San Lázaro), "Yâtzé" (San Marcos), "Tzigu-má" (la Ciénega), "Cuâ-cấ" (Arroyo Hondo), and "Cuâ-po-oge" (Santa Fé). Their inhabitants belonged to the tribe of the "Tanos," which spoke the "Tehua" language, and they thus formed the sixth linguistic and ethnographic district with which Coronado had become acquainted in May, 1541. To them belonged also the pueblos of "San Pedro," of "El Tuerto," the "Pueblo largo" (which the Apaches had destroyed five or six years before), and the villages south of "Tejon" ("Ojâna," "Quipâna") and "Tunque." All these are to-day deserted and destroyed.

Pecos was the headquarters of the Spaniards for a little while. Quivira appears to have been known there, for the people gave them a young Indian whom they called "Xabe," who was a native of Quivira. He said that gold and silver indeed occurred at his home, but not in such quantities as "the Turk" had pretended. Toward the middle of the month of May, 1541, Coronado started for Quivira and its supposed wealth of gold. The young Indian, "Xabe," shared with "the Turk" the function of guide.

Till then the Spaniards had had to endure only the dangers and hindrances offered by mountains. Now they encountered difficulties of another kind such as they had not before met on the American continent. They were to enter upon the boundless plains, the endless uniformity of which, fatiguing to body and mind alike, slowly and surely unnerved and finally crushed them. For, uncertain as was their aim, still more uncertain was the end. While till this time the expedition had borne a character of fascinating boldness, the stamp of useless adventure, of wanton risk, is plainly impressed on the march to Quivira.

CHAPTER V.

QUIVIRA.

It is a well-known fact that lost travellers involuntarily walk circuitously, generally toward the right, and so gradually return to the place whence they started. This phenomenon is especially frequent in wide, treeless plains, where prominent objects by which the wanderer can direct himself are wanting. It has an extremely dangerous effect upon the mind, and may, if it occurs repeatedly, easily lead to despair and frenzy. What happens to individuals may also occur to a larger number. This was the fate of Coronado and his company when they sought and found Quivira. They returned in a wide bend to their starting-point, after they had wandered for months on the desolate plains, "led around in a circle as if by some evil spirit."

Coronado, having completed all his preparations at Pecos, left that pueblo in the beginning of May, 1541, to go to the prairies. His general direction was northeast. On the fourth day he crossed a river that was so deep that they had to throw a bridge over it. This river was perhaps the Rio de Mora, and not, as I formerly thought, the little Gallinas, which flows by Las Vegas. The latter, an affluent of the Pecos, is too insignificant, while the Mora is tolerably rapid and deeper. But it was more probably the Canadian River, into which the Mora empties. Of the three accounts of the campaign which lie before me, Jaramillo's is very confused, and that of Pedro de Casteñeda, which was written long after the event, must be used with scrutiny and caution, while the third letter of Coronado to Charles V. was composed immediately after the expedition, and thus records fresh, clear recollections. Coronado and Casteñeda, besides, agree in the principal points. Herrera has compiled from all the materials, and has used, among other sources, the anonymous "*Relacion de los Sucesos de la Jornada*," etc. (1541). He is not less trustworthy as a source of information than Mota-Padilla.

The Spaniards soon found themselves in the plains, and were surrounded by herds of the American bison or buffalo. The first sight of these animals produced a great terror among the horses. They all ran away at the view of those large, hairy, ill-shaped beasts, which covered the plain by thousands, and whose hollow bellowing and glowing eyes still strangely affect those who see them for the first time. The plain aroused feelings of anxiety and gloom among the men by its immense monotony and the absence of any marks by which they could direct themselves. The conviction stands out in the writings of all the witnesses, that an oppressive feeling of helplessness soon made itself master of them. Casteñeda gives an excellent description of the llanos and their character: "All that one could see of these plains was entirely uninhabited. On a stretch of two hundred and fifty leagues one could discern neither the other mountain chains, nor hills, nor a single elevation of more than two or three fathoms. Occasional lagoons were found, as round as plates, which might have been a stone's-throw in diameter, while a few were a little broader. The water of some was fresh, of others salt. The grass grows high around these pools, but everywhere else it is extremely short. Trees stand only in isolated ravines, in the bottoms of which flow little brooks, so that one can see around him nothing but sky and plain, for he is not aware of these ravines till he gets to their edge. Descending them are paths, which the buffaloes have trodden in going to drink."

The feeling of helplessness which gradually crept upon the hearts of the Spaniards became critical by the growing conviction that their leader, "the Turk," was betraying them and purposely leading them astray. They began to believe that the inhabitants of the pueblos had induced him to conduct the Spaniards into the plains, in order that they might perish there and the sedentary tribes thus be rid of their troublesome guests. His companion, whom the Pecos Indians had associated with him, who was born at Quivira, and whom the chronicler calls variously "Sopete" and "Ysopete," talked quite differently from "the Turk." The feeling thus came upon the Spaniards, at the very beginning of the campaign, that the outcome of their enterprise was at least extremely doubtful.

The troop came upon the first Indians of the plains about seventeen days after leaving Pecos. Coronado pertinently designates these people as those "who go around the country with the cows."

The Prairie Indian, who lives on the bison, also, as it were, lives with him. These aborigines dwelt in tents of buffalo hide; they had no agriculture; they dressed in buffalo skins, and kept dogs, which they used as beasts of burden. The Spanish writers call them Querechos. There is no doubt that they were Apaches, and of the group which were called Vaqueros in the beginning of the sixteenth century, because they were associated exclusively with the "wild cow" (or bison). This tribe used the dog as a pack and draft animal as late as the middle of the last century. The species apparently belongs to the family of the Arctic dog, and probably came down with the Apaches from the north. I do not know whence the name of "Querechos" is derived, unless it is a pueblo name from the Jemez dialect, which was spoken in Pecos. It has some resemblance to "Oi-ra-uash," by which the Queres Indians designated a savage tribe that threatened the pueblos from the plains previous to the arrival of the Spaniards.

The Querechos, or Apaches, as I shall hereafter call them, were friendly toward the Spaniards; but they knew nothing of Quivira and its treasures. The whites then continued to follow their guides, but these soon lost their way; every landmark disappeared, and thirst began to afflict the adventurers, who wandered aimlessly over the plains. Reconnoissances led to no results, for the sky and bisons were all that could be discovered. The Spaniards had accustomed their horses to hunting the wild oxen, and inflicted the same useless slaughter upon them of which American and European hunters and travellers were guilty, till the animals disappeared from their haunts. At one of the camping places the troop were surprised by a violent storm, with hail, that frightened the horses, wounded many, and broke to pieces everything frangible in the camp. A whirlwind accompanied the hail, and carried away tents, coverings, and some of the horses. The storm fortunately came upon them in the bottom of a ravine; if it had been on the plain the damage would have been much greater.

Wandering around in this way upon the illimitable plains, they again came suddenly in contact with Indians. Like the Querechos, this tribe, which was called "Teyas," lived exclusively with and upon the buffalo. They were hostile toward the Apaches of the plain, had been troublesome to the pueblo of Pecos, and appeared frank and friendly toward the Spaniards. They were of large stature and well shaped, and painted their faces and bodies with various figures. I do not venture to express a definite opinion as to what tribe the Teyas belonged to. Some have thought they were the Comanches, but those Indians were not known to the Pueblos till about the year 1700, while the Teyas, as I have remarked, had had hostile (and also friendly) intercourse with them before the arrival of the Spaniards. They may have been Utes. They knew of Quivira and the eastern regions, and gave Coronado information concerning them. But they were ignorant of the stone buildings, of the treasures and wealth, and in general of all that "the Turk" had described. The dwellings in Quivira, they said, were of "straw and skins," and there was very little maize there.

These accounts produced great depression, but still greater was the irritation against the guide who had drawn them into this country. "The Turk" finally confessed that he had spoken falsely to the whites when he told them of stone houses; but he adhered to what he had asserted concerning the numerous population and the wealth in metals of Quivira. He was thereupon put in chains, and the company continued its arduous march with guides whom the Teyas supplied. Scarcity of water was the greatest privation they suffered. Intense thirst afflicted man and beast, and buffalo meat was all they had with which to appease their hunger, for the supplies of maize were exhausted.

The Teyas advised Coronado to return; they assured him that nearly forty days' march would still be required to reach Quivira, and that the scarcity of water and of vegetable food would destroy his little army on the way. Many soldiers had already disappeared by going from the camp to hunt, when they became lost and miserably perished. Nevertheless Coronado determined to satisfy at least himself personally with the sight of Quivira, but to risk the lives of only a few men on the chance. Against the entreaties and expostulations of his followers, he selected twenty-nine horsemen, put himself at their head, entrusted the command of the main corps to Tristan de Arellano, and went on under the guidance of the Teyas, together with the enchained "Turk" and the other Indian. According to Casteñeda's statements, the point where the Spaniards separated was thirty-seven days' march—of six or seven leagues or between sixteen and nineteen English miles each—from Pecos. If we suppose, what is, however, doubtful, because of their wandering around, that they marched toward the northeast, they were then near the eastern border of New Mexico, close upon what is now the Indian Territory. A passage in Coronado's report says that in thirty-seven days they only marched on twenty, so that the distance traversed would be about three hundred miles. It, however, appears very plainly that they had turned to the right and marched in a circle, and, instead of northeast, were east or east-southeast of Pecos.

The date of the separation can be fixed approximately. The Spaniards left Pecos on the 3d of May, and, according to Casteñeda, reached the place where the army remained on June 9th. On St. Peter and St. Paul's day—July 10th—according to Jaramillo, the little band of horsemen to which he belonged, and which was under Coronado's personal leading, had been thirty days on the march; the separation must therefore have taken place on the 9th of June—that is, on Ascension Day of 1541, as Mota-Padilla correctly gives it. The "army," as it was called, was now divided into two parts, and it is therefore necessary to follow the fortunes of each of them separately. Casteñeda belonged to the chief corps, and concerned himself, in his account, exclusively with it. Coronado and Jaramillo, on the other hand, speak only of the march to Quivira, in which they took part.

Arellano and the "army" proper remained fifteen days in the spot where Coronado left them, spending the time in slaughtering the buffaloes that ranged around them. This wasteful butchery was carried to such an extent that more than five hundred bulls were slain, with a number of cows. Several of the soldiers were lost in the hunt, and disappeared entirely. At last, on the 24th of June, a retreat was begun, in the course of which several salt lakes and numerous prairie-dogs were seen. More than thirty leagues (eighty-one miles) south of the spot where the bridge had been thrown across the Canadian River the band came to the Pecos, below "Anton Chico"; then followed the course of that river to the great pueblo, arriving in front of it on July 19th. The inhabitants had changed in feeling, and refused them provisions. So the weary company were obliged to go on, and came to a halt at Tiguex, near the present town of Bernalillo, in their former headquarters, at the end of July, 1541. The Tiguas had in the interval resumed possession of their pueblo, but left it on the approach of the Spaniards and fled to the mountains. It was still summer, and there was no lack of provisions. Arellano therefore busied himself actively with laying in stores for the winter.

So far as the main body of the Spanish "army" was concerned, the march toward Quivira had terminated, having borne only insignificant fruits. Except for the buffalo hunting, which supplied meat and hides in quantities, they had gained nothing in return for their unprecedentd toil and danger besides the conviction that they had been betrayed and misled, and that Quivira was in no sense the gold-rich land that it had been described to them to be. This conviction had been impressed upon every one of them, so that the men were unwilling to see Coronado start off on an adventure more hazardous than any they had passed through, and with only a few horsemen. They were truly devoted to their leader, and were reluctant to part from him; yet, although many took leave of him with a fixed impression that they would never see him again, they obeyed his orders; for his enterprise might ultimately lead to discoveries that would recompense them for all their sufferings in the past and the present.

They therefore readily disposed themselves to the commands of Arellano, who, starting from Tiguex, instituted further researches along the course of the Rio Grande. Francisco de Barrionuevo, with two soldiers, followed the stream toward the north. Passing through the country on the west side, he came to the group of the "Hemes." These are the pueblos of which numerous ruins lie in the neighborhood of the present Jemez. They are divided into two groups, numbering together ten villages, seven of which belong properly to Jemez, and three to the subdivision of Aguas Calientes (the present "Thermen"). The Jemez Indians entered at once into friendly relations with the Spaniards, and continued thus till 1680. Touching upon the Queres on the west, they were wedged in between them and the powerful hostile tribe of the Navajos. These were so troublesome to them that even the two churches which were built for them soon after the year 1600 were temporarily given up and the Jemez Indians were dispersed. About the year 1622 the Franciscan missionaries collected them again, and gradually united them into a single large village. This village, abandoned in 1680, is now merged in the pueblo of Jemez, which contains in all about four hundred souls.

Returning from Jemez to the Rio Grande, Barrionuevo seems to have followed the right (or western) shore of the river exclusively, for he mentions the pueblo of "Yuque Yunque," "the inhabitants of which, as well as those of another village situated on the river, fled to the mountains," where they had four other fortified villages. The place was inaccessible to horses. "Yuque Yunque" is the present deserted "Yuge-uinge" (village of the ravine), called briefly "Yunque." The town of Chamita on the Denver & Rio Grande Railroad stands on its ruins, and near by was built, in 1598, the first Spanish settlement in New Mexico, San Gabriel.* On the east bank is the pueblo of San Juan, in a charming situation, and the valley, which borders the course of the Rio Grande, although hardly twelve miles long, is the most fruitful and the loveliest in New Mexico, that of Taos, perhaps, excepted. The massive chain of the Sierra Madre overlooks it in the east, with peaks that rise to a height of 13,000 feet; in the west a gloomy front of volcanic mesas, intersected by awful clefts, projects close upon the riverbank; and behind them the mountains of Abiquiu and the Sierra del Valle crown the landscape. This beautiful region was, and still is, occupied by the Tehuas Indians. There yet stand two other of their pueblos, San Ildefonso ("Poo-joge") and Santa Clara ("Ka-Poo"), on the bank, which have existed since

* Santa Fé was not founded till ten years later.

1598. If Barrionuevo, as I suppose, went from Cochiti through the great cañon which the Rio Grande traverses between there and San Ildefonso, or on the east side of the river over the mesa of Toma and the "Cuervo," as it is called, to Chamita, he would have observed both these pueblos if they existed then. This, however, he seems not to have done, and the four villages situated on the mountain were, therefore, on the west side, "Tzirege" and "Triape," in a wild region difficult of access; and on the east side two pueblos in the neighborhood of "Nambé." The accuracy of the accounts of the Spanish writers often astonishes those who have become acquainted by long residence with the country they describe, and creates a feeling of high respect for them.

Barrionuevo pressed still farther toward the north. Twenty leagues, or fifty-four miles, beyond Chamita he came to a large pueblo called "Braba," which was built on both sides of a river, and contained very large estufas. General Simpson has identified this place with the present Taos, and I see no reason for not agreeing with him. The native name for Taos is indeed "Tegat-hâ," and I have never been able to find any name of a place in any of the pueblo languages that corresponds with "Braba" or "Uraba," or "Yuraba." Yet the situation and the whole description point to Taos as the place that is meant. Casteñeda says further on that Braba was the last village to the north that was built of stone and mortar, and that is actually the case with Taos.

Thus the Spaniards had found and specified, before the end of the summer of 1541, all the linguistic stocks of the pueblos of New Mexico, and had come in actual contact with all the groups of New Mexican aborigines, except the Jumanos and a few roaming hordes in the southwest, which once belonged to the Texan group. It is even possible that the Jumanos might be found among the painted Tejas, who were afterward called by the Spaniards, from their painting, *Indios rayados*, or striped Indians. This great tribe, which was extinguished in the insurrection of 1680, then inhabited the regions of eastern and southeastern New Mexico and northern Chihuahua. The Jumanos of New Mexico were in a state of constant feud with the Apaches, and this became the cause of their disappearance.

September was drawing toward its end, and the commander-in-chief had not yet returned from his hazardous journey to Quivira. The time which he had fixed for his return had passed, and Tristan de Arellano was anxious concerning the fate of the *Adelantado*. Leaving Barrionuevo in command at Tiguex, he went with forty horsemen to Pecos. The people there were still hostile, and he was obliged to bring his small artillery against their pueblo. The great houses resisted the attack, and he could not force an entrance. He was therefore encamped outside of the village in the valley, when the news came to him that the *Adelantado* was approaching with his company; and a few days afterward Coronado arrived, sound and in good health, but weary, empty-handed, and disappointed. He had found Quivira and explored it well, but discovered no signs there of a permanent settlement, or of gold or silver.

The Tejas Indians had informed the Spaniards, while the whole army was still together, that they had gone much too far south; Quivira was away in the north. When, therefore, Coronado started with his twenty-nine men, the Tejas led him directly north, for thirty days, through unlimited, treeless plains, covered with herds of buffaloes and traversed by small streams, till on August 9th they came to a river, which they named, in honor of the saints of the day, "Rio San Pedro y San Pablo." Jaramillo says that they had been able to march over only short distances each day, so that this river can have been no other than the Arkansas, and the spot where they struck it was probably near the Great Bend, for after crossing the river they followed its northern bank for three days toward the northeast, a direction corresponding exactly with the course of the Arkansas in that latitude.

It may be remarked, by the way, that Coronado speaks of this region as situated in the 40th degree of north latitude; that is, that it was five and a half degrees north of the Gila, according to the determinations of that time. The Gila River, however, runs, not in the parallel of 34° 30′, but of about 33°, while the Arkansas flows in the 38th degree, or five and a half degrees north of the Gila. Quivira should therefore be sought in the present State of Kansas, and in the central districts, about a hundred miles north of the Arkansas River.

It would be useless, however, to look for the ruins of a considerable permanent settlement of the natives. There is no such place, and the tribe that lived at Quivira was a roaming Indian horde that subsisted chiefly by hunting the buffalo, and casually followed a rude agriculture. Coronado says: "I had been told that the houses were made of stone and were several storied; they are only of straw, and the inhabitants are as savage as any that I have seen. They have no clothes, nor cotton to make them out of; they simply tan the hides of the cows which they hunt, and which pasture around their village and in the neighborhood of a large river. They eat their meat raw, like the Querechos and the Tejas, and are enemies to one another and war among one another. All these men look alike. The inhabitants of Quivira are the best of hunters, and they plant maize." There were no signs of gold or silver; some iron pyrites and a few pieces of copper were all the metal that was found. Jaramillo confirms these statements, adds that the huts were round, and clearly describes one of the medicine lodges that are common among the Indians of the prairies.

Coronado, with his company and "the Turk," arrived at Quivira on August 21st. "The Turk" was brought in chains, a prisoner, while the other Indian was able to prove that he had at least always told the truth. Through him the Spaniards had been well received at Quivira, and that embittered them all the more against the "the Turk." He confessed that the Pueblo Indians had engaged him to draw the Spaniards into the plains, in order that they might perish there. Implicit faith must not, however, be given to this assertion. When the prisoner could not deliver himself by such confessions and other pretences, he tried to stir up the people of Quivira against the Spaniards. The plan was quickly discovered, and the treacherous guide was hanged the same night.

Coronado stayed twenty-five days with the Indians of Quivira and the vicinity. He found the country fertile. "The soil," he says, "is the best that can be found for all the crops of Spain; besides being strong and black, it is well watered with brooks, springs, and rivers. I found plums like those in Spain, nuts, very fine grapes, and mulberries." To this description is added the testimony of Jaramillo, who praises the fertility of the soil, the abundance of water, and the absence of mountains, and gives special prominence to certain productions, such as flax, sumach, and grapes.

Notwithstanding all these advantages, which Coronado sufficiently pointed out, he could not remain in Quivira. Winter, if not immediately at his door, was not very far off, and the Spaniards, surprised by early frosts, and not being acquainted with the delightful autumn of Kansas and the Mississippi Valley, thought that cold weather would follow at once. They therefore began a retreat, accomplished it without accident in forty days, and arrived in the Pecos Valley on October 25th (1541). Thence Coronado returned with Arellano to Bernalillo, where he wrote on October 31st the report to Charles V., from which part of the facts we have related are taken.

It is remarkable that when Coronado told his men the full truth about Quivira, and confided to them the discouraging results of his expedition, they became all the more fixed in the idea that Quivira was a gold-rich country. They conceived that their commander had not gone far enough into the interior because, meeting a dense population, he was not willing to venture among them with his small following. Indians who had been with Arellano confirmed the Spaniards in these opinions, and promoted an inclination which was liable to lead on the one side to further expeditions, and on the other side to a breach with their leader. He found himself in a very difficult position. He was at all events convinced that another expedition beyond Quivira would not be likely to lead to the discovery of what they were seeking for, while it would be attended with great danger; for the whole army would have to follow him, and he would therefore be cutting himself entirely off from New Mexico and going out into the unknown without any base of operations. He felt, on the other hand, that such a campaign, if not of gold and silver, might lead to other important discoveries. He was sure that the great river which the Spaniards then called "Rio del Espiritú Santo," and which was nothing else than the Mississippi, must rise in those unknown regions. To reach this river from the west would be a great achievement, which would cover him and his men with honor, and be of much direct or indirect advantage to them. At the same time, his men were insisting so earnestly upon an attempt in that direction, that Coronado determined to yield to them, and, spending the winter in the valley of the Rio Grande, to leave New Mexico in the spring of 1542 and go eastward once more. Quivira, which had now been proved and acknowledged to be poor in metals, was no longer the sole object of the contemplated new expedition; it was to form the new base of operations, from which the step into the unknown should be made.

I have shown that Quivira was in central Kansas, in the region of Great Bend and Newton, and a little north of there. It is also clear that the name appertained to a roving Indian tribe, and not to a geographical district. Hence, when I say that Coronado's Quivira was there, the identification is good for the year 1541, and not for a later time. The tribe wandered with the bison, and with the tribe the name also went hither and thither. In the place where Coronado found Quivira, he was not more than seven hundred miles from the Mississippi. It is a remarkable fact that in the same year, and at nearly the same time, June 18, 1541, Hernando de Soto reached the Mississippi from the southeast and crossed it to the west. Had Coronado gone directly east or southeast from the point where he and his horsemen separated from the chief corps to go in search of Quivira, instead of in a northerly direction, he might have shaken hands with the discoverer of the Mississippi on the western shore of the great river.

On Coronado's return friendly relations were restored with the Indians of Pecos, and even the Tiguas at Bernalillo showed a disposition to inhabit their deserted villages again. Before the end of the year 1541 (not 1542, as Casteñeda says), in October, Pedro de Tobar arrived with reinforcements. The letters which he brought from Spain and Mexico caused Garcia Lopez de Cárdenas to leave the expedition and return home by way of Zuñi and Sonora. I mention this fact among others because it shows with what security a solitary Spaniard could then make the long journey, which is not wholly without dangers to-day, with only Indian guides. This security has been ascribed to the respect which the Spanish arms won from the tribes, and to intimidation caused by severe treatment. The explanation is not sufficient in the present case. The Pueblo Indian, or the Apache, or the Navajo would not have been afraid of individual Spaniards if he had been generally inclined to hostility. The relation between the Indians and the Spaniards was, on the contrary, a friendly one, to which only the excesses against the Tiguas formed a solitary and therefore a conspicuous exception. With all the other tribes (except the little frictions with the Pecos, which always smoothed themselves away) the Spaniards lived in peace, and the roads from and toward Sonora were more open and secure than they are now. Large tracts were uninhabited, it is true, in which at least a few human abodes may now be seen, and the savage Indians were much more widely dispersed than they are now; but the present increased population, with increased quiet, also furnishes occasions of greater peril to property and life.

Coronado was beloved by his men. He took the largest share in all their privations, and whenever there was an allotment of provisions and clothing, he was careful to protect the common soldiers against the greed of the officers. Such a division took place in the fall of 1541, but Coronado was not in a condition to exercise his accustomed authority. The bonds of discipline had become relaxed, and his own energy had been weakened. Undeceived concerning the value of his conquests, he perceived that they opened no future to him, and still less to his wife, whom he had left in Mexico. He longed to go back to this wife, without whom there was no home for him, and he could not give her a home in New Mexico. It was, therefore, not contrary to his secret wishes, as he remarked, that the soldiers began of themselves to object to the contemplated expedition and to talk of a return to Mexico. Nevertheless, he continued making his arrangements, and the winter of 1541-42 was quietly spent in the camp at Bernalillo in busy preparation. They were to start in the spring of 1542, and the time for breaking camp was approaching, when two events caused a change in their plans. As Coronado was one day tilting with Don Pedro Maldonado, while on the full run the girth of his saddle broke, and he fell upon the side of Maldonado's horse, which, being also at full speed, sprang over him, and inflicted a dangerous wound upon his head.

After long suffering he had begun to recover, when Garcia Lopez de Cárdenas unexpectedly returned from Sonora, bringing important news. He had gone to the Valley of Sonora without delay, and confidently hoped to meet the little colony in Suya. Instead of that he found the settlement a pile of smoking ruins, and the natives in full insurrection. After the death of Melchior Diaz, Diego de Alcaráz had continued in command at Suya. His character, which he had already revealed in Sinaloa, was not such as to qualify him for forming friendly relations with the Indians, while his subordinates were of the most unruly soldiers of the government of New Galicia. Their outrageous conduct excited the Indians to resistance. Some of the Spaniards fled to Culiacan; the rest, with a few exceptions, besides Alcaráz, were murdered in the night, their horses killed, all their cattle slaughtered or carried off, and their houses torn down and burnt. Cárdenas, in order to escape the poisoned arrows of the Opatas, hurried back to Zuñi, and thence to the Rio Grande.

This report provoked a relapse in Coronado's condition, which caused all thoughts of Quivira to be set aside for the time. How long his illness and convalescence lasted cannot be exactly determined. An error in counting the years has crept into Casteñeda's story, for he places the beginning of the expedition to the plains in 1541 and the return in 1542, but afterward corrects himself as to the date 1542, so as to fix the return to Mexico in the year 1543. This is certainly an error, unless Coronado's illness lasted a whole year and the Spaniards spent the winter of 1542–43 in Bernalillo. It appears clearly from the reports, however, that this was not the case, but that Coronado had fully recovered in March, 1542. The relapse which he suffered is suspected by Casteñeda of having been a pretence; but Jaramillo, who was an officer, and stood in closer relations with him than Casteñeda, says nothing of this. His wounded condition increased the weary commander's longing to return, and the insurrection of the Opatas in the rear of the little army made its situation very critical. He therefore proposed to his officers to take advantage of the feeling of the troops, and to have them prepare a petition to him for the evacuation of New Mexico. Signatures were easily procured for this petition, but Coronado had hardly begun the preparations for a retreat on the strength of it, when several of the signers asked to have their names withdrawn. It was, however, too late, and most of the soldiers adhered to their former decision. Casteñeda, whose morose nature dwells upon this division, says that Coronado had lost all authority and affection among the officers, who obeyed him after this, not out of respect, but only because of their oaths. Great discord prevailed in the little army; some wanted to stay at any cost; but they all agreed at last, and in the beginning of April, 1542, Tiguex was evacuated and the retreat to Zuñi begun.

Over a few members of the expedition Coronado had no power. These were the priests, who had come with him to this point; the Franciscan monks, Fray Juan de Padilla, Fray Juan de la Cruz, and the lay brother, Fray Luis de Ubeda, decided to remain in New Mexico, even without the protection of the army. It was indifferent to them whether there were treasures in the newly discovered regions or not; they thought only of the souls of the natives, and considered themselves pledged to devote their lives to the work of conversion. Coronado could not compel them to return with him, and they equally could not demand a large guard. Only volunteers, therefore, remained with them in Bernalillo. These were a Portuguese, Andrés del Campo; a mestizo; two Indians named Lúcas and Sebastian, who had been adopted by the monks in Michoacan; two Indians from Oaxaca; and a negro. They stayed voluntarily, as we have said, although there could hardly be a doubt as to what their fate would be.

Such heroic devotion finds favor even in Casteñeda's cynic judgment, for he says of Fray Juan de Padilla that "we must believe that his zeal was true and sincere."

After the "army" left the Valley of the Rio Grande the three priests apportioned the field of labor which they had chosen. Fray Juan de la Cruz remained among the Tiguas at Bernalillo, where he passed out of view. A story that he was murdered is little questioned in the church, and is very probably true. The other two priests went to Pecos, where Fray Luis de Ubeda settled, and likewise passed out of definite knowledge. The natives were, however, at least in the beginning, friendly in their demeanor toward him.

Fray Juan de Padilla, in his turn, chose Quivira as his field of work. Accompanied by the others who remained behind, and by guides from Pecos, he reached the tribe during the summer months of the same year. The wooden cross was still standing which Coronado had erected, with the words cut upon it: "Francisco Vasquez de Coronado, leader of a campaign, came to this place." This cross served him as the central point for missionary work, and the Quiviras received him gladly. Yet, notwithstanding the warnings of the people around him, he wanted to go farther. His first effort to travel toward the east brought him in contact with a hostile horde, which Casteñeda calls "the Guyas." The priest immediately perceived his danger, and ordered the Portuguese and his other companions to flee and leave him alone. Resistance was impossible, and it would be better to save their lives than sacrifice them uselessly. The advice was prudent and worthy of the devotion of the priest. His companions therefore left him, with bitter sorrow in their hearts, and saw him kneel to await the coming of the savages. There is no doubt that he was immediately killed.* It is thus not improbable that the first martyr of the church, in the Spanish attempts to settle in the southwest, fell in Kansas, not more than six hundred miles west of the Mississippi, and only fifty years after the landing of Columbus.

The story of this event could hardly reach posterity without including an adventure of great hazard and of the most marvellous character. The companions of Fray Juan de Padilla fled back to the Quiviras, and it is said that those savages received the not unanticipated news of the death of the priest with sincere mourning and deep grief. Neither the Portuguese nor the Indians who had accompanied him felt themselves longer called upon to continue the missionary work, but were anxious to return to Mexico. Yet they were disposed not to go back by the same route as they had come, but to see new regions. It was in the spirit of the time. Fearlessness and the constant expectation of finding something new and astonishing were so deeply implanted in those men that it was like a second nature to them to go recklessly forward into the unknown rather

* The legend stands in the Martyrology under date of the 30th of November, but Gonzaga ("*Orígen de la religion seráfica*," 1587, Part I., p. 105) is mistaken when he says that the event happened in the year 1560. Mota-Padilla depends on the manuscript of Don Pedro de Tobar, who fixes the date at 1542, which agrees closely with the statements of the monk's contemporaries—Casteñeda's error excepted.

than back into the known. Then, perhaps, a return to New Mexico might be more dangerous than an advance in the opposite direction. The Portuguese and the two Indians from Michoacan, who, as adopted children ("donados") of the order of St. Francis, wore the Franciscan dress, directed their course from Kansas toward the east and then toward the south. The fact is undoubted that they finally reached Pánuco (in the present State of Tamaulipas in the Mexican republic), after a journey comparable in its adventurous character with that of Cabeza de Vaca and his companions. I have not been able to fix the exact date, for the event, although verified in many ways, seems not to have attracted much attention. The fugitives did not see the Mississippi, but passed on the western side of the river, through the Indian Territory and perhaps a part of Texas, to Tamaulipas, whence the Portuguese went to the City of Mexico, and the two Indians, Lúcas and Sebastian, to their home in Michoacan, where Sebastian died a few days after his arrival. The details of this remarkable wandering are unfortunately very scanty. It is inferred, from the fact that Gomára mentions it, that it took place before the year 1550.

The main corps under Coronado had returned to Mexico. While the expedition had suffered in the beginning from the disadvantages occasioned by intense eagerness and haste to reach its object, the retreat afforded a spectacle of sad disappointment, discontent, and consequent insubordination. Between the Rio Grande and Zuñi disease broke out among the horses, under which more than thirty perished. It was, perhaps, the same disease which now prevails occasionally among horses in New Mexico, and is called *el mal*. The Spaniards rested in Zuñi, and some of the Mexican Indians remained there—a fact which should be carefully regarded in the investigation of the myths and usages of the natives. Although the people were friendly, they followed the troop for several days, and tried to compel some of the men to stay. The troop reached Chichiltic-calli without delay, and were met there by Juan Gallegas, who had come from Mexico with reinforcements and ammunition. He was very angry at finding the army on the retreat. The fabulous reports which, reinforced by the representations of "the Turk," had reached Mexico had produced a revival of speculative excitement respecting New Mexico, and the newly arrived soldiers were greatly dissatisfied. Some of the officers made use of this feeling to urge at least that a permanent settlement should be founded, but Coronado's soldiers opposed this, and insisted on continuing the retreat. Coronado himself pleaded illness, and seemed to have lost all his energy.

The troop therefore moved again, to make their way into Sonora. The Opatas opposed them, annoying the march daily, and killing men and horses with poisoned arrows. No pause occurred in the hostilities till Batuco was reached; thence the despondent company proceeded unhindered to Culiacan, and there all the bonds of discipline were broken. Coronado started from Culiacan for Mexico on the 4th of July, 1542. When he arrived at the capital he was followed by hardly a hundred soldiers.

The rest had scattered to the right and left on the way.

As the entrance into the capital was gloomy, so was his reception by the viceroy, Don Antonio de Mendoza, a hard blow for Coronado, from which he never recovered. This officer, the highest in authority in Mexico, declared to his former favorite that he was disappointed and angry that he had given up the north, and in such terms that Coronado withdrew to the present Cuernavaca, where he needed to give himself no more concern about his province of New Galicia, and died there in retirement. In the year 1548 the government was compelled, on account of his entire incapacity for business, to appoint a court of *audiencia* for the "kingdom of New Galicia." Little is known concerning the proceedings that were instituted against him. The once honored, now despised nobleman was deserted in early old age, and died neglected.

Was the disfavor into which he had fallen, and which cast a gloomy shadow over the whole of his after-life, deserved? As a leader Coronado was always worthy of distinction; he never spared himself, but always had a fatherly care for his subordinates; and if we regard the whole course of the campaign, we must acknowledge that he always acted prudently and yet decisively. Two dark features are visible in his intercourse with the natives: the abduction of the chiefs of Pecos, and the cruelties against the Tiguas at Bernalillo. In the former case Coronado followed an example which stood prominent at the time in the view of every Spaniard, and of many a champion in the rest of Europe—that of Hernando Cortés; and he afterward repaired his fault. The responsibility for the atrocious cruelties at Tiguex does not fall so much upon him as upon Garcia Lopez de Cárdenas. A proof that he did not, as a rule, behave badly toward the Indians is afforded by the fact that during the whole course of the expedition, which lasted two years and extended over so wide a territory, and in which so many different tribes were encountered, only four cases of real hostilities occurred, and only one of these was of great importance.

The conception which has been often formed of Coronado as a wicked adventurer is therefore unjust. Equally wrong and unfounded are the accusations which Mendoza formulated against him, and on the ground of which he treated the knight so severely. The following are assigned as the reasons by which the action of the viceroy was determined: first, while Alarcon wrote with the fullest detail in his reports, the letters of Coronado were short, and therefore unsatisfactory; second, Coronado wrote also directly to the emperor and king (Charles V.), which the viceroy considered a presumption on his part, and even regarded as bordering on treason; third, his evacuation of New Mexico and return seemed at least a gross violation of duty, for it was ascribed to disobedience, incapacity, and cowardice.

The letters of Coronado (of which I am acquainted only with those written to the emperor) are, indeed, not to be compared with the detailed daybook-like reports of Alarcon. But the latter, being most of the time on shipboard, had leisure and opportunity to prepare even more voluminous reports than he really made. It is not strange that he expanded his accounts. Coronado, on the other hand, was living under conditions which often made writing impossible, as I have many times experienced. No one is disposed to write long letters in the pueblo houses; moreover, in winter and on the road to Quivira the ink may have failed. Don Antonio de Mendoza understood none of these conditions, and did not realize the great difference between the situations of the seaman and of the officer in the heart of the continent. With all the traits for which he was distinguished, the viceroy was first of all things a European officer, who, however ably he could direct from his desk, had no comprehension of American camp-life. Coronado's letters to the emperor and king were, it is true, an imprudence on his part that bordered on insubordination, and (in view of the previous difficulties of Cortés with Diego Velasquez) might easily have aroused suspicion in the viceroy.

Respecting the evacuation of New Mexico, I have minutely examined the course of events, in order to make a judgment upon it possible. There was no cowardice. Coronado's wounds, and the result of the expedition to Quivira, with homesickness and a weakened bodily condition, probably contributed much to a discouragement which was based on the conviction that the country was not worth the effort which its control would cost. Coronado accused his predecessor, Fray Marcos, the discoverer of New Mexico, unjustly, as I have already shown, of having published exaggerated accounts of that country. He did not anticipate, he could not anticipate, that his own accounts, which fully agreed, so far as they concerned the same regions, with those of the monk, might afford occasion, to a superficial review, for the same reproaches against him as he made against the Franciscan, and supply material for distortions and mistakes the practical results of which would be as evil in the nineteenth century as were those of the exaggerated accounts of Cibola in the sixteenth century.

With the return to Mexico of the little army that Coronado commanded, the name of Cibola lost its fascination. The legend of the Amazons had, in the north, passed into that of the "seven cities," and these are accounted for by the seven pueblos or villages of Zuñi. But Quivira continued to exercise an unperceived influence on the imaginations of men. Notwithstanding, or perhaps because, Coronado had told the unadorned truth concerning the situation and conditions of the place, the world presumed that he was mistaken, and insisted on continuing the search for it. And although Juan de Oñate, in 1599, and Saldivar, in 1618, went out in the direction which Coronado had designated, and found only what he had found, yet was Quivira more persistently sought, and at a greater distance; and it became a phantom, like the Dorado, which hovered with visions of golden treasures before the fancies of the Spaniards, in the northeast and east of New Mexico. It was forgotten that the Quiviras were a wandering horde of Prairie Indians, who lived with the herds of bison, and not a sedentary people; that the mission of Jumanos, which Fray Francisco Letrado had founded, was visited by Quiviras, and the church there was the religious centre for all these wandering tribes after 1636; and that the Quiviras were then roaming around for a distance of forty leagues, or one hundred and eight miles, eastward, or in southeastern New Mexico, and that, therefore, they had moved southward. The insurrection of 1680 produced such a confusion in the ethnographic conditions of New Mexico that Quivira passed out of mind, and when the revolution extended to Chihuahua and Sonora in 1684, the only thought was of self-preservation. After the re-conquest of New Mexico by Diego de Vargas (1692 to 1694) followed the irruption of the Comanches from the north, greatly disturbing the former ethnographic conditions, in the east and down into Texas. The Jumanos had already vanished, and even the name of the Quiviras, if it was a real name, was lost; but not the recollection of the golden stories which had been associated with them. A golden kingdom had grown in imagination out of the tribe, and to this golden kingdom belonged, as did the city of Manoa to the South American Dorado, a great capital in New Mexico, called *la gran Quivira*. This treasure-city had lain in ruins since the insurrection of 1680; but its treasures were supposed to be buried in the neighborhood, for it was said there had once been a wealthy mission there, and the priests had buried and hidden the vessels of the church. Thus the Indian kingdom of Quivira of "the Turk" was metamorphosed in the course of two centuries into an opulent Indian mission, and its vessels of gold and silver into a church service. But where Quivira should be looked for was forgotten.

In the middle of the last century a Spanish captain of engineers, Don Bernardo de Mier y Pacheco, went upon a scientific and political mission for the Crown in New Mexico. He explored the ruins of the country, and the numerous pueblos of the Cañon de Chaca (in the present home of the Navajos) excited his interest in the highest degree. When he began to concern himself about the situation of Quivira, it was supposed that he had plans and documentary evidences to assist him in finding the place. The measurements which he made in the ruins of the Chaca convinced the people that Quivira was there, and this conviction grew and spread rapidly. There was living at that time in Socorro on the Rio Grande an old Indian who was called "Tio Juan Largo." When he heard of the search of the Spanish officer, he protested at once against the idea that Quivira could be found in the northwest, and insisted that the ruins of the former mission of the Jumanos and Quiviras were east of Socorro, on the "Mesa Jumana." He was a Jumano Indian—perhaps the last who passed for one. Attention was then turned at once to the region east of Socorro. The country beyond the Sierra Oscura, between the Rio Grande and the Pecos, had remained uninhabited after the insurrection of 1680, and the small settlements of Manzano and Abó, in the vicinity of the Great Salt Lake, were not founded till about 1841 and 1869. The Apaches Taraones and the Comanches had, as it were, frightened all life away from the region.

Ruins of pueblos and imposing stone churches, burnt out, with their enclosures open to the sky and the clouds, remains of the modest prosperity which the pueblo Indians enjoyed under the guidance of the Franciscan monks, before their unfortunate insurrection, lie scattered on the cliffs. Definite recollections are associated with all these ruins; the descendants of the Indians of Cuaray, Chililé, and Tajique still live at Isleta in Texas, and the posterity of the inhabitants of Abó at Senecú near El Paso del Norte. The existence of these ruins and a dim outline of their history were never absent from the recollections of the Spaniards.

Touching the Valley of Abó on the east and the basin of the Salt Lake on the north, rises a broad mesa, the borders of which are covered only on the north side with thin woods. The surface is inclined toward the south, and is treeless, though covered with good grass, but from the northern edge of the mesa south, southeast, and southwest, there is for from thirty to sixty miles not a drop of standing water. While I was there from the 4th to the 10th of January, 1883, melted snow was my only drink. This uninhabited plateau is the "Mesa de los Jumanos," and on its southeast side stand the ruins of a pueblo which, according to my measurements, contained about twelve hundred inhabitants, with two stone churches, one of which is thirty-four feet wide and one hundred and thirty-two feet long, and stands almost undamaged, except in the roof. The walls are six feet thick, and a few hewn beams are still left in the interior. Adjoining these ruins are the walls of a considerable presbytery. The other church has been reduced to crumbling walls. No running water is to be found anywhere near, but four large artificial pools afford enough water for drinking purposes. This is the ruin which the old Jumano Indian of Socorro in the last century described as the former mission of Quivira, and which consequently now bears the name of "*la gran Quivira.*"

The old man was right. In the year 1630 Fray Francesco Letrado undertook the conversion of the Jumanos after an earlier effort had failed. But instead of going directly among the Indians, he established himself in a pueblo of the Piros, and had them build a church for the use both of the people there and of the inhabitants of the surrounding country. This pueblo was called the "Tey-paná" in the Piro language, and was the present *Gran Quivira*, while the ruins of the little church are those of the smaller temple. The place was the most eastern mission in New Mexico, and was called *la mision de los Jumanos*. At the same time with the Jumanos, the Quiviras were visited by the priests; and a number of members were gradually associated from all these tribes with the people of the village, and thus the building of a new church became necessary. This was the newer, larger ruin, and the structure was never quite completed. The Apaches pressed so closely upon the remote and isolated village that the mission to the Jumanos was abandoned in 1679. A few surviving members of the Piros who once dwelt there still live in Jemez, but the Jumanos and Quiviras have died away.

The history of the mission, too, was lost in the eighteenth century, although it could be clearly learned from the annals of the church and in Spanish books and manuscripts. But instead of studying these, men have peopled the ruins with fanciful figures, and have entered them cautiously and timidly in superstitious treasure-hunting. Numerous excavations attest the stay there of persons who have searched for the golden cups, the candlesticks of solid silver, and all that the fables ascribed to the poor missionaries of the sixteenth century. Had the gold-hunters, and, in later times, the water-hunters, considered the history of the *Gran Quivira*, they might have spared themselves trouble, labor, much money, and much suffering.

What is true on a small scale of Quivira is true in far greater measure of New Mexico and its metallic wealth in general. Historical writers have dealt superficially with that country by taking only a few authorities (Espejo, for example), and those without adequate criticism, as the basis of their sketches. Practical life demands of research in the historical field that it make it acquainted with the experiences of the past for the use and advantage of the present. Had those experiences been represented as they are clearly and truthfully laid down in the Spanish documents, much useless expenditure of capital would have been spared in New Mexico alone. It cannot be said that those documents were inaccessible, for the reports of Fray Marcos and of Coronado were printed in Italy and in England in the sixteenth century, and the works of Gomara, Herrera, and Torquemada contained the truth in abstracts. A Spanish officer wrote as early as 1601 that New Mexico was not so bad as it was occasionally drawn, but was far from being as good as it was usual to represent the country; and Alexander von Humboldt explicitly denied ("*Histoire politique du royaume de la Nouvelle Espagne,*" vol. ii. cap. viii. 3d book, p. 246) the existence there of rich beds of ore. In spite of this he has often been brought forward as authority for the assertion that the richest mines in the world were once opened there and in Arizona. The truth as to the metallic wealth of the country lies between the two extremes, but considerably nearer the former; and a critical study of the documentary history of the region should have been enough of itself to convince inquiring mankind of the fact.

THE MASSACRE OF CHOLULA (1519).

The day on which occurred the massacre of Cholula—a very important event in the annals of the Spanish conquest of Mexico—has not been determined with certainty, but the month is known. It took place about the middle of Otcober, 1519, probably between the 10th and the 15th. The usual account of the tragedy—the conception of it regarded as historical—represents it as a causeless piece of treachery on the part of the Spaniards, an act of unjustifiable cruelty, an eternal blot on the fame of Hernando Cortés. Prescott gives the fairest and most exact expression to this view in his "Conquest of Mexico" when he says: "This passage in their history is one of those that have left a dark stain on the memory of the conquerors. Nor can we contemplate, at this day, without a shudder, the condition of this fair and flourishing capital thus invaded in its privacy and delivered over to the excesses of a rude and ruthless soldiery." At the same time Mr. Prescott excuses the proceeding as an act of military necessity, and censures only the excess of the chastisement which Cortés allowed to be inflicted upon the Indians of Cholula.

A long residence in Cholula has enabled me to become thoroughly acquainted with the scene of the massacre, and to collect and study the native traditions concerning it, and their pictorial representations of it. Many documents referring to the slaughter have also come to light since Prescott's work was published. These papers set the transaction in a new light, and illustrate how important to the composition of a correct historical account of an event is a previous study of its details and the local conditions.

Most incorrect and exaggerated ideas prevail concerning the condition of Cholula at the beginning of the sixteenth century, even in works admired for their apparent thoroughness; and of this Prescott is an example and proof. "The Cholulan capital," he says, "was the great commercial emporium of the plateau. . . . Not a rood of land but was under cultivation." From the top of the artificial hill (falsely called a pyramid) the spectator saw "the sacred city of Cholula, with its bright towers and pinnacles sparkling in the sun, reposing amidst gardens and verdant groves, which then thickly studded the cultivated environs of the capital." On the summit of what was called the pyramid "stood a sumptuous temple."

These passages are examples of the conceptions that are current, and specimens, as well, of inaccuracy and exaggeration. Concerning the pyramid so often mentioned, I appeal to the testimony of the authors whom Prescott is accustomed to cite. They agree that at the time of the arrival of the Spaniards this great artificial hill had long been in ruins and was overgrown with bushes. The top of the hill was then convex, and crowned with a "little ancient temple" dedicated to the god *Nahui Quiahuitl*, or nine rains. There was no trace of a large building, and the pyramid looked so much like a wooded hill that the conquerors regarded it as a natural elevation.

Cholula was not a capital, for it had no cities or villages attached to it, nor any rural population. I have investigated in the archives the development of the present district from the earliest period of Spanish rule, and have shown ("An Archæological Tour in Mexico") that all the Indian villages date from the sixteenth, seventeenth, and eighteenth centuries; that the few more ancient remains besides Cholula—except the sacrificial hill of Calpan—belong to a far more ancient period, and had been long deserted and forgotten when Cortés conquered Mexico; and that the whole tribe of Cholula dwelt together in six quarters, which were erected on the ground covered by the present city of Cholula and commune of San Andrés Cholula. The environs of these six quarters, which were separated from one another by open places, were cultivated; but the plantations extended no farther out. Three fourths of the present district lay fallow, where now forty villages with twenty thousand souls are supported by the cultivation of the soil.

The architecture of the natives did not include "sparkling towers." The one-storied, flat houses were whitewashed with plaster, and above them rose the rounded artificial sacrificial hill, on the narrow level spaces of the summit of which stood little tower-shaped chapels. The view of this whole complex, like that of the Indian pueblos of New Mexico, was very striking and very deceiving as to the real number of people, which appeared nearly twice as large as it actually was. Furthermore, as in the present villages of New Mexico, hardly more than two thirds of the houses are inhabited, and one is led to overestimate the population greatly.

Cholula was neither a specially sacred city nor an emporium of trade. The people had their gods, like any other of the tribes, and among them Quetzalcohuatl was held in high reverence. Pilgrims did not flock to his shrine from near and far, as to Einsiedeln or Mecca, and the lordly neighbors of Tlascala and Huexotzinco, as well as those of Mexico, regarded the idol of Cholula, accordingly as they felt friendly or hostile toward it, as representing a gallant hero, or a blasphemous image, or an evil spirit.

The trade of Cholula did not surpass that which other equally numerous tribes possessed. It was irregular and limited. As the Pueblo Indians used to go a few years ago to the Comanches, in well-guarded caravans, or, till 1859, to Sonora, sometimes to the loss of their goods and even of their lives, so in aboriginal Mexico they went in armed companies to the neighboring tribes for purposes of trade. Cholula was a good market, for its inhabitants were producers of cochineal, and as it was nearer the lowlands than the Mexican plateau and Tlascala, it was a place where traders could exchange their own products for tropical fruits and decorative articles. Feathers of richly colored birds were very much in demand. Parrots and *Trogon resplendens* came through Tehuacan to Cholula. The people of that region, on the other hand, had no salt. There is a considerable difference, however, between this primitive trade and a great inland market. What is great and important to an Indian people will appear to a European, as soon as the first impression of strangeness has worn off, often very insignificant. All the descriptions of the high civilization and the magnitude ascribed to Cholula rest upon the testimony of Spanish eye-witnesses, and have been composed without due regard to the sort of comparisons the Spaniards were able at that time to make. When, for example, Cortés compared Tlascala with Granada and Cempohual with Seville, we should not only consider how large those cities were in the year 1519, but should especially recollect that the comparisons only related to superficial extent. Every Indian town contains much more vacant space than any European city of the same area. All these accounts are therefore nearly as inexact as the political "campaign documents" of the present. Without really intending to state what was false, the authors of them involuntarily exaggerated in favor of their predilections. Everything was misunderstood at first, or not understood at all; the character of the people and their manners and customs were novel and bewildering. The population of a place was always greatly overestimated, for wherever the Spaniards showed themselves the people ran together, and the same throngs accompanied them all around, so that they met at every step a multitude that gave the appearance of great traffic.

Cholula had in its original condition not many more than 25,000 inhabitants, who were divided among the six quarters that surrounded, at considerable intervals, the chief sacrificial hill. The hill rose out of the usual walled court and stood where to-day stand the great Franciscan cloister of San Gabriel and the *capilla real*. At present not 10,000 people dwell in the city and in San Andrés, but the whole district contains at least as many Indians as inhabited it before the conquest, except that they live scattered over the land, and not, as formerly, together in an extensive pueblo.

The tribe of Cholula was tributary to no one; it belonged to the large number of settled groups which, wholly independent of one another, comprised the native population of old Mexico. Among these groups, which were all military democracies with elective officers, never hereditary monarchies or despotisms, three had joined in a confederation and had become very dangerous to all the others. They were the tribes of the Mexican Valley: Mexico, Tezcuco, and Tlacopan. Mexico took the lead in warlike affairs: Montezuma was simply the commander-in-chief of the soldiers of the three tribes, and not a crowned head. The allies were the most dangerous enemies of Cholula. Yet when the Spaniards had forced themselves into the present Mexico, Cholula had approached them, or rather the Confederation had approached the Cholulans, in order to obtain a support against Tlascala and against the powerful strangers who had just concluded an alliance with the Tlascalans.

Not much regard was felt in the neighborhood* for the shrine of the holy Quetzal-cohuatl, but its people were generally looked upon as cowards and knaves, and its idol as a "bad medicine"; and every appeal was made to Cortés to induce him not to go by way

---

* Tlascala is only twenty-five miles from Cholula.

of Cholula to Mexico. In Cholula the people were not pleased with the sojourn of the Spaniards in Tlascala, for that tribe stood in bad repute among them. It was inclined to favor Cholula's neighbors of Huexotzinco, between whom and Cholula bloody feuds prevailed at the time over a question of water-supply. Quarrels of this kind were frequent, for the Huexotzintecans controlled the upper course of the streams with which the Cholulans irrigated their gardens. If a Cholulan looked awry at a Huexotzintecan, or met him in hunting and reviled him, or a Huexotzintecan came to the market in Cholula and was overreached, the Huexotzintecans cut off the water from their neighbors, and war ensued. The dispute has lasted till the present day, with the difference that the Spaniards have suppressed the murders of former times, and have directed complainants to the courts.

Notwithstanding the strained relations which prevailed at that time between Cholula and Tlascala, four inhabitants of Cholula called upon Cortés and invited him to visit their tribe. The Tlascalans advised him not to go, and asserted that those men were not deputies, but unimportant personages. But little attention has been given to this episode; it has even been overlooked. It came about in the following way:

The Mexican Confederation regarded the friendly relations between the Spaniards and their hereditary enemies of Tlascala with great concern, and made more earnest efforts to come to a good understanding with Cholula. Through its envoys it stirred up the tribe of Cholula against the strangers, and succeeded in winning at least three of the quarters to its side. At the same time it was anxious that Cortés, in case he insisted on going on to Mexico, should not pass over the territory of Huexotzinco, for that tribe was decidedly hostile to the Confederation. Mexicans were present with the Spanish troops, both messengers and spies. They were ignorant of what was going on at Mexico and Cholula, but urged a march by way of Cholula, in order to withdraw the strangers as soon as possible from their alliance with Tlascala. The Spaniards knew nothing of this confusion; the thing of most importance to them seemed to be to secure the submission of one tribe after another. They felt sure as to Huexotzinco, and were anxious to have Cholula decide in their favor. Cortés therefore sent Indian commissioners thither.

What took place in Cholula cannot be learned from Spanish sources; but Indian paintings preserved at San Juan Cuauhtlantzinco, which were shown me, afford information on the subject. Their evidence is confirmed by the traditions which are still current in and around Cholula.

The summons of Cortés aroused much consternation in Cholula, where great fear prevailed concerning the mysterious visitors, and their presence was not desired at all. But a few, amongst whom were some men of influence, thought it would be better to ally themselves with the Spaniards. Against the voice of the majority, they went secretly to Tlascala and invited Cortés to go to Cholula. Cortés, urged by the Tlascalans, sent these men home, with a peremptory demand upon the tribe to send him officially a formal invitation, otherwise he would regard

18

them as enemies and make war upon them. The Indians conveyed this message to the council which constituted the chief authority of the tribe of Cholula.

The Indian sources which I have consulted represent the effect of this threatening message as a double one. The first effect was against the messengers, who were bound and imprisoned as traitors, then put into a *temazcalli* (or sweat-bath), for the purpose of smothering them with vapors of red pepper. This treatment was not successful, and the intended victims escaped. As much fear as anger prevailed against the Spaniards, and it was decided not to meet them with hostilities, but to respond to the demand of Cortés and send to Tlascala a formal invitation to him. When the strangers were once within the walls of Cholula then they could be disposed of. The Mexican envoys stirred the fire of excitement.

A large deputation from Cholula went to the Spanish headquarters, bearing gifts and messages of peace and hospitality, and attended the ceremonies which Cortés instituted to make them vassals to the Spanish Crown. Although the true meaning of this transaction was not apparent to the Indians, yet, as nothing was asked of them, they thought that if it did no good it would do them no harm, and conducted themselves as they were desired to do. The Spaniards considered that the Cholulans had voluntarily pledged themselves by the act to be subjects of the Spanish Crown. They did not know that a hundred formal oaths taken by the chiefs could bind the tribe only when they had been commissioned for that purpose by the tribe itself and armed with power to enter into the engagement in its name. The embassy from Cholula was delegated only to amuse the Spaniards, and as a decoy. The Tlascalans, while they, too, had no clear comprehension of this "submission to the Crown," recognized that the purposes of the Cholulans could not be sincere. They inferred this from their own usages. Certain religious ceremonies were essential to the obligation of a pledge, and when these were not observed, the engagement was without binding effect. Although discord now existed between the two tribes, they knew or could understand what was going on. The Tlascalans knew that the oracle at Cholula had said, "Let the strangers only come . . . ;" and they cautioned the Spaniards against treachery. Cortés, in order not to show weakness, and in order also to secure a new base against emergencies, decided, nevertheless, to continue his march through Cholula. He had less than five hundred men and his small guns. His new allies of Tlascala furnished him a few thousand men.* On the first day he came to the place where the little village of Xoxtla now stands, nine or ten miles north of the pueblo, and, according to the often very untrustworthy Bernal Diaz, one league, or $2\frac{7}{10}$ miles from the Indian plantations. These plantations were those of Coromanco, seven miles from Cholula, where the Indians had a few houses and fields—not a real village, but

* Five or six thousand according to his two letters, 2000 according to Bernal Diaz del Castillo, and 40,000 according to Andrés del Tápia.

temporary lodgings. A considerable delegation came to the Spaniards on the next morning in order to welcome them outside of the place. As usual, it included the chief officers—the two highest chiefs,* and the medicine-men, or priests, in ample robes, black, red and black, and all red. They carried incense-vessels in their hands, and perfumed the strangers. These attentions were interpreted by the Spaniards as signs of honor, submission, and even reverence; they were not aware that the Mexican Indians perfumed prisoners of war whom they expected afterward to sacrifice.

It could not surprise them much that the Cholulans demanded that as the Tlascalans were enemies they should not encamp within the circuit of the dwellings. The condition was reasonable, and Cortés agreed to it. The Indian allies remained near the present village of Santa Maria Coronanco, while the Spaniards went farther on, in the midst of a multitude that grew constantly more numerous. All Cholula came out to see the white men, their dress and weapons, and especially their wonderful horses. This multitude was not satisfied with seeing the strangers pass by; but the Indians followed them, as children run after a circus procession. Bernal Diaz says characteristically of the scene, "So great was the crowd that came to see us, that the streets and roofs were filled with them." The six quarters all turned out at once upon the line of march of the Spaniards, so that the same public was around them everywhere. There were, in fact, as Andrés de Tápia says, more than twelve thousand

---

* Called by Gabriel de Rojas, Aquiach and Tlalquiach.

THE MASSACRE OF CHOLULA (1519).

men and women of all ages, and they gave the impression of a population probably approaching a hundred thousand. Hence the "twenty thousand households" (*veintemil casas*) of Cortés. The word *casa* applied to an Indian settlement would not signify a single house, but a household.

Any one who has witnessed a dance of the sedentary Indians, with the throngs of spectators on the flat roofs, may form a conception of the diversified scene which this entrance of the Spaniards into Cholula afforded. I have seen in these dances women in their ancient dress, with the hair done up in the style of a turban, the short *uipil*, or sleeveless waistcoat, made of cotton cloth and embroidered with red, black, and white figures, through which the head and neck projected, and beneath it a long skirt, girt around the body; the men, excepting the officers, bareheaded, in white robes, and also in embroidered jackets; on the heads of the principal officers, the half-mitre, adorned with colored feathers, colored stones, and shells; the priests in black; all the faces painted in festive style, that is, hideously striped, those of the common people with cochineal on the cheeks and forehead, and those of the higher chiefs with green, blue, and yellow, and the faces of the priests black, with white rings round the eyes and mouth. Added to these features were the noise of large and small drums, the squeaking of pipes, the roaring, thumping sound of the "Tozacatl," and the clattering of many rattles. The Spaniards marched slowly along in the midst of this uproar, while the horses walked under their armored riders, not proudly and defiantly, but gently and rarely shying; for these horses had till now been engaged in hard and dangerous service, and much worse awaited them.

Of such character, according to the accounts of Indian writers of the sixteenth century, were the reception processions of the natives of Mexico. If we add to this picture the little company of Spaniards with their uniforms, their horses, and their small artillery, we can imagine the entrance of Cortés into Cholula as a festival far less formal and ceremonious than most of the historians have represented it, but still extraordinary, gorgeous, and strange enough. I have found the first impression in all the Indian dances well-nigh overpowering, but the eye gradually becomes accustomed to regard the spectacle with indifference.

The Spaniards, dazzled by the sight, wavering between heed to the warning of the Tlascalans and a favorable interpretation of the bearing of the people of Cholula, could not help regarding with wonder and suspicion whatever might reveal the real feeling of the people. They observed that the road was interrupted by ditches and depressions, and that slingstones were piled up on the flat roofs. The first sign seemed very suspicious and appeared to confirm certain statements of the Tlascalans. The depressions indicated pitfalls, or at least devices to stop their horses. The ditches, on the other hand, were not trenches, but simply the channels of the smaller irrigation rills such as run through the roads everywhere in the southwest. The Spaniards now saw them for the first time, and were naturally suspicious of them. To them, as to the Indians, whatever was new was doubtful. The piles of gravel on the roofs were at all events a warlike provision, but it is still questionable whether they were intended particularly for the Spaniards. Most of the Indian villages were open, and were defended directly from the houses, or, in case of extremity, from the sacrificial hills; and piles of sling-stones were always kept convenient and ready for this event. Cholula lay in a plain, with the heights of Tzapotecas three miles away. It had no walls, and an assailing enemy must of necessity be repelled from the roofs of the houses. The Spaniards not properly understanding the conditions, these hostile precautions seemed to them to be directly opposed to what had appeared a formal voluntary submission of the Cholulans. Cortés was moved by them to suspect treachery.

While thus many of the external signs were mistakenly interpreted by him, he was right in the main. The Indian paintings at Cuauhtlantzinco confirm the native story that the people of Cholula had prepared a trap for him; but not, as Bernal Diaz declares, with the aid of a corps of troops from Mexico. The Mexicans could not furnish such aid, for they had not the means; their own tribe numbered hardly 40,000 souls, and their allies hardly 60,000. Had they indeed ventured to appear in the neighborhood with 20,000 men, Cholula would not have permitted them to concentrate such a force on its territory; especially as they were its hereditary enemies. It was, besides, impossible to conceal even 10,000 men in that region so that, even though not visible to the Spaniards, they could escape the peering eyes of the Tlascalans who were encamped without. The tale of the auxiliaries from Mexico is a fable, like many other of the stories in the history of the Conquest of Mexico. The origin of the story, which the Spaniards really believed, is of great, of momentous significance.

The Spaniards were quartered in a large house surrounding a courtyard, which they supposed to be a public building. According to tradition, Cortés was lodged in the present southwestern quarter of the city, which is now called "Santa Maria Tecpan" —the "Tecpan" being the communal house where strange visitors were received. In the middle of the quarter there still stands, in the *Calle de Herreros*, an ancient portal, with the inscription, in the Nahuatl language and Latin letters, "Here stood the Tecpan, where now is the house of Antonio de la Cruz." The Spaniards were therefore really residing in a government building, but at the same time in private dwellings, for each quarter formed a connected complex, which had been temporarily vacated to give accommodation to the strangers. The people gathered in a crowd outside, and this gave the start to the story that a hostile force was lurking around Cholula.

In assigning a dwelling of this character to the Spaniards, the Cholulans enclosed them as if in a fortress, for the thick walls were proof against every attempt to break through them with native implements. The entrance indeed had no doors, but guards with guns and cannon were so planted that they covered the larger openings, and showed the Indians, or rather might have shown them, that an assault would be dangerous. The people of Cholula did not know what sort of guests they had invited, or what means they possessed for opposing any treachery.

THE MASSACRE OF CHOLULA (1519). 273

The behavior of the Cholulans was in direct contradiction to the popular view that they regarded the white men as gods. One does not entice gods into traps, and does not try, as was done after the coming of the Spaniards, to enfeeble them gradually by depriving them of food. Both devices were tried against Cortés and his companions.

The intercourse of the Spaniards with the natives was very limited. In the first place, neither could understand the other; and in the second place, Cortés restrained his men so far as he could from going outside of the quarter. Only the young Indian woman Marina, who had been given to the Spaniards at Tabasco, on account of her precious ability to speak both Maya and Nahuatl—who has been the theme of much descriptive writing and verse, and whose career as interpreter and mistress has been invested with a poetical nimbus not appropriate to it—went in and out, diligently using her eyes. A broad affection, which extended from the common soldiers to the commander-in-chief, attached the woman to the Spanish flag. It was said also in Cholula that the wives of those whom Cortés first visited in Tlascala, and who were threatened with death by strangulation, had talked in secret about their tribal kinsmen. Cortés was soon convinced that the people were removing their women and children, not only from the quarter assigned to him, but everywhere. Every one who is acquainted with Indians knows what that proceeding means. It is the incontestable evidence of hostile intentions, and only individuals can in such case, perhaps, escape. Had the Spaniards withdrawn upon the discovery of this fact, they would have been attacked in the streets, and might easily have been exposed to a slaughter far more disastrous to them than that which they afterwards suffered in the famous *noche trista*. They were secure where they were against an open attack. All Cholula could not have carried the quarter by storm in the face of the Spanish muskets and artillery. But the adoption by the Cholulans of the formidable instrumentality of gradual starvation compelled action. Cortés determined upon a measure which would have been wholly unjustifiable in time of peace. The Spaniards, however, knew that treachery, not peace, was in the air, and the Indians confessed it. The situation was such that only stratagem could deliver them from the snares that had been set for them.

Search was first made for the Mexican deputies who had been with the Spaniards, but they had gone away and had only left their attendants. The chief officers of Cholula were no longer to be seen in the Spanish headquarters, and Cortés had two priests called and questioned in his presence. Presents, cross-questionings, and threats were employed to extort a confession that the destruction of the Spaniards was contemplated. Cortés immediately sent word through these priests to the chiefs of the tribe to come to him, and they came. The Spanish commander reproached them courteously for their reserve, asked them why they had estranged themselves from him in such a way, and intimating to them that he would start for Mexico on the following day, asked for a number of their soldiers to escort him, and for porters. His request was very readily granted, even with professions of lively pleasure. But while Cortés was thus treating with them, messengers arrived from his Indian allies with urgent communications. Both Tlascalans and Indians from Cempohual, of whom a few hundred accompanied the Spaniards, brought reports that threatening proceedings were going on outside of the Spanish quarter. The people were collecting more stones on the roofs, and were barring and building up the passages. Pits had been discovered in the streets, or rather in the vacant spaces between the quarters, lightly covered with limbs of trees and earth. It was certain that all non-combatants had been sent away. Everything pointed to an impending outbreak of hostilities. The Spaniards, not being acquainted with the Indian custom of making no assault at night except under the most favorable circumstances, or in case of necessity, expected to be attacked immediately after dark. The number of men in the previously deserted space around the Spanish quarter was visibly increasing, and among them were some armed. As night came on, Cortés assembled his men for anxious consultation. Some proposed to evacuate Cholula and retire to Huexotzinco; but the majority, perceiving that it was too late for that, favored attacking the Cholulans on the next morning, before they could strike a blow.

While these measures were being determined upon, two Indians of the place, an old woman and her son, came secretly to the Marina whom we have mentioned. She was regarded, by virtue of her origin and her language, as belonging to the Nahuatls, and as she was, besides, a good-looking girl, and made considerable display of the presents which she had acquired from the Spaniards, she was regarded among her countrymen as desirable for marriage. The woman came to the girl in order to warn her and save her, and at the same time to secure her for one of her sons. Marina obtained from her a relation, to the minutest detail, of the whole plan of the conspiracy, how the Spaniards were to be attacked in the ravines and roads on their march to Mexico, and other particulars. Her story fully confirmed the statements of the priests. Marina detained the woman under the pretext that she wished to prepare to go away, and ran to Cortés to tell him all. The poor wife-hunter was consequently brought before the commander, closely questioned, and confined for the night with her son, while the Spanish soldiers prepared to march.

When morning broke, all was ready for departure, and armed Cholulans gathered around the lately deserted quarter, ostensibly to accompany the Spaniards, but really in order to attack them at the first opportunity. Both sides were alike ready, and the only question was, which should be first. The Spaniards had the advantage of knowing the designs of their perfidious hosts, while the latter had no suspicion that the whites were aware of their treachery. As soon as the Spanish guards permitted it, the court of the quarter was filled with Indians. They exhibited all the signs of satisfaction, in the false fancy that their success was assured. Cortés was already on his horse, with Marina by his side, the cavalry were mounted, and the infantry held their guns ready to fire. Orders had been sent to the

THE MASSACRE OF CHOLULA (1519). 277

Tlascalans during the night to hasten up on the first alarm. When the chiefs of Cholula had gathered around Cortés, he plainly told them through the mouth of the Indian interpreter that he had penetrated their designs. He said to them, without passion, that he knew all, and that, as they were bound to the Spanish Crown, having voluntarily made their submission to it, they should therefore be punished, according to Spanish law, as traitors and rebels. Before the Indians could recover from their astonishment, he gave the signal for attack, and the fight began with the firing of muskets into the throng. It lasted about five hours.

There was no slaughter of unarmed women and children. The non-combatants had been sent out of the way long before by the Cholulans to a place of security, with the exception of those in the remote quarters, who did not participate in the contest and were not harmed by the Spaniards. It was a house and street fight between armed whites who had anticipated likewise armed Indians, and had therefore secured to themselves the advantage of the assault. Many Indians were killed in the court—a relatively large number, it is said, perhaps more than a hundred men. This part of the affair occurred where the present Calle de Chalingo passes into the Calle Real, and the place is still called the "Ezcoloc," or the place of the flowing and crossing of meandering streams of blood. According to tradition, Cortés had his headquarters in the same system of houses. The action could not last long in the court, for the Cholulans, after the first volleys, rushed out of the trap into the open space, which they could easily do, as no doors prevented their exit. But they could not be allowed to go unpunished even outside, for the Spaniards were exposed to the danger of a siege by starvation. They also rushed out, and their enemies, driven by their guns, fled to the "Cerro de la Cruz," a sacrificial mound still partly standing, about 1100 feet east of the spot where the fight began. Here, according to the pictures at Cuauhtlantzinco, the principal engagement took place, in the storming of the artificial height. After this, all was over. The Cholulans who were involved in the conspiracy and were surprised belonged to three of the six principal quarters, while the three other quarters had been neutral and now interceded for peace. Cortés contented himself with this short chastisement, and did not permit his people to scatter— prudently, for that might have been very disastrous. In the afternoon he drew his troops back into the quarter, and the negotiations were begun which established peace and a good understanding.

In the meantime, when the fight was already on the wane, the Tlascalans rushed up in thick masses. They eagerly overran the empty houses in order to plunder them. It is self-evident that none of the inhabitants who fell into their hands were spared. But there were not many, for the unarmed had long ago betaken themselves to places of security; the soldiers were busy with the Spaniards, and the heroes of Tlascala did not venture against non-participants and their closed houses. Like genuine Indians, they contented themselves with robbery and the destruction of property: there was no extensive conflagration; the "smoking ruins" of Prescott could not exist where roof-beams loaded with earth and plaster were the only combustibles. Such a laying waste of Cholula as is represented by some authors would require pulling it down, and that could not be accomplished in so short a time as five hours. Yet five hours after the first shot was fired, Cortés stopped the proceedings of his companions. Many of them undoubtedly continued to steal privately; and on the next day reënforcements came from Tlascala for the purpose of recompensing themselves from the Cholulans and their property, but they were prevented from doing this by the strict orders of the Spanish commander. Andrés de Tápia speaks of a two days' destruction, but Cortés, in a letter which he wrote a year after the affair, affirmed that the place was again full of women and children on the next day.*

Cortés stated that about three thousand of the enemy were killed. In 1529 Nuño de Guzman accused him of having caused four thousand Indians to be slain in a large court in Cholula. The witnesses whom Cortés brought forward swore that a "few" Indians were indeed punished there with death. Las Casas, whose statements cannot be trusted on account of his strong passion, speaks of six thousand dead. The local conditions speak more definitely, and, above all, the duration of the battle. It is hardly conceivable that even if the conflict lasted five hours, five hundred Spaniards could have killed so large a number of Indians in that time.

* Tápia's account is of much later date, and Bernal Diaz composed his history nearly fifty years after the massacre of Cholula.

The first volleys may have been murderous, but after them the affair became a skirmish, with single brief and bloody combats at close quarters. The Tlascalans had no time to kill many.

I am very doubtful, especially when I recollect that the battle was fought on a space not an English quarter of a mile in length, whether more than five hundred men fell. Certainly nothing like what is called a "decline" of Cholula was caused by the massacre. The Indian population of the district is still as large as it was then, notwithstanding fatal epidemics have prevailed. The only difference between the past and present conditions of population is that the tribe has now dispersed into the country, while in the year 1519 it dwelt together in a group of complexes.

But even if only one Indian was killed without just cause, it would be a serious crime. Yet from a military point of view the conduct of Cortés is entirely justified. He was obliged to proceed in that way, to surprise the Indians, if he would not himself be surprised and destroyed. The reproach brought against him is not based upon the Cholula incident, but lies against the conquest in general, against every aggression of the kind, and against our own conduct toward the Indians.

Only the pretexts have changed with the times, while the means have become, through the advance of knowledge, surer and more destructive. The Spaniards took and held the land, and saved its inhabitants: in the United States we have destroyed the people to get their land. The Spaniards subdued the aborigines openly: we approach them in the disguise of neighbors, pursue them and vex them, often for years at a time, till the desired offence is committed which affords us a pretext for removing them or exterminating them. The history of Arizona since the United States forcibly incorporated that territory into its domain furnishes much worse and more blameworthy transactions than the "bloodbath" of Cholula. If we can excuse these and other wrongs, and can justify our whole systematic robbery and destruction of the Indians under the pretence of progress, then we cannot be judges against the Conquest. The Spaniards planted the European civilization of their time in the place of the rude semi-civilization that existed, and adapted the natives to it: we plant our present civilization without taking a thought for the continued existence of the Indians.

THE AGE OF THE CITY OF SANTA FE.

The belief has been fixed in the public mind for a considerable time that Santa Fé, the capital of New Mexico, is also its oldest Spanish settlement, and even the oldest city in the United States. It is obvious that the latter opinion is incorrect, for St. Augustine in Florida dates from 1560. After Coronado's retreat from New Mexico in 1542 no Spaniard entered the territory till 1580, consequently no city was founded there by them; and it is well known that Coronado left no settlers there. Santa Fé is therefore, in any event, younger than St. Augustine, for it was built after 1580.

Concurrently with the belief that Santa Fé is the oldest city in New Mexico prevailed the legend that it occupied the site of a populous Indian settlement, of a native seat of government for all the pueblos of the Province. This fable is wholly destitute of documentary proof, and is not supported by any traditional or archæological evidence. The present city covers the ruins of an Indian village, and the earthworks of old Fort Marcy have partly obliterated the remains of another, older one. The older village contained hardly five hundred inhabitants; the more modern one, of which one house besides San Miguel's Church is still standing, numbered seven hundred souls in the year 1630. The plateau of Santa Fé contains besides these two ruins only four sites of remains of Indian dwelling-places or pueblos. Five miles south are two, one smaller and one larger, on the banks of the usually dry "Arroyo Hondo." The small village contained not quite two hundred, the larger one—which is called "Cua-Kaa" by the Tanos, to whom it belongs—less than eight hundred souls. Both were deserted before the middle of the sixteenth century. Twelve miles southwest lie the ruins of "Tzigu-ma," near the place called "Ciénega." This village also, which was abandoned after 1680, never numbered one thousand inhabitants. Lastly, there is San Marcos, or "Yaa-tze," eighteen miles south-southwest of Santa Fé, near the so-called "Cerrillos." In the year 1680 it contained six hundred Indians, and the extent of the ruins leads me to the conclusion that this number was not at any time doubled. The plain of Santa Fé, which includes an area of hardly one hundred square miles, thus never held more than three thousand settled inhabitants before the advent of the Spaniards, and these were distributed among not more than four villages inhabited at one time. None of these villages could compare in population with Pecos, Hauicu, Pilabó (or Socorro), Teypaná (or Quivira), etc., or with the Zuñi of to-day.

Those villages were inhabited in the sixteenth century and from a long time before by the Indians called "Tanos." The Tanos were Tehuas; they constituted the southern half of that great linguistic stock; and their territory extended from Pojuaque ("P'ho-zuang-ge"), seventeen miles north of Santa Fé, to San Pedro ("Cua-Kaa"), forty miles southwest. Their traditions are fully confirmed by the archæological remains; but these traditions make not the slightest mention of a "center of population," or of a New Mexican "Indian capital," at Santa Fé.

The pueblo on the ruins of which Santa Fé stands is called "Cua-P'ho-o-ge," or "Cua-Pooge" (mussel-pearl-place-on-the-water). That the place, and even the district, played no prominent part in the sixteenth century, appears from the fact that no Spanish document specially mentions it till after the founding of the capital.

The plateau is dry and barren. The little Rio de Santa Fé sinks into the sand not far from the present capital, and issues from it again at the "Ciénega," or the entrance to what is called the "Bocas." The Arroyo Hondo is entirely dry; the village of Cua-Kaa, as well as San Marcos, get their water from a spring situated near them. The scarcity of water, which is still very much felt, would make any aggregation of native settlers around Santa Fé absolutely impossible.

The historians of Coronado hardly mention the region. Probably Cua-Pooge was one of the seven villages which Casteñeda mentions as lying near the snowy mountains.* The accounts of the eight Spanish soldiers who went in the year 1580 with the unfortunate Franciscan monks Fray Augustin Rodriguez, Fray Juan Lopez, and Fray Juan de Santa Maria to Bernalillo on the Rio Grande, prove that neither the escort nor the missionaries set foot upon the Santa Fé plateau.

In the year 1583 Antonio de Espejo, going east

* See the chapter on Cibola.

THE AGE OF THE CITY OF SANTA FÉ. 285

from the Queres villages on the Rio Grande, arrived at the Tanos and Galistéo. He called them "Ubates"—a corruption of the word "Puya-tye," by which the Queres now designate the Tanos. He there touched upon the southern part of the plain of Santa Fé. He mentions five Tanos pueblos, and estimates their population at 20,000 souls. Espejo was a careful and intelligent observer, except that his estimates of population are always exaggerated at least four times. The exaggerations arise from the fact that whenever the Spaniards visited a village not only the people of that village, but those also of the neighboring pueblos, were present to greet their strange animals, and this multitude followed them as long as they continued in the territory of the tribe. This was a result more of curiosity than of fear. Moreover, an Indian village, in consequence of the peculiar structure of its buildings, always appears at least twice as large as it really is.

The founding of Santa Fé has been ascribed to Espejo. The error is the result of inaccurate, extremely superficial historical inquiry. The mere reading of Espejo's account would satisfy any one that he marched all through New Mexico and northern Arizona with only fourteen soldiers; that his expedition was a mere reconnoissance and no scheme of colonization; and that he arrived again, with all his men, in Santa Barbara in southern Chihuahua on the 20th of September, 1583. The story of the founding of Santa Fé by Espejo in the year 1583, aside from the one which fixed the origin of the capital in 1550—which suggested the spurious "Tertio millennial jubilee" of 1883—furnishes a most emphatic proof of the want of thought and of scientific care with which the history of Spanish colonization is still written. After his return Espejo made a proposition to the Crown concerning the settlement of New Mexico (April 23, 1584), but he died in 1585, before the government had examined his plan.

The first Spanish settlement in New Mexico was founded in the year 1598 by Juan de Oñate. It was not, however, where Santa Fé now stands, but thirty miles north of that place, on the tongue of land formed by the junction of the Rio Grande with the Rio Chama, opposite the present Indian village of San Juan de los Caballeros. It was therefore very near the station Chamita, on the Denver & Rio Grande Railroad. Oñate marched from San Marcos to San Ildefonso on the Rio Grande, barely touching the southwest corner of the Santa Fé plateaus, and paid no attention whatever to the little village of Cua-Pooge. The well-watered, highly fertile valley near San Juan, on the contrary, attracted him at once, and he began the building, opposite that pueblo, of a chapel and a Spanish headquarters, which he called "San Francisco de los Españoles," on the 23d of August, 1598. The chapel was consecrated on the 8th of September of the same year. This first colony was called San Gabriel in 1599, and that has continued till now to be the name given to the place by the Mexicans, although every trace of the buildings disappeared long ago. Ruins were still visible about 1694.

San Gabriel remained the only settlement of Europeans in New Mexico till 1608. In that year the

Crown fixed the governmental regulations of the new possession and assigned a regular salary of 2000 ducats a year to the governor, and he immediately departed for Santa Fé. More exact statements concerning the date of this settlement are not accessible, although they probably exist in the Spanish archives; but it is certain that Santa Fé was not founded till after the year 1607. Twenty years afterward two hundred and fifty Spaniards dwelt there, including soldiers; and when the Indians rose and drove out the whites in 1680, the whole district contained not more than one thousand Europeans, about half of whom lived in Santa Fé.

All the other towns in New Mexico, the Indian villages excepted, are of much later origin than Santa Fé. Albuquerque, for example, dates from 1701, Las Vegas from 1835, Bernalillo from 1701, Socorro—the old pueblo was destroyed in 1681—from 1817. The oldest Indian missions in Arizona —"Tubac," "Tumacacori," etc.—date from the close of the seventeenth century. Tucson was still in 1772 a small village of the Pimas. Santa Fé is therefore the oldest existing city in the two Territories, and the second oldest European town in the United States that is still inhabited.

The first church in Santa Fé was begun in 1622 and completed in 1627. It stood on the site of the present cathedral, and the remains of the walls of the old "Parroquia," or parish church, probably belonged to that oldest temple. Of San Miguel, the walls are of the middle of the seventeenth century. The roof and towers were built after 1694. The old house by the side of it is of the same age. The oldest churches in New Mexico still standing and in use are those in the Indian villages San Ildefonso and Santa Clara; the oldest abandoned houses of worship are those of Pecos, San Diego de Jemez, and perhaps Abó and Cuaray. All these buildings were erected in the beginning of the seventeenth century.

JEAN L'ARCHEVEQUE.

The Indian village—or, as it is usually called in New Mexico, the pueblo—of Santa Clara lies thirty miles north of the city of Santa Fé, on the Texas, Santa Fé & Northern Railroad. It is inhabited by about four hundred agricultural Indians of the Tehua tribe, whose one- and two-storied houses form two irregular quadrangles, surrounding two open places, called plazas. A large church of adobe, now in decay, stands at the northeastern end of the village. It dates from the middle of the last century (1760). The priests' houses have fallen to ruins, the interior of the temple is strikingly bare and bald, and the few paintings are either unrecognizable on account of the dirt and the advanced decay of the canvas, or they are specimens of the unskilful works of the domestic art industry so often met with in New Mexico. The best kept of the appurtenances are two wooden side-altars, marked with the date of 1782. The bell bears the year-mark of 1710. Everything savors of neglect; only a few dwellings are outwardly new, but within the habitations are comparatively clean; while the population, through frequent mixture with wandering Indians—the Utes, Apaches, and Navajos—are taller and more slenderly built, if not stronger, than the ordinary pueblo Indians of New Mexico.

Santa Clara is situated on a sandy prominence

which overlooks the course of the Rio Grande del Norte from a height of about fifty feet. The village is not more than five hundred paces in a straight line from the river-bank. The view from the dune on which it stands is therefore not without attractions, but the immediate vicinity is bare and treeless. Fields, green in summer, desolate in winter, lie around it, while in the west the side of a barren tableland rises to shut off every view in that direction. Only the highest peaks of the mountains of Abiquin look down furtively, as it were, upon the barren hillside of rubbish and gravel.

A broad view is spread out toward the east. The course of the Rio Grande is visible from north to south for a length of ten English miles. A dark mesa, the Mesa de la Canoa, shuts off the northern horizon, while the river is lost sight of in the south at the foot of a grand isolated rock of dark lava—the Mesa de San Ildefonso. A narrow but fertile valley forms the eastern shore, on the other side of which stretches the chain of the high mountains—the wild Sierra de la Truchas, the massive flat dome of the Sierra de Nambe, and the Pico de la Laguna. The range descends in terraces to the south, where the city of Santa Fé lies hidden at its foot. All these peaks exceed twelve thousand, the Truchas thirteen thousand, feet in height, and they are often crowned by snow-fields in summer.

If one stands, in the evening, when the sun is setting and the shadows are already cast over the valleys, on the swell above the church of Santa Clara, he will see the snow-peaks glowing for a little while in fiery red. The crags of the Truchas blaze like flowing ore. An Alpine lustre is displayed, less soft in colors than that of the central mountains of Europe, but much more intense and longer lasting. The mountains stand out ghostly pale as soon as the last glow is extinguished, and a white shroud appears to rest upon the landscape.

In this homely Indian village has lain concealed for many years a treasure of historical knowledge, an archive rich for America, so poor in archives, of the history of New Mexico. The Indians preserve and guard the treasure with superstitious care. It was entrusted to them years ago; and although their care for it has been limited to a superstitious guardianship and a cautious preservation, and no catalogue exists and no thought is taken of the greedy mice, the papers are still tolerably well preserved, and might safely lie there for yet many a year, suspiciously watched by men to whom the text is still a puzzle—for to them reading is a mystery, and the art of writing seems a kind of magic.

The collection is the remains of the archives of the Franciscan order in New Mexico, the "*Custodia de la conversion de San Pablo de la Nueva-Mexico*," which have lain here for more than thirty years, or since the time when the old military chapel (called *Castruenza*) of Santa Fé was condemned as unsafe. Such of the documents and church-books stored there as were not immediately needed were securely deposited in Santa Clara; for a priest then lived in the pueblo, and Santa Clara formed a parish by itself. When the parish was discontinued and the seat of the pastorate was removed to Santa Cruz, the archives were left. No one having any use for them, they remained in an old cupboard of the ruined convent till an Indian, who could neither read nor write, but had a clear head and respect for the old and venerable, proposed to commit the care of the papers to private hands. It took long and solemn meetings for consultation before the *Principales* of the pueblo would agree to such an innovation. They would keep the documents, indeed, as something having an incomprehensible sanctity, but to remove them from the ruins, where they were given up to mold and decay, seemed at first a doubtful step. Those above, the "Shiuana," might be displeased at it. The spiritual powers were finally consulted, and their decision was in favor of the innovation. The Franciscan archives were thus carried into the dark back-room of an Indian house, where a blind man was their first guardian; but they are now in charge of an intelligent, tolerably clear-seeing citizen of the village.

I tried in 1886 to obtain access to these old manuscripts, but was at once refused. It is of no use to importune an Indian. If he denies a request he is fixed in it, and one must wait. I waited two years, provided myself with a most urgent letter of introduction from the archbishop and an order from the priest of Santa Cruz, and went again. At last the prohibition was withdrawn, and after three protracted visits to Santa Clara, the last of which lasted twenty days, I was able to say that I had exhausted all the material and had accurate and complete copies of all the documents which had any important bearing on the history of New Mexico. It was no easy work, for the hand-writing was often nearly illegible, and the ink had faded and the paper grown yellow, and become almost rotten. The contents of the archives of Santa Clara may be divided into three classes. The first class consists of documents not strictly ecclesiastical, among which I found much that was valuable; the second, of the special church books, including registers of baptism, marriage, and death, many of the last of which begin with the date of 1694. Many valuable facts were also found in these. The papers called *Diligencias Matrimoniales*, or *Informaciones*, official inquiries to determine the civil standing of the contracting parties, which preceded every marriage, were the most numerous. Many of these are very long; some of them are of the seventeenth century, and they unfold an extremely instructive picture of the customs of those times. There are hardly any documents left in New Mexico of the period before the great insurrection of 1680, and I have the few that have been saved. But I found in Santa Clara a large number of details concerning the years preceding the insurrection, although contained in manuscripts that were composed one or two years after the troubles broke out. There have come to light little "court histories" of the governor of the time, scenes from the private life of long-vanished families which were then playing an important part in the troubled world called the Spanish Colony of New Mexico; notices of many an event which is never mentioned in the printed annals, and which was still of great importance. The real life of the people has taken shape out of these obscure writings of the monks, and many a striking revelation has been obtained from them. One of the discoveries made in them has given occasion to the present paper.

Among the *Diligencias* or *Informaciones* was one the superscription of which read, "Information of Pedro Meusnier—a Frenchman—1699." It was strange to meet with a Frenchman in New Mexico in 1699; and on reading the document it appeared that Pedro or Pierre Meusnier, or Meunier, at the time a soldier in the garrison at Santa Fé, born in Paris, had come to America in the year 1684 with the flotilla commanded by Monsieur de la Sala. Meunier brought forward two witnesses, one of whom was named Santiago Grolee, the other Juan de Archeueque. Both were French, and both declared that they had come across the sea with Meunier in the flotilla which the same "Monsieur de la Sala" commanded; and Grolee said that he was born at La Rochelle.

"Monsieur de la Sala" could have been nobody else than the famous brave discoverer of the mouths of the Mississippi—Robert Cavelier, Sieur de La Salle. The date agrees with this supposition, for La Salle crossed the Atlantic Ocean for the last time in 1684, to found a French colony on the coast of Texas. There came also with the expedition Jacques Grollet, a sailor, and a certain Jean l'Archévèque. It was the latter who, on March 18, 1687, led the unfortunate commander into the trap which his confederates Duhaut and Liotot had set, and in which La Salle was killed. Grollet was in the plot, but took no part in the murder. The supposition seems at least well founded that Juan de Archeueque was the traitor L'Archévèque, and Santiago Grolee was his accessory in a lesser degree, the sailor Grollet. I wrote at once to Mr. Francis Parkman, the historian of Canada, and received the answer that my supposition seemed to him perfectly well founded, although all that is known concerning the fate of the two men after La Salle's death is that they were found among the Indians in 1689 by Alonzo de Leon, commanding a Spanish expedition to Texas, and were taken to New Mexico. They were sent from Mexico to Spain, where they were supposed to have ended their lives in the galleys.

The last supposition was soon shown to be erroneous. The Jesuit father Andrés Cavo, author of the work "*Los tres siglos de Mexico,*" says: * "After a number of days the messengers [whom Leon had sent to the Indians] came back with two Frenchmen, whose names were Jacob Grollet and Juan l'Archiveque. . . . After Monclova returned, the governor [Leon] sent the two Frenchmen to the viceroy, and they legitimated themselves before him. The Conde de Galve, convinced that the affair was of particular importance, sent them both to the court of Charles II. under the care of Captain Don Andrés Perez.† . . . In this year [1691] Don Andrés Perez came back from Madrid with both of the Frenchmen." This is now also confirmed by the deposition of Santiago Grolee himself, which I found in Santa Clara in the investigation (*Informacion*) concerning his own person. It is of the year 1699, and he said in it: "We remained lost in that country five years among the wild infidel Indians, and after we had at

* Page 230.   † Page 236.

last escaped from their power we went to Spain by the order of the Viceroy Conde de Galve, in order to give an account of our persons and of that country." He said nothing of La Salle's death and of his own participation in the murder.

Satisfied that in the persons of Archeueque and Grolee I had found the notorious L'Archévèque and the sailor Grollet, two of the accomplices in the killing of La Salle, I made further investigation in the case. Members of a family named Archibeque still live in different parts of New Mexico; and as this one wrote his name that way in the later papers, I thought that these Archibeques might be descendants of the ill-famed Frenchman. In Santa Clara, and with the help of the general surveyor's archives at Santa Fé, I succeeded in restoring a tolerably complete picture of the life of Jean l'Archévèque. I shall now limit myself to this picture, and avoid the tedious details of documentary research. With the exception of the participation in the death of La Salle and the voyage to Spain, the facts are new and the results of local investigations.

Jean l'Archévèque was born in Bayonne, in southern France, in the year 1671. His parents were Claude l'Archévèque and Marie d'Armagnac. Both died in 1719. When thirteen years old, in 1684, he went with Robert Cavelier de La Salle to the coast of Texas and shared the fortunes of that unfortunate expedition. He entered the service of the notorious Duhaut, who, equally with the surgeon Liotot, was chief of the conspiracy to which La Salle fell a victim. His relation to Duhaut and his youth, he being only sixteen years old in 1687, explain, or at least partly excuse, the criminal part which he performed on the morning of the 18th of March. It was he who stood on the river-bank and when La Salle came over and inquired for his nephew, who was already murdered, answered the commander in insolent tones, and led him towards the ambush, where Duhaut and Liotot were hidden in the high grass. Mr. Parkman has described the scene from the best sources and with his accustomed vividness; and I therefore refer to his work, "La Salle and the Discovery of the Great West," for the details of the affair. This historian also gives a very intelligible account of L'Archévèque's behavior immediately after the murder. Whether repentance or a sudden coming back to his senses after the act or uncertainty concerning the real intentions of his associates determined him to it, L'Archévèque seems to have afterward gradually separated himself from the murderers. He thus escaped the vengeance which the freebooter Hiens inflicted on Duhaut and Liotot. The adherents of the murdered man also seem to have considered him less guilty. But he did not join the little company which set out on its extensive wanderings northward under the lead of Joutel. With Grollet and some others, among whom was Meunier, he stayed among the Indians of Texas till 1689, when Alonzo de Leon ransomed him. Fray Isidro Espinosa gives the details of this ransoming in his "*Crónica seráfica y apostólica*" (first part); but he does not mention L'Archévèque, although he names Pedro Muñi (or Meunier).

I have not been able to determine the date when the three Frenchmen went from Mexico to New

Mexico. It was probably with Don Diego de Vargas, the reconqueror of the province. L'Archévèque and Meunier were soldiers, while Grollet came as a settler. All three were in Santa Fé as early as 1696. In the next year L'Archévèque was married to Antonia Gutierrez, who was born at Tezonco, near the City of Mexico, and was the widow of a certain Tomas de Yta, who had been murdered three years previously near Zacatecas. In the year 1701 he bought a land estate in Santa Fé, but still continued a soldier, and in that capacity visited in the next year the distant Indian villages of Acoma, Laguna, and Zuñi. His wife died in the first year of the eighteenth century, and he continued a widower till 1719, when he married as his second wife the daughter of the Alcalde Mayor Ignacio de Roybal. The second marriage was solemnized in the church of the pueblo of San Ildefonso, and the governor of New Mexico at the time, General Don Antonio Valverde Cosio, was one of the witnesses. L'Archévèque, or, as he now began to call himself, Captain Juan de Archibeque, stood in high credit. He had left the military service with honor, and had become a successful trader, or peddler. His trading journeys extended to Sonora, and he occasionally visited the City of Mexico on business. His notes* were current everywhere, and were even accepted and endorsed by men connected with the government. He was a man in easy circumstances—for New Mexico, a wealthy man. His son by his first marriage,

* I saw the head of one of them, which was for 800 pesos—a large sum for the conditions in New Mexico at that time.

Miguel de Archibeque, assisted him faithfully in his business affairs, and a natural son, Augustin de Archibeque, likewise helped, by his labor and his watchful care of his interests, in the accumulation of his wealth. Everything went on according to his desire. Jean l'Archévèque celebrated his second marriage on the 16th of August, 1719, with a daughter of one of the first families of New Mexico. A year afterward, on the same day of the same month, Jean l'Archévèque was a bleeding corpse.

The "Captain" and former soldier, Juan de Archibeque, enjoyed with the Spanish military officers no less a degree of confidence than was reposed in him as a merchant by the same officers and the people in general. He was consulted concerning all important enterprises; and the minutes are in my hand of several war councils in which his views were influential. When, therefore, in the spring of 1720, Governor Don Antonio Valverde Cosio was contemplating the preparation of an expedition by order of the viceroy to the far northeast, in order to establish commercial relations with the Prairie Indians of Kansas, as well as to make a military reconnoissance in a direction in which an approach of the French was apprehended, L'Archévèque gave his opinion that the expedition should be dispatched at once. Among the reasons which in his view should commend it to the Spaniards, he emphasized the approach of "his countrymen, the French." The campaign was organized; Don Pedro de Villazur was given the command of the fifty armed men who formed the corps, and Jean l'Archévèque, or Archibeque, went along as one of his staff. The march led through the great plains to the banks of the Arkansas River, which the force reached about August 14th. There they confronted a large camp or village of the Pananas (Pawnees). When the Pananas returned an obscure and therefore suspicious answer to a peaceful message of the Spanish commander, Villazur went back with his men and crossed the Arkansas, in order to have the river between himself and his presumed enemies. During the night between the 15th and 16th of August, the Spanish guards and the Indians of the company heard a splashing in the river, as if men were swimming across; and the guards were captured. A dog barked, but no attention was paid to that sign. At daybreak, when the horses had been collected and the command was about to mount, an attack was made upon them from the high grass. The horses took fright at the first shots, which were fired from a very short distance, and were aimed mainly at the tent of the commander. Some of the soldiers succeeded in catching the fugitive animals, but only for their own deliverance. The effect of the enemy's fire was so quick and murderous that nothing else than flight was thought of. Five or six of the fifty armed men escaped. Among the dead were the commander, Don Pedro de Villazur, and Jean l'Archévèque. It is probable his own countrymen, the French, of whom there were several with the Pananas, shot him. His personal servant, although himself bleeding from six wounds, stayed with him till he ceased to breathe, and then saved himself "by a miracle," as he declares, with one of the horses of the deceased.

The betrayer of La Salle had fallen, on the anniversary of his second marriage, at the hands of his own countrymen or their allies.

L'Archévèque left a property of 6118 pesos, a considerable sum for the time. Besides his sons—his legitimate son Miguel and his natural son Augustin—he left a daughter, Marie, by his first marriage. His widow three years afterward married Bernardino Sena. From the two sons are derived the present families of Archibeque in New Mexico.

It is hardly possible to determine how far L'Archévèque was knowingly accessory to the murder of La Salle. His youth lends favor to the supposition that he may have acted ignorantly or thoughtlessly when he led the great discoverer into the ambush. But his whole character, as it was afterward unfolded, indicates an early maturity of mind, a considerable capacity, and great resolution, as well as unusual sagacity. His hand-writing, which I have often read, shows that he had been taught in school; and he could have received his instruction only in France. The manner of his death is very suggestive of a later requital for his earlier offence.

Of Meunier I could learn nothing further; and of Grollet only that he settled at Bernalillo, on the Rio Grande, there married Elena Galuegos in the year 1699, and was still living six years later.

The three persons on whose fate a light has been so curiously thrown by the archives of Santa Clara were the first French settlers on New Mexican territory. Driven there in consequence of a murder, one of them at least, L'Archévèque, played a notable part in the history of the country. His descendants know little or nothing of the deeds and adventures of their ancestor, and are quiet, modest people; who yet seldom fail to insist that they are of French origin. The church in which Archévèque was married a second time, a year before his tragical death, cannot be seen from the barren dune on which Santa Clara stands. The high mesa of San Ildefonso hides the pueblo, although it can be barely five miles from Santa Clara. That isolated lava cliff also, with the perpendicular precipices around its summit, bears a memory of the betrayer of La Salle. As a Spanish soldier he made several unsuccessful attempts to take the Black Mesa, as it was called, by storm.

From Santa Clara the view is very beautiful; but a taint of blood adheres to the rocks and to the valley which thence the eye looks down upon. Elsewhere throughout New Mexico, in places of ancient habitation, it is the same: for the history of this region is darkened by a sombre melancholy, the inevitable outcome of its blood-stained past.

THE END

D. APPLETON & CO.'S PUBLICATIONS.

THE HISTORICAL REFERENCE-BOOK, comprising a Chronological Table of Universal History, a Chronological Dictionary of Universal History, a Biographical Dictionary. With Geographical Notes. For the use of Students, Teachers, and Readers. By LOUIS HEILPRIN. Fourth edition, revised and brought down to 1893. Crown 8vo. 569 pages. Half leather, $3.00.

"One of the most complete, compact, and valuable works of reference yet produced."—*Troy Daily Times.*

"Unequaled in its field."—*Boston Courier.*

"A small library in itself."—*Chicago Dial.*

"An invaluable book of reference, useful alike to the student and the general reader. The arrangement could scarcely be better or more convenient."—*New York Herald.*

"The conspectus of the world's history is as full as the wisest terseness could put within the space."—*Philadelphia American.*

"We miss hardly anything that we should consider desirable, and we have not been able to detect a single mistake or misprint."—*New York Nation.*

"So far as we have tested the accuracy of the present work we have found it without flaw."—*Christian Union.*

"The conspicuous merits of the work are condensation and accuracy. These points alone should suffice to give the 'Historical Reference-Book' a place in every public and private library."—*Boston Beacon.*

"The method of the tabulation is admirable for ready reference."—*New York Home Journal.*

"This cyclopædia of condensed knowledge is a work that will speedily become a necessity to the general reader as well as to the student."—*Detroit Free Press.*

"For clearness, correctness, and the readiness with which the reader can find the information of which he is in search, the volume is far in advance of any work of its kind with which we are acquainted."—*Boston Saturday Evening Gazette.*

"The geographical notes which accompany the historical incidents are a novel addition, and exceedingly helpful. The size also commends it, making it convenient for constant reference, while the three divisions and careful elimination of minor and uninteresting incidents make it much easier to find dates and events about which accuracy is necessary. Sir William Hamilton avers that too retentive a memory tends to hinder the development of the judgment by presenting too much for decision. A work like this is thus better than memory. It is a 'mental larder' which needs no care, and whose contents are ever available."—*New York University Quarterly.*

A CHRONOLOGICAL TABLE OF UNIVERSAL HISTORY. Extending from the Earliest Times to the Year 1892. For the use of Students, Teachers, and Readers. By LOUIS HEILPRIN. 12mo. 200 pages. Cloth, $1.25.

This is one of the three sections comprised in Heilprin's "Historical Reference-Book," bound separately for convenience of those who may not require the entire volume. Specimen pages sent on request.

New York: D. APPLETON & CO., 1, 3, & 5 Bond Street.

D. APPLETON & CO.'S PUBLICATIONS.

COLONIAL COURT-HOUSE, PHILADELPHIA, 1707.

"This work marks an epoch in the history-writing of this country."—*St. Louis Post-Dispatch.*

THE HOUSEHOLD HISTORY OF THE UNITED STATES AND ITS PEOPLE. For Young Americans. By EDWARD EGGLESTON. Richly illustrated with 350 Drawings, 75 Maps, etc. Square 8vo. Cloth, $2.50.

FROM THE PREFACE.

The present work is meant, in the first instance, for the young—not alone for boys and girls, but for young men and women who have yet to make themselves familiar with the more important features of their country's history. By a book for the young is meant one in which the author studies to make his statements clear and explicit, in which curious and picturesque details are inserted, and in which the writer does not neglect such anecdotes as lend the charm of a human and personal interest to the broader facts of the nation's story. That history is often tiresome to the young is not so much the fault of history as of a false method of writing by which one contrives to relate events without sympathy or imagination, without narrative connection or animation. The attempt to master vague and general records of kiln-dried facts is certain to beget in the ordinary reader a repulsion from the study of history—one of the very most important of all studies for its widening influence on general culture.

"Fills a decided gap which has existed for the past twenty years in American historical literature. The work is admirably planned and executed, and will at once take its place as a standard record of the life, growth, and development of the nation. It is profusely and beautifully illustrated."—*Boston Transcript.*

INDIAN'S TRAP.

"The book in its new dress makes a much finer appearance than before, and will be welcomed by older readers as gladly as its predecessor was greeted by girls and boys. The lavish use the publishers have made of colored plates, woodcuts, and photographic reproductions, gives an unwonted piquancy to the printed page, catching the eye as surely as the text engages the mind."—*New York Critic.*

GENERAL PUTNAM.

"The author writes history as a story. It can never be less than that. The book will enlist the interest of young people, enlighten their understanding, and by the glow of its statements fix the great events of the country firmly in the mind."—*San Francisco Bulletin.*

New York: D. APPLETON & CO., 1, 3, & 5 Bond Street.

D. APPLETON & CO.'S PUBLICATIONS.

JOHN BACH MCMASTER.

HISTORY OF THE PEOPLE OF THE UNITED STATES, from the Revolution to the Civil War. By JOHN BACH MCMASTER. To be completed in five volumes. Vols. I, II, and III now ready. 8vo, cloth, gilt top, $2.50 each.

In the course of this narrative much is written of wars, conspiracies, and rebellions; of Presidents, of Congresses, of embassies, of treaties, of the ambition of political leaders, and of the rise of great parties in the nation. Yet the history of the people is the chief theme. At every stage of the splendid progress which separates the America of Washington and Adams from the America in which we live, it has been the author's purpose to describe the dress, the occupations, the amusements, the literary canons of the times; to note the changes of manners and morals; to trace the growth of that humane spirit which abolished punishment for debt, and reformed the discipline of prisons and of jails; to recount the manifold improvements which, in a thousand ways, have multiplied the conveniences of life and ministered to the happiness of our race; to describe the rise and progress of that long series of mechanical inventions and discoveries which is now the admiration of the world, and our just pride and boast; to tell how, under the benign influence of liberty and peace, there sprang up, in the course of a single century, a prosperity unparalleled in the annals of human affairs.

"The pledge given by Mr. McMaster, that 'the history of the people shall be the chief theme,' is punctiliously and satisfactorily fulfilled. He carries out his promise in a complete, vivid, and delightful way. We should add that the literary execution of the work is worthy of the indefatigable industry and unceasing vigilance with which the stores of historical material have been accumulated, weighed, and sifted. The cardinal qualities of style, lucidity, animation, and energy, are everywhere present. Seldom indeed has a book in which matter of substantial value has been so happily united to attractiveness of form been offered by an American author to his fellow-citizens."—*New York Sun.*

"To recount the marvelous progress of the American people, to describe their life, their literature, their occupations, their amusements, is Mr. McMaster's object. His theme is an important one, and we congratulate him on his success. It has rarely been our province to notice a book with so many excellences and so few defects."—*New York Herald.*

"Mr. McMaster at once shows his grasp of the various themes and his special capacity as a historian of the people. His aim is high, but he hits the mark."—*New York Journal of Commerce.*

". . . The author's pages abound, too, with illustrations of the best kind of historical work, that of unearthing hidden sources of information and employing them, not after the modern style of historical writing, in a mere report, but with the true artistic method, in a well-digested narrative. . . . If Mr. McMaster finishes his work in the spirit and with the thoroughness and skill with which it has begun, it will take its place among the classics of American literature."—*Christian Union.*

New York: D. APPLETON & CO., 1, 3, & 5 Bond Street.

D. APPLETON & CO.'S PUBLICATIONS.

A BOOK FOR THE QUADRI-CENTENNIAL YEAR.

CHRISTOPHER COLUMBUS.

THE STORY OF COLUMBUS. By ELIZABETH EGGLESTON SEELYE, edited by Dr. Edward Eggleston. With 100 Illustrations by Allegra Eggleston. 12mo. Cloth, $1.75.

This book is the result of most extensive investigations, which have been carefully verified by the eminent historian and novelist, Dr. Eggleston. It is not too much to say that the whole world has been drawn upon for material by the author and the artist. The fruits of these investigations are presented in a popular, readable, always entertaining form. While the book contains all the results of modern inquiry offered in the bulkiest biographies, the story is here condensed and the material selected with a view to an always interesting narrative. To a considerable extent the plan of both text and illustrations is like that of Eggleston's "Household History of the United States." It is hardly necessary to say more regarding the fitness of this volume for a place in every American private, public, and school library.

CARAVEL.

"A brief, popular, interesting, and yet critical volume, just such as we should wish to place in the hands of a young reader. The authors of this volume have done their best to keep it on a high plane of accuracy and conscientious work without losing sight of their readers."—*New York Independent.*

"In some respects altogether the best book that the Columbus year has brought out."—*Rochester Post-Express.*

"A simple story told in a natural fashion, and will be found far more interesting than many of the more ambitious works on a similar theme."—*New York Journal of Commerce.*

CATAPULT.

"This is no ordinary work. It is pre-eminently a work of the present time and of the future as well."—*Boston Traveller.*

"Mrs. Seelye's book is pleasing in its general effect, and reveals the results of painstaking and conscientious study."—*New York Tribune.*

"A very just account is given of Columbus, his failings being neither concealed nor magnified, but his real greatness being made plain."—*New York Examiner.*

"The illustrations are particularly well chosen and neatly executed, and they add to the general excellence of the volume."—*New York Times.*

IMAGE FOUND AT SANTO DOMINGO.

New York: D. APPLETON & CO., 1, 3, & 5 Bond St.

D. APPLETON & CO.'S PUBLICATIONS.

AROUND AND ABOUT SOUTH AMERICA: Twenty Months of Quest and Query. By FRANK VINCENT, author of "The Land of the White Elephant," etc. With Maps, Plans, and 54 full-page Illustrations. 8vo, xxiv + 473 pages. Ornamental cloth, $5.00.

No former traveler has made so comprehensive and thorough a tour of Spanish and Portuguese America as did Mr. Vincent. He visited every capital, chief city, and important seaport, made several expeditions into the interior of Brazil and the Argentine Republic, and ascended the Paraná, Paraguay, Amazon, Orinoco, and Magdalena Rivers; he visited the crater of Pichinchas, 15,000 feet above the sea-level; he explored falls in the center of the continent, which, though meriting the title of "Niagara of South America," are all but unknown to the outside world; he spent months in the picturesque capital of Rio Janeiro; he visited the coffee districts, studied the slaves, descended the gold-mines, viewed the greatest rapids of the globe, entered the isolated Guianas, and so on.

IN AND OUT OF CENTRAL AMERICA; and other Sketches and Studies of Travel. By FRANK VINCENT. With Maps and Illustrations. 12mo. Cloth, $2.00.

BRAZIL: Its Condition and Prospects. By C. C. ANDREWS, ex-Consul-General to Brazil. 12mo. Cloth, $1.50.

"I hope I may be able to present some facts in respect to the present situation of Brazil which will be both instructive and entertaining to general readers. My means of acquaintance with that empire are principally derived from a residence of three years at Rio de Janeiro, its capital, while employed in the service of the United States Government, during which period I made a few journeys into the interior."—*From the Preface.*

CHINA: Travels and Investigations in the "Middle Kingdom." A Study of its Civilization and Possibilities. With a Glance at Japan. By JAMES HARRISON WILSON, late Major-General United States Volunteers and Brevet Major-General United States Army. 12mo. Cloth, $1.75.

"The book presents China and Japan in all these aspects; the manners and customs of the people; the institutions, tendencies, and social ideas; the government and leading men."—*Boston Traveller.*

New York: D. APPLETON & CO., 1, 3, & 5 Bond Street.

D. APPLETON & CO.'S PUBLICATIONS.

*A*BRAHAM LINCOLN: *The True Story of a Great Life.* By WILLIAM H. HERNDON and JESSE W. WEIK. With numerous Illustrations. New and revised edition, with an introduction by HORACE WHITE. In two volumes. 12mo. Cloth, $3.00.

This is probably the most intimate life of Lincoln ever written. The book, by Lincoln's law-partner, William H. Herndon, and his friend Jesse W. Weik, shows us Lincoln the man. It is a true picture of his surroundings and influences and acts. It is not an attempt to construct a political history, with Lincoln often in the background, nor is it an effort to apotheosize the American who stands first in our history next to Washington. The writers knew Lincoln intimately. Their book is the result of unreserved association. There is no attempt to portray the man as other than he really was, and on this account their frank testimony must be accepted, and their biography must take permanent rank as the best and most illuminating study of Lincoln's character and personality. Their story, simply told, relieved by characteristic anecdotes, and vivid with local color, will be found a fascinating work.

"Truly, they who wish to know Lincoln as he really was must read the biography of him written by his friend and law-partner, W. H. Herndon. This book was imperatively needed to brush aside the rank growth of myth and legend which was threatening to hide the real lineaments of Lincoln from the eyes of posterity. On one pretext or another, but usually upon the plea that he was the central figure of a great historical picture, most of his self-appointed biographers have, by suppressing a part of the truth and magnifying or embellishing the rest, produced portraits which those of Lincoln's contemporaries who knew him best are scarcely able to recognize. There is, on the other hand, no doubt about the faithfulness of Mr. Herndon's delineation. The marks of unflinching veracity are patent in every line."—*New York Sun.*

"Among the books which ought most emphatically to have been written must be classed 'Herndon's Lincoln.'"—*Chicago Inter-Ocean.*

"The author has his own notion of what a biography should be, and it is simple enough. The story should tell all, plainly and even bluntly. Mr. Herndon is naturally a very direct writer, and he has been industrious in gathering material. Whether an incident happened before or behind the scenes, is all the same to him. He gives it without artifice or apology. He describes the life of his friend Lincoln just as he saw it."—*Cincinnati Commercial Gazette.*

"A remarkable piece of literary achievement—remarkable alike for its fidelity to facts, its fullness of details, its constructive skill, and its literary charm."—*New York Times.*

"It will always remain the authentic life of Abraham Lincoln."—*Chicago Herald.*

"The book is a valuable depository of anecdotes, innumerable and characteristic. It has every claim to the proud boast of being the 'true story of a great life.'"—*Philadelphia Ledger.*

"Will be accepted as the best biography yet written of the great President."—*Chicago Inter-Ocean.*

"Mr. White claims that, as a portraiture of the man Lincoln, Mr. Herndon's work 'will never be surpassed.' Certainly it has never been equaled yet, and this new edition is all that could be desired."—*New York Observer.*

"The three portraits of Lincoln are the best that exist; and not the least characteristic of these, the Lincoln of the Douglas debates, has never before been engraved. . . . Herndon's narrative gives, as nothing else is likely to give, the material from which we may form a true picture of the man from infancy to maturity."—*The Nation.*

New York: D. APPLETON & CO., 1, 3, & 5 Bond Street.

D. APPLETON & CO.'S PUBLICATIONS.

***A**PPLETONS' CYCLOPÆDIA OF AMERICAN BIOGRAPHY.* Complete in six volumes, royal 8vo, containing about 800 pages each. With sixty-one fine steel portraits and some two thousand smaller vignette portraits and views of birthplaces, residences, statues, etc.

APPLETONS' CYCLOPÆDIA OF AMERICAN BIOGRAPHY, edited by General JAMES GRANT WILSON, President of the New York Genealogical and Biographical Society, and Professor JOHN FISKE, formerly of Harvard University, assisted by over two hundred special contributors, contains a biographical sketch of every person eminent in American civil and military history, in law and politics, in divinity, in literature and art, in science and in invention. Its plan embraces all the countries of North and South America, and includes distinguished persons born abroad, but related to American history. As events are always connected with persons, it affords a complete compendium of American history in every branch of human achievement. An exhaustive topical and analytical Index enables the reader to follow the history of any subject with great readiness.

"It is the most complete work that exists on the subject. The tone and guiding spirit of the book are certainly very fair, and show a mind bent on a discriminate, just, and proper treatment of its subject."—*From the* Hon. GEORGE BANCROFT.

"The portraits are remarkably good. To any one interested in American history or literature, the Cyclopædia will be indispensable."—*From the* Hon. JAMES RUSSELL LOWELL.

"The selection of names seems to be liberal and just. The portraits, so far as I can judge, are faithful, and the biographies trustworthy."—*From* NOAH PORTER, D. D., LL. D., *ex-President of Yale College.*

"A most valuable and interesting work."—*From the* Hon. WM. E. GLADSTONE.

"I have examined it with great interest and great gratification. It is a noble work, and does enviable credit to its editors and publishers."—*From the* Hon. ROBERT C. WINTHROP.

"I have carefully examined 'Appletons' Cyclopædia of American Biography,' and do not hesitate to commend it to favor. It is admirably adapted to use in the family and the schools, and is so cheap as to come within the reach of all classes of readers and students."—*From* J. B. FORAKER, *ex-Governor of Ohio.*

"This book of American biography has come to me with a most unusual charm. It sets before us the faces of great Americans, both men and women, and gives us a perspective view of their lives. Where so many noble and great have lived and wrought, one is encouraged to believe the soil from which they sprang, the air they breathed, and the sky over their heads, to be the best this world affords, and one says, 'Thank God, I also am an American!' We have many books of biography, but I have seen none so ample, so clear-cut, and breathing so strongly the best spirit of our native land. No young man or woman can fail to find among these ample pages some model worthy of imitation."—*From* FRANCES E. WILLARD, *President N. W. C. T. U.*

"I congratulate you on the beauty of the volume, and the thoroughness of the work."—*From* Bishop PHILLIPS BROOKS.

"Every day's use of this admirable work confirms me in regard to its comprehensiveness and accuracy."—*From* CHARLES DUDLEY WARNER.

Price, per volume, cloth or buckram, $5.00; sheep, $6.00; half calf or half morocco, $7.00. Sold only by subscription. Descriptive circular, with specimen pages, sent on application. Agents wanted for districts not yet assigned.

New York: D. APPLETON & CO., 1, 3, & 5 Bond Street.

D. APPLETON & CO.'S PUBLICATIONS.

MILITARY TEXT-BOOKS.

THE NEW ARMY DRILL REGULATIONS. As approved by the Secretary of War. Superseding Upton's Tactics, previously the authorized standard for the United States Army.

 FOR INFANTRY.—One volume. Bound in leather, with tuck, 75 cents; in stiff paper covers, 30 cents.

 FOR CAVALRY.—One volume. Bound in leather, with tuck, $1.00.

 FOR ARTILLERY.—One volume. Bound in leather, with tuck, $1.00.

MANUAL OF GUARD DUTY, for the United States Army. Paper, 25 cents; leather, 50 cents.

HANDBOOK OF MILITARY SIGNALING. Prepared by Captain ALBERT GALLUP, Signal Officer First Brigade, National Guard, New York. Illustrated. 16mo. Flexible cloth, 50 cents.

This manual has been approved by the Signal Office at Washington, and its use has been prescribed for the National Guard of the State of New York.

THREE ROADS TO A COMMISSION IN THE United States Army. By Lieutenant W. P. BURNHAM, Sixth U. S. Infantry, author of "Manual of Outpost Duty," etc. 12mo. Cloth.

PROMPT AID TO THE INJURED. A Manual of Instruction designed for Military and Civil Use. By ALVAH H. DOTY, M. D., Major and Surgeon, Ninth Regiment, N. G. S. N. Y.; Attending Surgeon to Bellevue Hospital Medical Dispensary, New York. With 96 Illustrations. 12mo. Cloth, $1.25.

New York: D. APPLETON & CO., 1, 3, & 5 Bond Street.

D. APPLETON & CO.'S PUBLICATIONS.

MODERN SCIENCE SERIES.

Edited by Sir JOHN LUBBOCK, Bart., F. R. S.

THE CAUSE OF AN ICE AGE. By Sir ROBERT BALL, LL. D., F. R. S., Royal Astronomer of Ireland, author of "Starland."

"Sir Robert Ball's book is, as a matter of course, admirably written. Though but a small one, it is a most important contribution to geology."—*London Saturday Review.*

"A fascinating subject, cleverly related and almost colloquially discussed."—*Philadelphia Public Ledger.*

THE HORSE: A Study in Natural History. By WILLIAM H. FLOWER, C. B., Director in the British Natural History Museum. With 27 Illustrations.

"The author admits that there are 3,800 separate treatises on the horse already published, but he thinks that he can add something to the amount of useful information now before the public, and that something not heretofore written will be found in this book. The volume gives a large amount of information, both scientific and practical, on the noble animal of which it treats."—*New York Commercial Advertiser.*

THE OAK: A Study in Botany. By H. MARSHALL WARD, F. R. S. With 53 Illustrations.

"An excellent volume for young persons with a taste for scientific studies, because it will lead them from the contemplation of superficial appearances and those generalities which are so misleading to the immature mind, to a consideration of the methods of systematic investigation."—*Boston Beacon.*

"From the acorn to the timber which has figured so gloriously in English ships and houses, the tree is fully described, and all its living and preserved beauties and virtues, in nature and in construction, are recounted and pictured."—*Brooklyn Eagle.*

ETHNOLOGY IN FOLKLORE. By GEORGE L. GOMME, F. S. A., President of the Folklore Society, etc.

"Many scholars have drawn upon various classes of folklore as illustrative of problems in mythology, but no attempt has been made until lately to formulate the principles and laws of folklore in general. This labor the learned President of the English Folklore Society has undertaken, and has accomplished his task, as might have been expected, in a scholarly and entertaining volume."—*New York Evening Post.*

"The author puts forward no extravagant assumptions, and the method he points out for the comparative study of folklore seems to promise a considerable extension of knowledge as to prehistoric times."—*Independent.*

THE LAWS AND PROPERTIES OF MATTER. By R. T. GLAZEBROOK, F. R. S., Fellow of Trinity College, Cambridge.

Each, 12mo, cloth, $1.00.

New York: D. APPLETON & CO., 1, 3, & 5 Bond Street.

APPLETONS' LIBRARY LISTS.

Libraries, whether for the school, home, or the public at large, are among the most important and wide-reaching educational factors in the advancement of civilization. Modern intellectual activity, keeping pace with modern invention, has added to the earlier stores of literature myriads of books, and a still greater mass of reading-matter in other forms. Unfortunately, much of the material put into print is not of an educational or elevating character. It is important, then, in the selection of books for public use, especially for the young, that great care be exercised to secure only such kinds of reading as will be wholesome, instructive, and intrinsically valuable.

For more than fifty years Messrs. D. Appleton & Co. have been engaged in the publication of the choicest productions from the pens of distinguished authors of the past and present, of both Europe and America, and their catalogue now comprises titles of several thousand volumes, embracing every department of knowledge. Classified lists of these publications have been prepared, affording facilities for a judicious selection of books covering the whole range of Literature, Science, and Art, for individual book-buyers or for a thorough equipment of any library.

Lists A, B, and C are of books selected especially for School Libraries. The other lists are of books grouped according to subjects. The classifications are as follows:

List A.—For Primary and Intermediate Grades.

List B.—For Grammar and High School Grades.

List C.—For College and University Libraries.

List D.—HISTORY.
" E.—BIOGRAPHY.
" F.—PHYSICAL SCIENCE.
" G.—MENTAL AND MORAL SCIENCE.
" H.—POLITICAL AND SOCIAL SCIENCE.
" I.—PHILOSOPHY AND METAPHYSICS.
" K.—HYGIENE AND SANITARY SCIENCE.
" L.—FINANCE AND ECONOMICS.
" M.—TECHNOLOGY AND INDUSTRIAL ARTS.

List N.—ANTHROPOLOGY AND ETHNOLOGY.
" O.—LITERATURE AND ART.
" P.—BOOKS OF REFERENCE.
" R.—TRAVEL AND ADVENTURE.
" S.—PEDAGOGY AND EDUCATION.
" T.—FICTION.
" U.—AMUSEMENTS AND RECREATIONS.
" V.—EVOLUTION.
" W.—ARCHÆOLOGY AND PALÆONTOLOGY.

Also, Special Lists of Legal, Medical, and Religious Works.

We respectfully invite the attention of public and private book-buyers everywhere to these lists, confident that they will be found of interest and profit. Either or all will be mailed free on request.

New York: D. APPLETON & CO., 1, 3, & 5 Bond Street.

www.ingramcontent.com/pod-product-compliance
Lightning Source LLC
Chambersburg PA
CBHW030807230426
43667CB00008B/1108